THE DEVELOPMENT OF WORLD ECONOMY
1975-1991

THE DEVELOPMENT OF WORLD ECONOMY
1975–1991

EDITED BY
ALAIN GÉLÉDAN

SOCIAL SCIENCE MONOGRAPHS, BOULDER
DISTRIBUTED BY COLUMBIA UNIVERSITY PRESS, NEW YORK

1994

CONTENTS

PREFACE

A NECESSARY, SMALL DOSE
OF STATE INTERVENTION

Despite the financial, monetary and energy crises of the last fifteen years (1975-1990), the world economy has witnessed spectacular growth. In global terms at the beginning of the 1990s, humankind produced in one year nearly twice the volume of goods of the early 1970s. But this progress has not solved the world's problems, as can be seen in this volume, based on Economic and Social Reports produced by the economics department of *Le Monde*.

This growth occurred amid a series of crises which are recounted in this book: the oil shocks of 1973 (resulting in the quadrupling of the price of petroleum), and of 1979 (the doubling of the price of petroleum), the monetary chaos of the mid-1980s (the rise and fall of the dollar in 1985), the collapse of oil prices in 1986, then the stock market crash of 1987, to name the most important. The general enrichment, however, did not benefit all in the same way, as is evinced in the persistence of mass unemployment in most industrialized countries and the problem of famine which affects some of the underdeveloped countries.

THE END OF IDEOLOGY

If we look beyond the official record, what lessons can we draw from the past fifteen years which will help us in the future? Historians will probably consider this period as the death knell of ideology. At the beginning of the 1970s, academics could discern the same division in politics and in public opinion. The world was divided into two camps: the conservative free marketeers on one side, the socialists/communists on the other. Each side had their theorists (Adam Smith, Hayek... on one side, Karl Marx, Lenin... on the other), their gods (the market for the former, planning and state monopoly (statism) for the latter), their places of worship and their histories. At the beginning of the 1990s these categories collapsed. Few of today's leading economic advisers follow Hayek or Marx.

Conservatism, socialism: these keywords have all but disappeared from economic jargon. During the 1970s many economists, political leaders, and others believed socialism could work. Then in the 1980s a wind of conservatism swept through the global economy. Both strands have, however, seen many a bitter defeat during the last fifteen years. Academics, politicians, and people seem to prefer nowadays a "pragmatic" approach which combines the efficiency of the market with social welfare assured by the state. This is what the French president, Francois Mitterand, calls a "mixed economy." The phrase has no theoretical grounding. It describes the situation which may well prevail in the world economy during the 1990s. The last fifteen years have been marked by economic policy failures, which drew on the traditional theories, grounded in the antithesis between state planning and the free market. This is evident in North and South, as well as in the East.

A CONSERVATIVE... KEYNESIAN

To start with the North, in the industrialized countries. The year 1981 was very significant. During that year, two politicians with diametrically opposed views, especially in economics, became the leaders of two great democratic countries: the United States and France. They were the conservative Ronald Reagan in Washington and the socialist Francois Mitterand in Paris. To overcome the crisis brought about by the second oil price hike, the former promised to roll back state intervention, the latter on the contrary announced he would reinforce it. If they did, in fact, both manage to get their economies back into gear, it was because they rapidly abandoned their ideological postures and ended up adopting very similar policies.

So, even if he reduced direct taxes as he had promised, Ronald Reagan did not lay down the foundations of economic conservatism, but followed a neo-Keynesian line, massively increasing defense spending and stimulating demand by increasing the budget deficit. The economic recovery was a direct consequence of the tight monetary restrictions imposed by the president of the Federal Reserve, Paul Volcker, in the early 1980s. Paradoxically, the arch conservative Ronald Reagan proved that Keynesian theories worked.

A SOCIALIST... CONSERVATIVE

By contrast, the socialist Francois Mitterand's experience proves the value of following a conservative line. The former leader of the French Socialist Party certainly gave the state more power to manage the economy by nationalizing the banking sector and several large industrial groups. But, two years after becoming president, after 1983 he completely reversed his economic policies, under pressure from abroad. His new doctrine included lowering taxes and tax deductions. This conservative policy, which spread to numerous other areas and gathered momentum in France because of the prospect of a single European market in 1993, led to a spectacular strengthening of the French economy.

In the North, therefore, reactionary conservatism and doctrinaire socialism were both discarded. During these crisis-ridden years, West Germany became a role model. Its economy sustained the economic shocks better than other countries. Its secret was "the social economy of the market," as the Bonn leaders put it. In fact it was a subtle mixture of market and state, free of dogma.

In the South the last fifteen years also saw the failure of the two ideologies. Many large Third World countries tried to escape underdevelopment by following the socialist path: Algeria,

Madagascar, Vietnam .... The results were very disappointing. Conservatism fared no better. In the Third World, the success stories are those of the countries which knew how to combine subtly the different options available from conservatism and socialism. The economic takeoff of South Korea, and also of Southeast Asia (Thailand, Malaysia, Indonesia ...), was led by the state, but sustained by market forces.

Finally, in the East, the collapse of communism at the end of the 1980s was mainly the result of economic incompetence. From 1970 onward, growth petered out in Eastern Europe and the Soviet Union. Some countries tried piecemeal reforms. However, the economy was still based on the same foundation, collective ownership of the means of production, and there were many difficulties. By 1989 most people in the East agreed that central planning and the highly bureaucratic system had to go: all the new leaders, communist or not, advocated the road to the market economy -- more or less fast. The failure of "communism" seemed in the early 1990s like a victory for market economics. The transition will be hard. The new East European democracies seem more likely to follow the German model of "social economy of the market" rather than the more conservative one, espoused by Margaret Thatcher of Great Britain.

PRAGMATISM SUPREME

The conservatives rediscovered the state, the socialists the market. It was the end of ideologies and the return of pragmatism. This was also true of the world economy. For twenty years it had functioned without an international monetary system. In the mid-1980s American leaders still maintained that the market was supreme. French leaders insisted that what was needed was a truly "French" system. In fact, since the monetary agreements of September 1985 (called the Plaza agreements, after the New York hotel in which they were signed), the leading world nations have moved in concert. The money markets are partly controlled by the state. Will this pragmatism help find a solution to the problems facing the world economy in the 1990s? There are three major problems to be solved: unemployment in the richer countries, debt for the intermediately wealthy countries, and famine in the poorer countries.

Despite the return of strong economic growth and massive job creation at the end of the 1980s, industrialized countries continue to face unemployment: at the end of 1989 more than 25 million people (6.6 percent of the working population) were unemployed in the Organization for Economic Co-operation and Development (OECD) countries (made up of the 24 leading rich countries of the world). It is lower than the figures for 1983: there were then 32.4 million (9 percent of the working population). But it is still too many. Especially since they will soon be joined by all those made redundant by the transition to market economics in the East.

The second problem: debt in the developing countries. At the end of the 1980s Third World debt amounted to $1400 billion dollars. This is a time bomb for the world economy. Since the summer 1982 crisis (when Mexico declared that it could not meet its scheduled debt repayments), governments and international bankers have congratulated themselves on having avoided a crash. No solution has been found to the problem of paying off debt without damaging the debtor nations' development.

The third problem: famine in the poorer countries. Despite the spectacular developments in agricultural production and for certain countries the achievement of self-sufficiency in food (notably in China and India), feeding the world remains a problem. According to the FAO (the United Nations body dealing with food and agriculture), out of over five billion humans on the planet, there are one billion underfed. In the early 1990s 35,000 children died every day for lack of food.

Will the pragmatism, which is espoused by all economists and those they advise, allow us to find answers to these terrible problems in the 1990s? There are many others, including protecting the environment. At the end of the summer of 1990, there was another menace on the horizon: a third oil crisis. State intervention seems just as necessary today as it ever was.

Erik Izraelewicz
Paris, August 1990

THE DEVELOPMENT OF WORLD ECONOMY, 1975-1991

1. 1975 — The Crisis

THE PIT OF RECESSION

THE THREE ILLS OF A SICK ECONOMY

"The worst peacetime year in two generations!" How many governments would have dared say this in the first few weeks of 1975? Even in the United States, which had been in recession for a year, the government claimed there was "light at the end of the tunnel." In the rest of the world no leader admitted to being afraid of catching a "flu because of the American cold," and *Le Monde* shocked everyone when, in February, it predicted "zero growth" for France.

The official smugness gradually disappeared. One after another, the industrialized countries admitted failure as unemployment rose and production collapsed. The industrialized capitalist countries had more than 15 million unemployed, failing industries, and inflation that was barely under control. The year 1976 had hardly begun when the most astute commentators attacked the politicians' renewed confidence in an imminent recovery as groundless: the number of unemployed continued to rise, as the OECD explained, debt repayments were falling behind, and inflation was being stoked up. The non-capitalist countries also felt the shock waves: price increases, slowdown of growth, international trade under threat....

"Keynesian," "Friedmanian," "arch-conservative," neo-Marxist... no one knew which label would be attached to the architect or architects of economic recovery. For the moment, the search was on for a way to allow humankind to be dragged out of the "pit of recession," in the hope that 1976 would not be like 1975. No one wanted to get used to the three ills of that year.

* The combination of recession and unemployment, first of all. Everyone agreed that the captains of industry were to blame because of their mistaken confidence in the stability of the system — they had not kept an eye on their order books. Industry had built up its stocks, and when the panic set in, had sold them too quickly, throwing many workers onto the scrap heap. As the recession set in, subcontractors also laid off their workers. Classic economic theory could not explain why consumers preferred to save rather than buy, and industrialists refused to accept public help for investment. With hindsight, "the economy of self-sufficiency" which was prevalent in most industrialized countries, was unable to trigger off the same mechanisms as the "consumer oriented" economy of the past. There was the risk of deferring the recovery, causing lasting damage to growth, and worsening structural unemployment.

* The persistence of inflation was perhaps caused by similar factors: the concentration of industry flattened out competition; technological developments reduced the returns on investments; the unbridled stimulation of consumption led to waste.... There was no need of poor harvests or price hikes by cartels of raw material producers to perpetuate inflation: in 1975 harvests were on the whole good and commodity prices on the whole dropped; however prices continued to climb.

* Finally, the recession restored the rich countries' balance of payments — $27 billion for the OECD members — so that they were no longer beholden to the oil producers. But the poorer countries became even poorer suffering a $38 billion deficit on trade (four times the figures for 1973), mainly due to $14 billion price increases on goods bought from the industrialized countries. They were forced to get further into debt or else beg from the better off nations. It was the same the world over as the recession hit the most vulnerable — African Americans, immigrants, young people, blue collar workers, those nearing retirement..., — similarly the less well off nations lost out in their dealings with the richer countries — in terms of cash, trade, fuel, and even food.

The recession dragged on unexpectedly long for five reasons: massive destocking, decline in trade, fear of unemployment meant consumers saved rather than spent, governmental caution led to a refusal to kick-start the economy for fear of inflation, lack of investment.

HOW TO COPE WITH RECESSION

The cycles of slump and boom which had been staggered between richer countries, but not so markedly at the peak of the crisis, returned to the original pattern, when things seemed to look up. It was no longer a minor, local problem of the Western economies, but two or even three different phenomena. The drop in industrial output, which began in the middle of 1974 — after six months' stagnation at the levels achieved at the end of 1973 — did not stop at the beginning of 1975, as most governments and official experts had anticipated. It was worse: the decline persisted and even worsened during the first months of the year, causing the biggest drop in industrial output, in peacetime, for 40 years.... Most of the OECD countries saw a 15 percent drop in production during the first half of 1975, compared with the second half of 1975.

PERFORMANCE INDICATORS: FROM BAD TO WORSE

Gross National Product (GNP), which was closely related to industrial output, fell in all the large industrialized countries without exception during the first half of 1975: in Japan by 0.2 percent, in the United States by 7.7 percent. Between the two extremes lay a whole series of poor performances, including West Germany (fell by 7.2 percent), Italy (fell by 5.8 percent), France (fell by 5 percent), and others. Despite an improvement in the second half, GNP figures were bad in 1975 in comparison with the previous year: -3 percent in the United States, +1.2 percent in Japan, -2 percent in France, -3.7 percent in West Germany, -4.5 percent in Italy, -2.2 percent in Great Britain.... An average drop of -1.2 percent for OECD countries. Sales prices collapsed: 30 to 40 percent down for exports, 15 to 20 percent down within the

European Economic Community (EEC) (much less in the United States and Japan, where companies were able to retain their profitability). In Europe, and especially in France, the trading account was in the red.

UNEMPLOYMENT: A GRIM YEAR

In France the number of registered unemployed passed the million mark, and for all the OECD countries the record total of 15 million, reached in May 1975 (5.5 percent of the working population), was maintained until December. Even in smaller countries, like Switzerland, where until 1974 unemployment was almost unknown, the number of unemployed grew rapidly, going from a few hundred in the middle of 1974 to more than 20,000 in November 1975 (the previous year's total had been 618).

If you compare the increase in unemployment year on year the average increase was 60 percent. Within the EC the biggest increases were in Denmark (+103.5 percent), Great Britain (+81.4 percent), Belgium (+79.5 percent), and France (+71 percent). Unemployment would have been even higher if two factors had not succeeded in bringing it down: many people decided to quit work when they realized they would not be able to find jobs because of the recession; the return of many Third World people to their country of origin: in Switzerland more than 100,000 left.

RESPONSES TO THE RECESSION
INDUSTRIAL UNREST

On the whole, with the exception of Italy, industrial disputes were not as prevalent as they had been in previous years. As in Great Britain and Belgium, wage demands in Italy produced much unrest. However, gradually the need to work became more important: there were strikes against redundancies or the closing down of factories, such as car plants in Britain and glassworks in Belgium. There were also demands for state intervention to keep factories open and guaranteed work as in Italy, where Fiat had agreed on 8 November not to lay off any workers for a year. Even in Germany, which had very few strikes during the year, there were two industrial disputes caused by redundancies: there was a three-week sit-in at a cement factory in Ervlitt, near Dortmund and seven workers went on hunger strike at a plastics factory, owned by Mannesmann, in Dortmund .

Japan had a relatively quiet year, although there was a dispute at the end of November over the public sector workers' right to strike. The United States had several industrial disputes: in New York and other states there were strikes and demonstrations over the laying off of state employees.

GOVERNMENT INITIATIVES

The main problem in 1975 for the large industrialized countries was how to stimulate the economy without provoking inflation. Some stimulated consumption (mainly by reducing imports, as in the United States), others encouraged investment both by the state and the private sector.

* West Germany increased state investment and relaxed controls. For a country which depended on exports, it was difficult to prosper during a worldwide recession. Government policy worked. Even before the oil shock, West Germany had imposed an austerity program. It was one of the first to dismantle those controls. After December 1973, Bonn relaxed most of the anti-inflation measures introduced the previous spring.

* The United States reduced imports to stimulate consumption. In early 1975 the American government did a U-turn in economic policy. On 13 January the White House announced $16 billion's worth of tax cuts, which Congress increased to $23 billion. There was a $8.1 billion cut in income tax, $7.8 billion cut in pay as you earn; the amount companies could set aside for investment was raised from 7 to 10 percent. The idea was to increase personal spending power by 2 percent and stimulate consumer spending.

During the first few months of 1975 consumers increased their spending and the US economy rose from its lethargy. Many American economists thought this should be maintained in 1976 but the government also had to limit the budget deficit, which was running at $70 billion (about 5 percent of GNP). With the presidential elections looming on the horizon, the government needed to uphold demand and fight inflation. However householders became worried about high levels of unemployment and price increases, and spending petered out. In any case, increased sales only meant the economy was catching up, it did not indicate growth.

* Japan relaxed its hold on the economy in four stages. After prioritizing the fight against inflation, it gradually loosened its grip.

ANTI-INFLATION MEASURES

Despite the depths of the recession, the governments of the large industrialized countries were more careful than in the past before embarking on inflationary programs and fueling a new round of price increases.

* The monetarist straitjacket of 1974 was only gradually loosened in most countries. In the United States, Mr Burns, president of the Federal Reserve System (Fed), avoided any expansion in the money supply. Japan, West Germany, and France adopted similar policies. Also, a drop in interest rates reduced the cost of borrowing for many companies.

* Public spending cuts were planned for 1976 in Bonn, Washington, and Paris to prevent any further increases in budget deficits. Bonn financed its 1975 deficit by encouraging savings through public borrowing and not through increasing the money supply.

* Pay rises were halted in many countries by worsening unemployment. Incomes suffered as a result of the recession. Many governments used all their power to impose this policy. For example, West Germany asked all its workers to forego an annual pay rise "for fear that wage increases would trigger off inflation."

* Price controls: In France, where there was no deal between employers and workers to scrap pay rises, the government controlled import prices and prices in shops, but left industrialists freer to set their own price levels.

THE RESULTS
INFLATION SLOWED DOWN

During the six months up to October 1975, retail prices in most industrialized countries increased by the equivalent of a 9 percent annual rate. This inflation rate was still very high compared with 15 percent in 1974. So 1975 ended with a partial success since the governments of the industrialized countries had succeeded in bringing inflation rates down to under 11 percent.

This is an average encompassing widely differing rates. In France, for example, the inflation rate fell but not as much as the government hoped it would: the second half of 1974 saw a 14.5 percent increase in the annual rate of inflation; this dropped to 11.6 percent in the first half of 1975, and 9.2 percent in the second half. In the United States the comparable figures were: 11.9 percent, 6.9 percent, and 6.2 percent. Japan and Italy achieved the best results. Japan saw prices increase by an annual rate of 17.6 percent in the second half of 1974, then drop to 11.3 percent in the first half of 1975, to finish at 8.7 percent in the second half of 1975. Italy went from 25.6 percent, to 16.9 percent, then 9 percent during the same period. Other countries were jealous of West Germany's annual rate of inflation, which was a very modest 6 percent. Great Britain's rate of inflation at 22 percent was 16.8 points higher than West Germany's and was a worry to all — but there was a discernible trend behind them: rates were gradually falling after enormous hikes in 1973, 1974, and early 1975.

SIGNS OF RECOVERY

Spring saw signs of increased production in the United States, led by consumer spending which was fueled by tax cuts. On the other side of the Atlantic the recovery looked like being strong. The Japanese recovery started before that in Europe but was less strong. The upturn began to show in the figures. But no one was sure whether it could be maintained or whether it would gain strength over the next few months. It was not certain that increased demand (from households, factories and other countries) would materialize and stoke the engines of recovery. In fact demand fizzled out or stopped in mid-1976.

The six heads of state of the United States, Japan, Great Britain, Italy, West Germany, and France decided to reaffirm their commitment to free trade and not fall into the isolationist trap.

Experience shows that during recessions, many countries tried to cut their losses by adopting an isolationist policy. This happened in the 1930s, and it deepened the severe depression in the Western countries. In 1975, however, international rates of exchange were more important than they were 40 years previously. In 18 months world trade shrank at a greater rate than it should have done given the drop in production. Any return to protectionism in these circumstances would have been disastrous.

THE FIRST DROP IN EXCHANGE RATES SINCE 1958

The first surprise of 1975 was the improvement in the US balance of trade. The OECD experts had forecast a $250 million deficit but according to the estimates it was only $10 million. Other countries produced similar results. This occurred against a backdrop of recession and a drop — especially in the first half of the year — in world trade, which fell for the first time since 1958. During 1975 OECD countries experienced a drop in imports of 10 percent — more than industrial production (-7 percent) — and exports of 5 to 6 percent.

THE BALANCE OF PAYMENTS CRISIS: DEFICITS WITHOUT TEARS

After the quadrupling of petroleum prices in October-December 1973, everyone was convinced that the Western countries would be unable to balance their budgets. This was not as bad as forecast in 1974 and by 1975 it hardly figured as a problem. The OECD found that the total level of its members' deficit did not exceed $6 billion.

Wiped out. In a situation where the rich countries remained unscathed, while the poor came out in a worst plight, what had happened to the balance of payments crisis? By looking at the level of reserves during the 1973-75 period, only the oil producing countries increased their holdings, as was forecast. What was unexpected was that other countries' reserves stayed more or less the same. Many thought that there would be winners and losers, that the industrialized countries and the developing countries which did not produce oil would lose some of their reserves.

This did not happen. Why? As Jacques Rueff noted governments were able to have "deficits without tears," as had occurred in the United States in the previous ten years. It was as if the extra bill for oil was paid by credit, the debtor countries took out massive loans on the Eurodollar market, which was swelled by deposits from the oil-producing countries, or from those countries which put their capital, the surplus petrodollars which they could not use at home, on the international market. The accumulated debt became so large that it would have been almost impossible to pay off. This was a source of worry to oil producers, who hoped to get their loans guaranteed, particularly through a dialogue between North and South.

RAMBOUILLET AND THE FOURTH WORLD

It was not surprising that the "poorest of the poor" should try to benefit from rivalry between the old wealth and the nouveaux riches. From Algiers, Dakar, Cuba, and Lima, they came with their grievances. They were listened to... but to no effect. When it came to decisions, the pronouncements of the International Monetary Fund (IMF) at Washington or of the Rambouillet summit in December, 1975 showed they had made no impact.

"A starving empty stomach cannot hear." Rather it carries little weight. When it came to sharing out the spoils, the creditor nations decided on: a weak recovery for fear of inflation; free trade so they could still sell overseas. The Fourth World people continued to miss out because they seemed irrelevant.

2. 1976 — Disappointed Hopes

FEEBLE GROWTH
THE UPSWING FALTERS

FEARS OF OVERPRODUCTION

Was it a cold or a fatal sickness ? This was the question on everyone's mind as the specter of the 1930s loomed. The economic indicators of 1976 showed signs of both problems. In spring many thought the sudden drop in output in the autumn of 1974 had been a passing phase mainly due to irregular supplies. After a year of decline, output recovered more or less everywherc with figures approaching the record levels of yesteryear. The doom merchants could not get any mileage out a 12 percent average rise in industrial production.

But the summer brought further worries. Previously the government had encouraged investments through subsidies, tax relief, and budgetary incentives, now these had to stop because production was out of step with demand and the political future was unclear (particularly in France). Exports had boomed during the recovery — world trade had increased by 10 percent — but they fizzled out as countries tried to sell their surplus goods to their neighbors and protect their home markets. Consumption, the engine of the Western economies, faltered under the triple threats of increased unemployment, a decline in purchasing power, and an increase in savings after the hopes of a recovery in spring.

Production slumped as businesses tried to avoid the overstocking of 1974. After fall industrial growth which had been cut by half in the previous six months, remained stagnant. The motor industry was immune to this, but there was a string of bankruptcies in the textile and construction industry. The most severely affected sector was the iron and steel industry. The OECD downgraded its July pessimistic forecasts. In four years the most important capitalist countries had only managed to increase their production by 8 percent, that was less than 2 percent annually as opposed to 5 percent annually before. Feeble growth had now become the norm, after being merely academic. It seemed to point to the inability of the system to respond to people's material aspirations.

STAGFLATION ALL ROUND

In the industrialized countries unemployment rose: almost six million jobless in Europe and about 15 in all the developed countries. This was worse than one could have imagined and some leaders feared there would not be any pick up until 1978 — productivity gains would ensure some growth and wipe out any possibilities of creating jobs. This general malaise did not kill off inflation in the OECD countries. Although the inflation rate had fallen from 10.6 percent in 1975 to an average of 8 percent, it was vulnerable to any change. In France the rate crept up to 12 percent and killed off the Fourcade plan. The inflationary pressures, such as waste, wage demands, money supply problems, the need to restore profits, raw material price rises, spending on social welfare, were such that they did not respond to ordinary treatment.

The more determined governments (Bonn, Washington) were able to gain a few victories; others (London, Rome) were exhausted by the fight against the social cancer. Between these two extremes, France and Japan tried out some of the necessary medicines: credit squeeze, budgetary controls, import restrictions without being able to eradicate inflation. The weakest suffered as they were less able to withstand price increases than those with secure financial means. The disease even spread to the communist countries, where prices climbed but shortages persisted.

The effects of the economic slowdown were far-reaching among the less affluent countries. Many countries were so in debt

— to the tune of $150 billion — that they had no choice but to borrow in order to finance the trade deficits ($24 billion this year). The industrialized countries had pinned their hopes on a recovery of world trade. This proved precarious, leaving them slightly worse off each year but the winners in the trade game — the oil producers and to a lesser extent West Germany and Japan — gave them a few crumbs of comfort. Stagflation meant that each country was looking after their own interests. Conservatives — arch or not — threw their principles by the board and asked the state to intervene. Even those who favored more socialist methods put national interest first.

WHY WAS THERE A HALT AFTER THE SPRINT?

In mid-1975 economic growth took off under the double impact of an end to destocking and government measures. Yet this slowed down more quickly than had been anticipated in 1976. OECD statistics showed that the recovery lasted for 10 months when there was an average annual rate of 11 percent growth but by the first quarter of 1976 it had died out. National output in many countries grew, on average by 5 percent in 1976 compared with a drop of 1.2 percent in 1975. There were two factors behind this slowdown in economic growth in 1976.

1) *Personal consumption* in almost all the industrialized countries grew slowly from the second quarter of 1976. This was the result of low wage increases, increased taxation, the stabilization of savings rates, a slower than predicted build up of stocks — the captains of industry no longer believed in strong and inevitable economic growth, as was the case in the early 1970s.

2) *Business investments* in most capitalist countries were at a low level because of lack of confidence. The captains of industry preferred to improve their profit margins rather than pass on to the customer what they gained from improving productivity.

A GENERAL MOBILIZATION AGAINST INFLATION

Many industrialized countries became mesmerized by the fight against inflation. The idea was to shore up businesses at the expense of the consumer.

West Germany: profits came first

The annual wage negotiations agreed to a ceiling of 6 percent on pay rises. Employees lost out — their share of national income fell from 72 per cent to 69.5 percent — industry profited. The Bundesbank maintained strict controls on the money supply, which grew by 8 percent. The national debt was reduced from 68 to 57 billion Deutschmarks, thanks to spending cuts, increased taxation, and social security contributions.

Great Britain: public spending cuts

The government launched another incomes policy and got the Trades Union Congress to agree to a ceiling of 4.5 percent on annual pay rises from August 1976 to August 1977. However the threat of a seamen's strike caused the pound to collapse, thus increasing the price of imports and stoking up inflation. The government responded with a tough monetarist policy — the minimum lending rate was raised from 11.5 to 13 percent — and a request for a $3.9 billion loan from the IMF. To get this help Britain introduced an austerity program aiming at reducing the budget deficit by £1.5 billion in 1977-78 and £2 billion the following year. The government sold off then £500 million worth of shares in British Petroleum.

United States: credit controls

The preferred weapon in the fight against inflation were tight credit controls. The Federal Reserve continued to keep the growth of the money supply within the bands of 4.5 and 7 percent. By the end of the year credit controls were relaxed slightly. The government did not intervene allowing its 1975 tax incentives to make their impact. Budget spending was pruned and wage demands became more moderate.

MEDIOCRE AND INADEQUATE RESULTS

In the industrialized, capitalist countries retail prices increased by 8.7 percent in 1976 as against the annual increase of 10.9 percent in 1975, 13.4 percent in 1974, and 7.9 percent in 1973 (from 1962-72 the average annual increase was 3.9 percent). It seemed as if inflation was continuing to slow down in 1976. But this was mainly due to measures taken the previous year. Differences in the rates of inflation were ironed out in 1976. The rates in the United States (5 percent in 1976) and West Germany (4.7 percent) were three times less those of Italy and Great Britain (17 and 15 percent respectively). France and Japan were in between at 10 percent.

These figures highlighted the split of the industrialized, capitalist countries into two groups: the strong, like West Germany and the United States, which had overcome inflation and could stimulate demand at home, particularly household spending (Jimmy Carter cut taxes in 1977); the weak, including France, which had to follow an austerity program and put a halt to raising the standard of living.

WORKERS FEARED UNEMPLOYMENT

"In spite of the increased economic activity of the first months of 1976, the labor market remained sluggish in the OECD zone"; and at the end of the year "in some countries the situation worsened," declared the OECD. At the end of the year unemployment rose in most of the OECD countries, mainly West Germany and the United States, even if the rate was less than that of the previous year.

The economic upturn in most OECD countries did not lead to wage disputes, as might have been expected. There were more than in 1975, but that had been a particularly quiet year. In fact the number of days lost through strikes was everywhere — apart from Belgium and Italy — lower than before the crisis. Unemployment continued at a high level, except in West Germany, and kept the workers under control. The increased economic activity did not reduce unemployment but it allowed those in employment to recover their purchasing power after the severe setback of 1975.

WORLD TRADE PICKED UP

According to the Paris Chamber of Commerce and Industry, world trade grew by 10 percent. In 1975 it had, for the first time since 1958 (a 1 percent drop then), shrunk by 5 percent to $880 billion. This was caused by the upturn and increased trade between industrialized countries. The producers of raw materials and the Eastern Bloc countries had difficulty meeting their bills and oil producers spent less, so the industrialized countries increased their imports rather than their exports.

BALANCE OF PAYMENT PROBLEMS PERSISTED

The 1975 recession had hidden many industrialized countries' trade imbalance but the upturn of the first quarter of 1976 allowed them to reemerge. The oil bill was paid late. Among the larger countries only Japan and West Germany had a trade surplus.

* Every year Japan's surplus doubled: from $5 billion in 1975 to $10 billion in 1976. The West German surplus hardly shrank from $17 billion to $16.5 billion. The German economy dominated world markets: the revaluing of the Deutschmark did not hurt exports and made imports cheaper.

* This was in marked contrast to other countries. The United States had had a trade surplus in 1975 of $9 billion but in 1976 there was a deficit. Three Western countries traded in the red. Great Britain's deficit barely changed in 1975 and 1976, hovering at $7 billion marks. Both Italy and France had improved their trade balance in 1975 but this was reversed in 1976.

DEBTS

The main threat to world trade was the increased level of international debt. In Europe, countries like Italy, Great Britain, and Denmark had an exterior debt which was greater than their annual exports. Other countries, particularly France (which owed more than $10 billion), were in a weak position. However West Germany had a huge currency reserve. The Eastern Bloc countries owed nearly $40 billion and developing countries which did not produce oil had around $150 billion in debts. The Third World countries were asking for a moratorium on debt payments if not the cancellation of debts.

3. 1977 — Loss of Confidence

SLUMP

THE RECESSION PERSISTED

The fourth year of the Western world's recession ended without any apparent signs of improvement. The Western economy was still in a slump, making it difficult to separate cause and effect. Investments stagnated or dropped because there were not enough customers; this in turn affected consumption by hitting manufacturing industry — and workers' wages. Demand at home was damped down by a general loss of confidence — which affected pay — as well as by the government austerity programs against inflation. The market had still not recovered the vigor of the pre-1973 oil shock years.

Previously international trade had grown at three times the rate of GNP, but in 1977 this also petered out at a 6 percent increase, compared with 14 percent in 1976. The failure of this third motor of economic recovery was the new feature of the year. The reason for this was that every country tried to sell its surplus goods abroad but this merely stimulated protectionist measures, making it even more difficult to sell. Anti-protectionist declarations did not prevent the barriers — tariff or other — from going up. The loss of confidence affected the running of the economy as well as output and turnover. There were fewer social reforms and less industrial action. The few attempts at the restructuring of industry were led by the government (Swedish, British, French) rather than the business community.

NOT THE USUAL KIND OF RECESSION

The recession was unusual in that it had lasted longer but been less acute. The year 1977 produced more distinctive features: price rises slowed down, but only marginally; profits recovered slowly; interest rates dropped at the beginning of the year, then markedly everywhere; the countries with a strong currency (Deutschmark, yen) continued to amass their trade surpluses, while the currency of countries with deficits, mainly the United States, collapsed (from 13 to 18 percent in a year for the dollar).

Was this "weak growth" predicted by many commentators over the last 10 years or "steady growth" as President Valery Giscard d'Estaing of France put it? Neither. It could be argued maliciously that in fact it was the classic recipe for sluggish growth — monetary weaknesses, massive under-employment, and persistent inflation without any structural changes.

More dispassionately the recession can be said to have continued and even beginning to affect the Eastern Bloc countries. It was due in part to the impact of Third World production on the world markets (often financed supranationally), and the ineffectiveness of the regulatory forces of yesteryear. The Western countries had controlled their economies and eradicated certain old-style social ills but they had also deprived them of their resilience.

Some countries were better able to cope than others and greater disparities between them emerged. The United States which should have suffered most from the consequences of the oil price rise, since it imported more and more "crude" from OPEC countries, paradoxically was able to weather it, because the currency instability it encouraged meant it did not have to pay its debt and the fall of dollar protected jobs at home, to the detriment of other countries. The slide of the dollar had the undeclared side effect of exporting unemployment. There was a need for a new approach to growth, maybe finding new targets for development, or at the very least a change of emphasis in the objectives sought by the developed countries' economies and a change in the behavior of rich people so far too indifferent to waste.

INVESTMENT AND INDUSTRIAL STAGNATION

Industrial recovery, which began in the mid-1975 and continued in 1976, hung fire in 1977, just as the pre-recession rates of growth were being achieved. Demand failed to sustain the 1976 recovery: individual consumption dropped, even though fiscal policy was less restrictive in 1977; investments continued to be mediocre, except in the United States and Great Britain; and exports grew by a mere 5 percent, compared to 10 percent in 1976. Of the three elements fueling demand, it was the failure to invest that led to the 1977 stagnation.

ATTEMPTS TO KICKSTART THE ECONOMY

* The United States was one of the first to try and kickstart its economy. In early January, the newly elected president, Jimmy Carter, announced a $30 billion reflationary program spread over two years of tax cuts (tax rebates, raising tax thresholds, reductions in company taxes) and public works. However, in view of the recovery, in April Jimmy Carter canceled much of his program, particularly the tax rebates and company tax reductions, which fell from $15.7 billion in 1977 to $3.4 billion.

American economic policy thus returned to orthodox principles. In April a strict anti-inflation program was announced, which eschewed all forms of control and rested on cooperation between employers and employees, as well as balancing the budget. Jimmy Carter was holding himself back for an energy conservation program, which was still being blocked by the oil companies. In August the president proposed a 1980 reform of the welfare system, which would reduce the number of recipients.

* West Germany spent 1977 resisting pressure from other industrialized countries, particularly at the G7 summit in London

in May, to launch a reflationary policy. In March the Bonn government adopted a series of measures designed to sustain the recovery and improve its finances: a 16-billion Deutschmark public investment program spread over four years; raising Value Added Tax (VAT) from 11 to 12 percent on 1 January to increase its revenues by 10 to 15 billion Deutschmarks and thus finance tax cuts.

In September 10 billion Deutschmarks of tax incentives were introduced — , tax thresholds were raised on productivity bonuses, basic tax allowance and depreciation costs. However, because of the lack of demand abroad and overconsumption at home, economic growth in 1977 hovered at 3.5 percent, rather than the forecast 5 percent. In December the minimum lending rate was at its lowest since fall 1972. But by the end of the year West Germany still refused to reflate, as it had done consistently since January, while on four occasions after 1973 this course had been taken.

* Great Britain reduced its minimum lending rate six times, so that it fell from 12.25 percent in January (15 percent in October 1975) to 5 percent in October. In November it was raised to 7 percent. However in October the government launched a £1 billion' worth reflation. Tax thresholds were raised by 12 percent, so that 900,000 people did not have to pay income tax and everyone paid less. There was a special payment to pensioners for Christmas, £400 million' tax concessions to the building industry, and tax incentives for small businesses (worth £100 million). Further tax cuts were promised for the spring as long as income did not exceed the official limit of 10 percent. After a few skirmishes, the social contract held and in December the miners' union agreed to defer its wage demands until 1978.

* In Japan, despite international pressure particularly from the United States and from Japanese employers, the government led by Takeo Fukuda refused to stimulate demand at home. It did not want to stoke up inflation and thought household consumption would be no substitute for export-led demand. On top of that, the

revaluation of the yen (which gained almost 20 percent against the dollar in one year) wiped out most of the measures taken by the Japanese government to show its good intentions vis-à-vis the Western countries. Finally the Japanese economic growth rate never achieved the 6.7 percent forecast for the financial year (31 March 1977 to 1 April 1978), it barely reached 4.9 percent.

DISAPPOINTING RESULTS
THE FAILURE TO CREATE JOBS

In 1977 many Western governments launched job creation programs, aimed particularly at those under 25 years of age, who had very poor prospects of finding work. These measures, which some international experts denounced as "stopgap solutions, often improvised, which do not get to grips with the fundamental problems," did decelerate the increase in unemployment but by the end of the year there had never been so many out of work: in OECD countries there were 16.3 million unemployed, of whom 7 million were young, that is 5.4 percent of the working population; in the EEC (9 countries) 6 million, of whom 2 million were young, that is 5.7 percent of the working population. At the end of 1977, the 24 OECD countries had half a million more unemployed than they had had at the height of the recession in 1975 and 700,000 more than in the first quarter of 1977.

Signs of an upturn in the economy in 1976 had allowed wage earners to improve their purchasing power, but they were not in evidence in 1977. The result was that not only had unemployment risen but wage rises had slowed down. This was part of a government policy to make companies profitable again and improve exports' competitiveness.

The commodity prices dropped in 1977. There were a few exceptions, tin had rarity value, lead was very much in demand, and cocoa was subject to speculation. Those most affected by the price collapse were copper and zinc among the minerals, which were hit by the worldwide recession, but also cereals and soya, because of abundant harvests. The price of coffee rocketed but then fell to well below the level at which it had started the year. The slowdown in wage rises, the drop in commodity prices reduced manufacturing costs. However the slowdown in economic growth in the industrialized countries in 1977 reduced profitability; especially since in most countries (apart from the United States) employers preferred to keep on their employees rather than lay them off. There were social as well as economic reasons for this: it was more and more expensive to make workers redundant (in Sweden, for example), it was also expensive to take on new people and train them.

THE ANTI-INFLATIONARY POLICIES OF JAPAN AND WEST GERMANY

The year 1977 was notable because most of the important, industrialized countries decided to take on board the need to keep down inflation. Japan and West Germany, which both had trade surpluses, resisted all kinds of pressure to stimulate demand at home for fear of inflation. This paid off for the capitalist countries: after a shaky start, 1977 ended well. Previously they had used inflation to cushion the shock of the oil price increases.

The slowdown in growth, often the result of restrictive government policies, improved the trade balance of many important, industrialized countries. This was possible because the rate at which foreign goods were bought dropped from 14 percent in 1976 to 6 percent and exports grew. A notable exception to this was the United States: imports increased by 12 percent, swelled by oil imports, and exports dropped. The American balance of trade deficit trebled in one year. By way of contrast the Japanese trade surplus almost doubled between 1976 and 1977. West Germany had an equivalent surplus to the Japanese one, despite the revaluation of the Deutschmark. So both countries retained their advantage in the trade wars.

THE POORER COUNTRIES' DEBT GREW

According to UNCTAD (United Nations Conference on Trade and Development), the total debt of the non-oil-exporting, developing world stood at $240 billion at the end of 1977, as opposed to $200 billion at the end of 1976 (+4 percent). Of this $30 billion belonged to the poorest countries. Interest payments on the debt in 1978 would account for a quarter of export receipts, and for some countries even more than that.

For most developing countries, interest payments represented 3 percent of GNP in 1976, while the debt itself accounted for 20 percent — that is double the level; of 1965. More than half the interest payments came from eight countries: Argentina, Brazil, Egypt, Israel, Mexico, North Korea, Spain, and Yugoslavia. The interest rate on these debts was relatively low at 6 percent, compared with 5 percent in 1973.

OVERSEAS AID

While the developing countries' debts quadrupled in nine years, the richer countries' overseas aid budgets (from the CAD-Aid Committee of the OECD) totaled $13.7 billion in 1976 ($13 billion in 1975), that is 0.33 percent of GNP as opposed to 0.35 percent. The aim was to reach 0.7 percent but only the Netherlands, Sweden, and Norway achieved this. By contrast the three countries which represented two-thirds of the CAD's GNP, West Germany, the United States, and Japan, only contributed 0.32, 0.26, and 0.21 percent of their GNP. OPEC contributions dipped slightly from $5.5 billion to $5.2 billion, that is 2.14 percent of GNP as opposed to 2.7 percent in 1975. Until then they had always increased. The Communist Bloc countries also reduced their aid budgets from $0.8 to $0.5 billion, 0.03 percent of GNP as opposed to 0.09 percent in 1973.

4. 1978 — Further Depression

CHANGING TACK

RECOVERY AND SLUGGISHNESS

With many a change of tack, 1978 gave rise to heightened feelings of economic insecurity. The countries which seemed to be doing well in the spring — the United States, Japan — did not end the year so hopefully. By contrast those which were performing sluggishly — particularly West Germany — picked up in fall. Others, like Italy, Great Britain, France, went up and down according to the season, performing poorly, in the grip of the depression which the Western world had found impossible to shake off for four years. The increase in unemployment was the most serious sign of this.

Each country's performance indicators gave fragmented and contrasting results. On the whole inflation was on the wane (especially in Italy and Great Britain), but not in France, where the Barre plan's radicalization fueled price increases, once the elections were over. In the industrialized countries, inflation differentials went varied between one and four. Similarly underemployment went down in the United States and West Germany, but worsened in France and in most developed countries — the experts claimed there were one hundred more jobless every minute. The economic news headlines were redundancies, regional blight, and industrial unrest (depending on how resigned employees were and how well wages were keeping up).

There were also great differences in the balance of trade. Japan's surplus shot up by $9 billion in 1978, West Germany's went up by $2 billion, Italy $3 billion; France increased its takings by $5 billion and went back into the black. At the same time the oil producers' surplus on trade dropped by $20 billion and the underdeveloped countries without oil increased their deficit by $10 billion. The Western countries had regained their place in world trade but the debt of the Third World non-oil producers has risen to $300 billion (an increase of 15 percent in one year). This dwarfed the $6 billion of debt written off the previous year by nine countries (this did not include the United States or France).

Industrial production in developed countries rose slightly in 1978 compared with the previous year. The annual average growth rate reached 4.1 percent, while the 1977 average for the OECD countries had been 3.7 percent in 1977. It should be noted that this approached the levels achieved during 1965 and 1975, when the annual average was 4.2 percent growth. In fact the seven leading industrial nations achieved 4.5 percent growth in 1978, which surpassed the 4 percent growth achieved in 1965-75, mainly because of the United States' rapid growth and a strong recovery in Japan.

REFLATIONARY POLICIES

THE THEORY OF THE CONVOY
REPLACES THAT OF THE LOCOMOTIVE

In 1978 everyone expected West Germany to lead the world out of recession but it was the United States that did so. During 1977 and early 1978 the Western world subscribed to the theory of the "locomotives." With their massive currency reserves, West Germany and Japan were supposed to stimulate growth in order to pull the international train out of recession.

In the event neither were willing to follow this policy for fear of price increases, which they had staunchly resisted in the past. Also, at the OECD meeting in Paris at the end of February and the G7 meeting at Bonn on 16-17 July, the theory of the locomotive was replaced by that of the "convoy," that is concerted recovery. For the first time at an international conference, concrete pledges were made. Nonetheless, for the time being, the United States, which had enjoyed steady economic growth since 1975, led the field. The US economy was booming more quickly than those of other countries, but this in turn provoked an increase in the US trade deficit as well as in prices. Then in fall the US government had to slow down growth, running the risk to cause a slump in the economy.

The Western world was unable to combine growth, monetary stability, and full employment. If it concentrated on the fight against inflation, then business suffered and employment rose. If it launched a boom, there was the prospect of price increases. If it led an export-driven boom, then production costs had to be squeezed and there were factory layoffs.

AN INDUSTRIAL BATTLEGROUND

Each country followed a monetarist, conservative line thus helping the powerful. Everywhere — particularly in France — profits rose at the expense of wages. The famous "German theorem" that "increased profits leads to more investment, which creates jobs," did not prove correct. Generally companies preferred to increase their profits and lay off workers. They realized that in a time of bitter competitiveness in world trade it was easier to employ cheap Third World workers than demanding First World ones. Workshops at home were closed down and new plants were opened overseas.

This process, which rectified the international division of labor, took place in the absence of any international outcry. The industrial reorganization soon resembled a battleground, as industries and regions bore the brunt, without there being any prospects of replacing the lost jobs. The workers replied, where they could, by demanding shorter working hours so that the work could be shared out without their standard of living dropping too much.

In the economic war, currency remained a powerful weapon. The dollar fell by 20 percent against the yen during the year and it helped the United States to regain its share of the world market.

The Deutschmark had, up till now, been used to save on the cost of raw materials without making exports too expensive to sell abroad.

INSECURITY AMONG THE MOST POWERFUL COUNTRIES

IMPROVEMENTS IN PROFITS AND WAGES

In 1978 companies' finances improved in almost all the industrial countries. For example, in the United States profits during the second quarter would have contributed to an annual total of $78.4 billion (using the 1972 dollar rate as a constant), compared with $68.4 billion in the first quarter and $71.9 billion in the last quarter of 1977. Before the world recession of 1974-75, profits in the United States had stood at $70.8 billion for the year. So the second quarter of 1978 showed an 11 percent increase on the pre-recession figures.

This increase in profits in most of the industrial countries, especially in France, did not prevent workers' purchasing power from increasing — sometimes considerably. While the Western world and Japan were able to maximize both profits and wages, it was at the expense of the Third World countries which depended on oil and raw materials exports, whose price dropped. This transfer of resources, which was known as a deterioration in the terms of trade, allowed the producers and consumers of the industrial countries to gain. The projected 1979 increase in oil prices might well have reversed — or slowed down — this trend. The improved companies' financial results stimulated investments in the United States, particularly in the housing market. In West Germany and Japan the recovery was more modest and in France there was no improvement in results.

EMPLOYMENT: IMPROVEMENTS FOR THE BETTER OFF

In the OECD countries there were nearly 18 million unemployed by the third quarter of 1978 — 10 million from the

United States, Canada, Great Britain, West Germany, and France. The EEC had 6 million unemployed, that is 5.6 percent of the working population. Globally, unemployment in the industrial countries did not increase during 1978.

Analysts even claimed that during the first quarter of 1978 OECD countries saw a "rapid expansion of employment," mainly due to the strong growth in the United States, an above-average increase in employment in Japan, and stabilization in several European countries. They also pointed out that this expansion occurred in non-manufacturing industries. In most countries the number of new jobs remained at a low level or in the manufacturing industries employers continued to lay off workers as production fell. This was the case in the industries most vulnerable to the recession: textiles, shipbuilding, and iron and steel.

IMPROVEMENTS IN THE BALANCE OF PAYMENTS

The OECD balance of payments had shown a $27.5 billion deficit in 1977 but in 1978 it was almost even. This masked great differences between countries' results: the Japanese surplus almost equaled the US deficit at $20 billion, which according to the OECD "lay at both extremes of the trade imbalance. The improvement of $25 to 30 billion in the OECD current account could be accounted for partly, according to OECD experts, to increased trade with OPEC countries ("half from the volume of trade and half from improved terms of trade"). Some $10 billion came from the change in the terms of trade with developing countries. Thus the oil-producing states' current account surplus went from $30 billion in 1977 to $10 billion in 1978. However the Third World deficit grew by $10 billion (an increase of 40 percent) to a total of $35 billion.

The big losers in this bitter world game were Third World countries. Those who had oil were not so badly affected but they lost out over the drop in the dollar's value. Some countries were able to "takeoff," but not all of them. Those without oil became poorer with every year: the raw materials they produced were worth less and less in real terms, and the industrial goods they bought became more expensive. The rule was get into debt — if it was possible — or fall further behind. The harsh laws of the modern world decreed increased dependence and greater inequality between countries.

5. 1979 — New Shocks

THE SECOND OIL CRISIS

FROM HOPE TO DEPRESSION

The year 1979 began with the hope of further recovery but ended in disappointment and the generally held fear of depression. As always there were great discrepancies between countries: some avoided the worst to the detriment of others. Globally, the Western world ended the year having achieved a pitiable growth rate of 2 percent (as opposed to more than 3 percent in the first quarter) and was faced with the prospect of general depression in 1980. The communist countries, members of the Council for the Mutual Economic Aid, or Assistance (Communist Nations) known as COMECON, found themselves in great difficulties: the leading country, the Soviet Union, barely achieving half the projected 4 percent growth. The developing countries without oil suffered from the general depression as well as the increased oil prices, and for the most part did not have the resources to cope. China, which had hoped in 1979 to "takeoff," had to revise its ambitions downward.

Only the oil producers and a few of their clients enjoyed a year of prosperity with healthy growth and a trade surplus (OPEC had a $104 billion surplus, double that of 1978). The rest had huge deficits in 1979: $30 billion for OECD countries, treble the deficit of 1978 and a bit more than the 1974 deficit, the "terrible year" of the Yom Kippur War; $47 billion for the developing countries without oil (double the total for 1977); $8 billion for the COMECON countries, whose foreign debt increased by a sixth in one year and exceeded the cost of a quarter of the Soviet Union's exports or half of Poland's exports. Everywhere countries had to increase their debt in order to subsist at ever increasing rates. Also banks were beginning to wonder about some of their customers' ability to pay.

There were a few beacons of hope in the middle of this uncertainty. Italy increased its rate of growth by a half — this despite a poor performance in the first few months of the year — and maintained its current account in surplus. France finished the year with improved results: inflation — which increases consumption and stockpiling — and government policy stimulated demand and for a time halted the rise in unemployment. The newly industrialized nations — Algeria, Brazil, Mexico, South Korea — made spectacular leaps in performance.

THE IMPACT OF OIL

After a pause of five years, the price of oil — which had dropped in value, given the increase in the price of manufactured goods and the drop in the dollar's value between 1974 and 1978 — more than doubled in a year. This was partly the result of OPEC policy but also because the oil producers acting on their own, in concert with market forces, forced the price up. Oil consumption did not drop — in fact stockpiling stimulated it — and this knocked a hole in the budget of the user countries, whose growth rates were cut by 1.5 percent for the year, according to the OECD. This trend continued into 1980 since the final oil price increases took place in the last quarter of 1979. This accounted for the prospect of "zero growth" in the Western world in 1980.

West Germany, the United States, France, and Japan (which agreed to make real efforts to adjust the imbalance in trade with the West) were all able to pay for the increase in their oil bill by digging into their trade surpluses. Those who could not afford to do this got further into debt: $300 billion of debt for the developing countries, $55 billion for COMECON countries. The experts predicted that 1980 would be even worse and the OECD countries could anticipate a global debt of $50 billion.

The increase in oil prices — as well as having an impact on worldwide inflation — accelerated price increases everywhere by engendering an atmosphere of uncertainty. This was not helped by the Iranian revolution and fear of war. Restocking also "dragged" prices upward in spite of an overall picture of economic stagnation. The worsening of inflation (an increase of three points to 10 percent in the EEC; an increase of five points to 12.5 percent in the United States) produced the second shock which shook up the currency markets, put public spending in the red, led to massive increases in the interest rates... and speculation pushed the price of gold up to more than $500 per ounce (and even up to $600 in early January).

INCREASING THIRD WORLD COMPETITION

Further shocks emanated from the Third World. The newly industrialized countries, with their newly built factories and low-paid workers, threatened to take away the First World's markets. This was not new but it forced traditional manufacturers in iron and steel, textiles, electrical goods, to pull out or change completely. The large multinationals followed — often led — this new industrial strategy by moving productive capacity, particularly in car manufacturing. Many companies, such as, Chrysler, Sidelor, Usinor, British Leyland, British Steel, AEG, Telefunken, were forced to restructure by improving their productivity, moving, or closing down.

DEPRESSING RESULTS

To get an idea of the seriousness of this second oil shock a comparison between oil bills and GNP is necessary. For France the ratio went from 1.18 percent in 1970 to 3.54 percent in 1974; it then dropped, but by 1980 was estimated to be 3.6 percent before the conference of Caracas. For the United States the ratio went from 0.23 percent in 1970 to nearly 3 percent in 1979.

Similarly oil represented only 6.9 percent of US imports in 1970 but by 1980 it approached 30 percent; in France the proportion went from 9.3 percent in 1970 to 20 percent in 1979. The industrial countries had spend a growing part of their wealth on oil and read about OPEC's decisions with fear. There was no ceiling on oil prices, but the Saudi Arabian price of $24 a barrel was the lowest, while Libyan oil went for as much as $35.

Apart from the price increases, there were also fears of political instability in the Persian Gulf during the last quarter. The freeze of Iranian assets in US banks, the refusal (limited in fact) to accept dollars for oil payments, the embargo on oil purchases only convinced the oil producers to restrict their production to a level only high enough to finance their development.

INCREASING INFLATION

Price inflation dramatically increased in 1979. The OECD countries experienced an average increase of 11 percent. In 1978 it had been 7.9 percent — a jump of more than three points in a year. The year 1979 was notable for the sharp increase in prices, pushed by two factors: American inflation and the fact that the countries with strong currencies such as West Germany and Switzerland were no longer immune. The increase in oil prices was thought to have added 4 percent to prices by the end of 1980. This figure included the catching up of the price of other forms of energy and the secondary effects on wages — workers wanted some compensation. The massive increase in the money supply, stimulated in several countries (the United States, Great Britain) by an explosion in bank credit, led to a reduction in the purchasing power of money. A drop in productivity gains, notably in the United States, also increased the unit costs of production.

CREDIT OUT OF CONTROL

Inflation in the industrial countries (not to speak of the others) led to massive increases in credit which reached new heights in some countries. In the United States, the money markets' rate went from 10 percent on January 1 to almost 14 percent in November, this precipitated an increase in the costs of bank credit. The

American banks' base rate remained at the 11.5 percent rate from January to July (not counting a slight increase in June), but after that shot up to reach a record 15.75 percent. To stop the fall in the dollar, the president of the Fed, Paul Volcker, appointed at the end of July by President Carter, had to dig deep. On October 6, he announced a new program: an increase in the minimum lending rate to a record 12 percent, and an increase in the amount banks had to hold in reserve with the Fed.

Gold as a Refuge

In 1979 the price of gold hit the roof to reach record levels. Even in 1974 there had been a great deal of speculation in the second half and prices had risen spectacularly — this occurred because the market thought the price would rise after January 1, 1975 when American citizens would be allowed to buy gold after 40 years of prohibition.

From January to December 1974 gold's price in dollars on the international market in London had gone up by 70 percent. For a time on October 31, 1978 it had hit $244 an ounce with the news of the Carter Plan. In early 1979 the price fell to $227. On December 19, during the OPEC conference at Caracas, it hovered below $500 — an increase of almost 120 percent — before overtaking it on December 27. In the first days of 1980 the price rocketed to $600 and above.

The rise in the gold price has often been compared to the oil price: the price of "black gold" doubled in 1979 and that of gold went up by 100 percent. There are more significant comparisons to be made. Since the beginning of the 1970s the volume of Eurocurrencies had increased tenfold and the price of gold had gone up fourteen fold. The price of gold increased with the means of paying for it, which in turn led to a depreciation in the value of currency.

ASTONISHING INDUSTRIAL GROWTH

In the OECD countries industrial output grew in 1979, averaging a 4.7 percent growth rate compared with 4.1 percent in 1978. This was better than the average rates recorded from 1965 to 1975 and occurred despite a slowdown in the United States (4 percent in 1979 compared with 5.8 percent in 1978). It was mainly due to spectacular growth in Japan (8.2 percent compared with 6.2 percent in 1978), West Germany (5.5 percent compared with 1.9 percent in 1978), France (3.3 percent compared with 2.8 percent in 1978), and Italy (5 percent compared with 1.9 percent). However many smaller countries also saw rapid growth. The year 1979 was not characterized by depression as many feared it would be after the oil price increases and the slowdown in growth in the United States. With strong discrepancies inside the current cycle, countries like Japan and West Germany, which were undergoing a strong recovery, were able to compensate for the negative effects of the United States' downturn on international trade.

Variations between the economies of industrial countries were a boon for the Western world in 1979. Had it not been for oil price increases which had a depressing effect on investments at the end of the year, mainly because of the violent increases in interest rates, 1979 might well have seen strong economic growth. The growth occurred in unhealthy circumstances, propelled in many cases by precautionary purchases of goods (particularly plastics) by manufacturers. They wanted to protect themselves from further price increases and build up their stocks. The effects of destocking were probably harmful to the economic situation , which many predicted would go into reverse in 1980. The annual figures for 1979 masked a downward trend which occurred in the summer.

THIRD WORLD PROBLEMS

The Cambodian famine temporarily reawakened the Western world's bad conscience in respect of poverty in the Third World. The year 1979 was, after all, the last year of the second decade of development. The "strategies" adopted in October 1970 at the

United Nations had almost completely failed. Some 800 million people lived in "absolute poverty" and 50 million died of starvation. In the light of these statistics, the North and South leaders continued to meet at pointless conferences, while building up their stocks of weapons. In May 1979 UNCTAD held its 50th session in Manila. It was a talking shop and there was no progress in setting up a fund to stabilize the prices of raw materials, a policy which had been adopted in Nairobi in May 1976. At Manila, the Third World faced secure countries anxious to protect their positions.

The renewal of the Lome Convention was less depressing. It was a trade agreement between 58 African, Caribbean and Pacific countries with the nine members of the EEC. It agreed to the extension of the system of stabilizing export receipts for 14 agricultural products and introduced a new mechanism to protect prices of mineral ores. At the end of October, in the Togo capital, Lome II was unenthusiastically signed. The poorest countries became poorer, as the oil price increases affected them badly. At the OPEC conference at Caracas in December, Algeria proposed the creation of a Third World Bank, with over $20 billion of capital, to lessen the cost of their energy dependency and to prevent the outbreak of the "77" front. The appeal fell on deaf ears. In 1978 the OECD countries donated $20 billion in aid, about 0.35 percent of their GNP and half the amount agreed on in the early 1970s. Nonetheless military spending continued apace, having reached $420 billion in 1978, of which $120 billion was spent on arms. Third World countries spent $90 billion on arms and their foreign debt climbed to over $300 billion.

6. 1980 — The Relapse

A THRILLER

LOST ILLUSIONS

By the end of the year there were many unanswered questions. The OECD experts had no difficulty writing "in recession" in their end of year report on the industrialized countries: a year of relapse. It was also a year of lost illusions. Sometimes the economic medicine administered by governments did not work or, as in Great Britain, produced indifferent results and a great deal of suffering. Pronouncements on the need for austerity no longer had any impact. No one was in any doubt about the seriousness of the situation but there was no clear direction to follow. The two traits of this period of transition were lack of confidence in political leaders and the inability to see the future, even the near future, as a continuation of the present.

The year began like a thriller: everyone waited for the frightening stranger to knock on the door. In fact orders, production, company results continued to improve as if there had been no oil price increases (130 percent up in 1979) and there was no problem with inflation. The American economists, both government and private sector, were the most confused. The recession they had predicted for more than a year had still not materialized. It was in fact around the corner. In the end it was precipitated by excessive spending by Carter's administration (which was exacerbated in the following months by a desperate attempt to buy votes with public spending), the Fed's dogmatism and the banks' improvidence.

INTEREST RATES CLIMBED

In almost all countries the notable feature of 1980 was that the fight against inflation was prioritized. The main weapon in this fight was interest rates. In the United States they reached record levels. Thus anti-inflation policies created a huge gap between the US and German interest rates, increasing the cost of money and having a negative effect on the industrialized countries' economic health.

The most extreme swings upwards occurred in the United States in spring and toward the end of the year. The Fed, under Paul Volcker, imposed a series of restrictive measures to combat inflation because it was worried by the excessive demand for credit and an increase in the money supply. At the end of January there was a crisis on the US money markets, similar to those that have littered 20th-century US history. The bond market went into an unprecedented nosedive. Panic set in on Wall Street.

For years the economy had been kept going by inflation. The government, companies, and those who needed money kept the demand for credit high, until it went out of control. The new monetarist doctrine had dictated that interest rates should float. After Volcker's restrictions were introduced on March 14, interest rates rocketed to 20 percent in April. (Interest rates had previously gone out of control in October 1979.)

This sudden increase in the rates of interest had disastrous consequences for the automobile industry, already vulnerable to foreign (mainly Japanese) competition because of oil price increases, as well as the building industry, which depended on mortgage loans to finance house purchases. Builders in Detroit lost between 30 and 40 percent of their business; the number of housing starts dropped rapidly. By the end of the first quarter, the effect of both these sectors' vulnerability meant the US economy was in full recession. This downturn, which lasted until June, was worse than that of the last quarter of 1974 or the first five months of 1975. Yet again it was clear that interest rates were linked to the turning around of economic cycles. This had always been the case, under various guises, since the early days of the industrial revolution.

The American recession only lasted for the first quarter, and was very localized, mainly affecting the highly industrialized states (particularly those with iron and steel plants). However it did not produce any beneficial results. This is perhaps because the Fed and the White House, whose main concern was the November presidential election, were terrified. Chrysler got into trouble so the government bailed it out. Less publicly thousand of smaller companies were kept afloat. Meanwhile Volcker dismantled all the credit controls that had been so hastily introduced in March and April. This called into question the Fed's constitutional independence. Within a few weeks, interest rates dropped until they hit 10.5 percent in July. After that they began to rise again because there was still a lot of inflationary pressure. The statistics on which the authorities based their action — or inaction — also went crazy. It seemed as if the recovery was under threat but the GNP figures for the third quarter showed a 2.4 percent growth rate as opposed to the 0.9 percent that had been predicted during the recession.

THE POLITICAL PRESSURES ON ECONOMIC POLICY

Great Britain experienced the same problems. Perhaps this was due to the fact that both countries had the same blind faith in monetarism, and therefore confused a squeeze on credit with high interest rates. This occurred in Margaret Thatcher's Britain where a long period of high interest rates exacerbated inflation and failed to kill it. Margaret Thatcher, like Raymond Barre in France, was inspired by Milton Friedman but also by the West German model, which was no longer the pride of Chancellor Helmut Schmidt. In Britain the price of sterling was forced upward, partly as a result of the North Sea oil receipts. However, the higher value of sterling increased foreign competition and many British companies found themselves in difficulty. Redundancies proliferated and unemployment hit the two million mark, that is 7.4 percent of the working population.

Even though their politics were very different from that of the US democrats (social democrats inspired by John Maynard Keynes), Margaret Thatcher and her Industry Minister, Sir Keith Joseph, propped up British Leyland just as Jimmy Carter had Chrysler. The "iron lady's" key doctrine was a reduction in public spending but the government deficit soared uncontrollably.

On the European mainland the downturn was staggered. In both West Germany and France there was relative optimism until the spring. After that things went downhill. As 1981 approached both countries faced stagnating or declining industrial output, and a downgraded investment program. In France the failure of Raymond Barre's "gradual" fight against inflation was patently clear. Prices increased by nearly 14 percent. West Germany had up till then enjoyed a low level of unemployment at around 4 percent but a few disillusions lay in store. The OECD experts had predicted as usual that price increases would fall and they did not go any higher than 5.1 percent. However there were many problems by the end of the year. Why would West Germany escape the fate of all the other countries? With a weak currency (the Deutschmark trailed in last position in the European Monetary System for most of 1980) and a huge deficit on public spending and its balance of payments, all the indicators pointed towards inflation.

Industrial output in the Western countries had accelerated strongly after the summer of 1979 and in the early months of 1980 this momentum was maintained but in the second quarter the delayed and indirect effects of the oil price increases took their toll. This reversal happened more suddenly than in 1974, following the first oil shock. However the subsequent recession was not as severe as the 1974 one. If industrial production in the OECD countries fell by 6 percent from March to July, there were signs of recovery, especially in the United States, or stabilization in some countries after the summer. Even if these were only momentary upswings — mainly in the United States and Japan — the worst seemed to be over at the end of 1980. One thing was certain: leaving aside disasters, the downward economic trend had ended.

However it was likely that recovery in the second half of 1981 would be much more feeble than in 1975-76.

THE SEARCH FOR SELF-SUFFICIENCY IN ENERGY REQUIREMENTS

At the OPEC meeting in Bali in December 1980 an 8 percent increase in oil prices was agreed and it was clear that the era of price hikes was not over. Shocked by the successive price increases of the previous 18 months, the oil-consuming countries were able to avoid a third oil shock, which could have occurred because of the Iran-Iraq War. The worst did not happen. The combination of a reduction in energy consumption and a slowdown in the Western economies, in truth a recession in the United States for most of the year, led to a considerable drop in demand of almost 7 percent in the more important industrialized countries and 5 percent for the world.

The industrialized countries became concerned with changing the structure of consumption. The G7 heads of state met at Venice at the end of June and agreed to increase coal and nuclear power production so that in ten years time oil would represent 40 percent of energy needs rather than the current 53 percent. The American Senate also agreed to the taxing of the oil companies' super-profits, which brought in $227 billion — part of which would go to the development of synthetic fuels , such as alcohol, liquefying coal and others.

All these decisions would not bear fruit until the end of the 1980s. In the meantime, the oil-consuming countries were at the mercy of any internal crises which might occur in the Gulf, bringing about the downfall of those in power, or at the mercy of frontier disputes between countries, particularly the explosive relations between the two leading powers in the area.

RUNAWAY INFLATION

The increase in prices, which had accelerated in 1979, continued to run away in 1980. For most industrialized countries prices increased by more than 10 percent, as in 1974 and 1975. At the end of 1980, increases of 12 percent were predicted.

The Effects of the Second Oil Shock

The second oil shock, which began in successive waves in 1979 (the average price of a barrel went from $15.2 in the spring to $32.3 at the end of 1980), provoked increases, insofar as it was possible to measure them, of 3 to 3.5 percent in prices, including indirect effects. Therefore without the oil price increases, prices would have risen by 8.5 to 9 percent in 1980, an increase on 1978 (7.9 percent). The rhythm of inflation did not slow down in the industrialized countries, in fact it accelerated. This was a sad commentary on the inability of Western governments to come to grips with the problem.

Wages and prices went up in 1980, in varying degrees in different countries. However the year ended almost everywhere — despite an increase in the nominal value of wages — with a decrease in workers' purchasing power, or with a drop in the upward trend. Purchasing power dropped — during the eight or ten first months of the year — for the second consecutive year in the United States. The OECD predicted that only Japan would enjoy an increase in workers' purchasing power in 1980.

GREATER INTERNATIONAL COMPETITIVENESS

At the same time as international competition intensified, the slowdown and increased unemployment led to renewed protectionism. Two-thirds of world trade was governed by tariff and non-tariff barriers. According to a UN study, the United States had 400 non-tariff obstacles on some 1,000 goods from Latin America, Japan had 100 on 430 goods, and the EEC 300 on 480 goods. In any case the industrialized countries lost ground in international trade and their terms of trade suffered from the increases in oil prices. The upward trend in world trade was reversed. In 1979 world trade represented $1,625 billion, an increase in volume of 6 percent compared with 1978. In 1980 the increase slumped to half that total at 3 percent.

INDUSTRY

The first year of the 1980s went down in history as the most fruitful in the restructuring of industry. Investments and disinvestments are common in industry: each year there occur mergers, bankruptcies, and diversifications. However in 1980 this reached new heights. The map of world industry was noticeably changed by the recession, technological progress, and the internationalization of trade.

The recession, and its corollary called "rationalization," affected the traditional, industrial giants, including those which had been the motors of growth for decades. Along with textiles and shipbuilding, the car industry faltered with the tire industry in its wake.

Unemployment had stabilized in 1979 but in 1980 it climbed rapidly in the OECD countries: some 23 million jobless, of whom almost half were under 25 years old. The G7 countries, the United States, Canada, Japan, West Germany, Great Britain, Italy, and France, had between them 16.5 million unemployed at the beginning of the fourth quarter as opposed to 13.5 million in the same period of 1979. By the end of the month of November, there were 7,600,000 unemployed within the EEC, that is 6.9 percent of the working population, as opposed to 6,063,000 (5.4 percent) in October 1979.

7. 1981 — New Deals

A MISERABLE RECORD

The year 1980 was a year of relapse: 1981 was not the year of recovery. Apart from Japan, the main industrialized countries barely grew, mainly owing to the quasi-stagnation of industrial output, and unemployment shot up. The EEC had ten million jobless, the United States more than nine million: this was a miserable record which an increase in agricultural production and a slowdown in inflation could not wipe out, especially since many countries faced the problem of paying the welfare bill. Things were no better in the East. The Soviet Union's economy did not meet its performance targets, Poland's results were as poor as expected. Only East Germany and to a lesser extent Bulgaria emerged with decent results. Among the developing nations, the poorest had become a bit poorer and more in debt at the same time as the more dynamic, like Brazil and Mexico, had run out of steam. Even the oil exporters had suffered, forced to reduce production and prices.

SUPPLY SIDE ECONOMICS

This seventh lean year in a row was notable for the accession to power of Ronald Reagan in the United States and François Mitterand in France, both of them elected on economic programs which were radically different from those of their predecessors. At the beginning of the year the dollar took off to reach its highest point in August. This was a sign of the international financial world's expectations of Reagan's presidency. The new president had among his advisers a team of young ultraconservative economists keen to prove the benefits of supply side economics. This was a very simple theory: to revive the economy, production must be stimulated by encouraging individuals and companies to produce and invest by reducing taxes, the loss of government income was offset by a reduction in its budget and interventions, to be followed by an acceleration in growth.

In accordance with his electoral promises, Reagan got Congress, after a bitter fight, to adopt a budget of tax relief and cuts in all areas particularly welfare, but military spending was increased. The first Reagan budget was a disappointment. One of its primary objectives was to cut the budget deficit, but this seemed risky given that the economic downturn was turning into a recession, the result of the policy of high interest rates. It was hardly surprising that the financial world and even David Stockman, the director of the budget and the new administration's economics adviser, were sceptical, even though observers had to reserve judgment.

THE NEW AMERICAN POLICIES
THE RETURN OF CONSERVATISM

Reagan thought the US tax burden was too great as it was a disincentive for investment, or savings, or even work. Income tax and tax on companies' profits represented 48 percent of public revenue in 1979 compared with 35 percent in West Germany, and 17 percent in France. Without any corrective mechanisms, taxpayers were continually pushed by inflation into the next income bracket.

LIGHTENING THE TAX BURDEN

* For companies Reagan had no problem getting his way, but he had to concede further demands. The budget was retroactive to January 1, 1981. The amortization of goods period was reduced and procedures simplified. Companies gained from better tax credits for investment and other concessions for research and

development costs. Congress also imposed special measures for small companies: reduction in the tax rates on companies and a new inventory accounting.

* For individuals a dozen measures were introduced. The most important was the reduction by 25 percent over three years (the White House wanted 30 percent) of income tax, that is, 5 percent from October 1, 1981 (a delay of nine months on Reagan's initial program), 10 percent from July 1, 1982, and 10 percent from July 1, 1983. The marginal rates were changed: the tax bracket increases from 11 to 50 percent compared with 14 to 70 percent. A family of four saved $218 on an annual income of $10,000, but $12,744 on an income of $100,000.

* Other measures included the removal of the marriage penalty: where couples who worked had to pay more tax if they were married than if they were single. The maximum rate paid on investment income was reduced from 70 percent to 50 percent. Taxpayers benefited from various other deductions or tax credits. The major innovation was that Congress tied the tax brackets to an index of price increases; but this measure would not take effect until 1985.

According to US Treasury figures, the tax concessions would cost the government $28.8 billion in lost revenue in 1982, $75.7 billion in 1983, and $120.5 billion in 1984. Reagan also set a target of reducing the part of the GNP represented by government spending from 23 percent in 1981 to 19 percent in 1984. Spending should only increase by 6.5 percent in 1982 (half the previous rate), 3.4 percent in 1983, and 4 percent in 1984. Defense spending was the only sector of the budget to escape cuts. According to Reagan's initial program, the Pentagon would get an extra $1.3 billion in 1981, $7.2 billion in 1982, $20.7 billion in 1983 .... Military spending would increase its share of the budget from 24 percent in 1981 to 32 percent in 1984. Congress did not complain and gave the Pentagon $200 billion in the 1982 budget, more or less what the White House had requested.

The new fiscal measures were debated, amended, and passed by Congress and on August 13, 1981 signed. They encompassed tax relief for companies and individuals, measures to encourage saving, and less tax on inheritance and donations. The reduction in social spending went against the social policies following the New Deal and there were bitter protests from welfare recipients, more numerous than one would have thought in the land of free enterprise. The president insisted that he was not penalizing the worst off but he tightened the rules on a host of payments: food coupons, free meals for some schoolchildren, student loans, early retirement, medical subsidies....

The Budget Deficit Crept Up

In the middle of the summer the budget deficit for 1982 was forecast to be $42.5 billion. In November the estimate was revised to $96.7 billion. The next month it went up to $109.11 and gloomy prospects for the following years. Without an increase in taxes or new cuts, the deficit would hit $152 billion in 1983 and $162 billion in 1984. This mistake came about for a number of reasons. Firstly, Reagan used his predecessor's figures, which were distorted. More importantly the new administration miscalculated its sums. To begin with it predicted a GNP increase of 4.2 percent in 1982 and a reduction in unemployment. Ten months later, growth was a meager 0.2 percent in 1982 and the number of unemployed was at a record high. Faced with harsh reality the presidential advisers backtracked. In fall some said they were in favor of increased taxation and reduced military spending. They had to review and correct their theories. Thus Murray Weidenbaum declared that the fight against inflation was more important than balancing the budget. William Niskanen contradicted this saying that the budget deficit had nothing to do with inflation. Bill Jordan said he saw no relation between the deficit and the high interest rates.... There was no sign of Reagan's proclaimed beliefs.

There were also substantial cuts in export credits, overseas aid, local subsidies, the production of liquid fuel, the space program as well as transportation, postal services, scientific and medical research, arts subsidies. Without counting the cancellation or reduction of public works (road building, airports, etc.), the abolition of two government departments (Education and Energy), the reduction in the number of government officials, and the limit of 4.8 percent in their annual pay rise.

The proposed budget was fairly well received. Only the trade unions showed any opposition. Following his electoral victory and knowing how to win over Congress, Reagan's program was passed. The only hiccup was over pension reform, which the White House had to abandon temporarily. The early euphoria evaporated slowly and Reagan soon found himself up against the skepticism of the business community as well as some Republican Congressmen and women, concerned about the growing deficit. The strong consensus of the spring had weakened by fall and even the Administration was visibly divided.

In the middle of these difficulties, budget director Stockman got into trouble. The young and brilliant economist had voiced in private to a journalist his doubts about his own economic policy. In November an article in The Atlantic about these conversations was the talk of the town. Stockman seemed to have little faith in a balanced budget and suggested that Reagan's program was a sham aimed at restoring the classical Republican "trickle down theory," by which the rich have to be encouraged to revive the economy. The Democrats could not believe their luck. Stockman was hauled over the coals at the White House on November, 12. He had to make a fairly humiliating public apology, but his resignation was rejected as it would have given substance to his comments and he was still indispensable. This strange affair confirmed the growing doubts of Congressmen and women, of trade unionists, and of business people about the success of the government program.

VOLCKER'S MONETARISM

Who made this combative statement at the beginning of May 1981? President Reagan or one of his advisers? Not at all: it was Volcker, the Fed's inflexible president. Previously, Volcker had restated his belief that strict control of the money supply was of great importance in the fight against inflation.

These declarations were followed up by action. Intervening on the open market, that is buying and selling Treasury bonds (which adds or detracts from liquidity) on the money markets, the Fed engineered a rise in the cost of credit in 1981 to reach the same heights as at the end of 1980 (21.5 percent base rate for the most secure banks; and much more for others). After a dip in the spring, interest rates climbed up, a process which was only reversed after September.

This reverse was due to a slowdown in the growth of the money supply, which in May grew by an annual rate of 14 percent to drop to 6 or 7 percent at the end of the summer. There was also predictably the beginning of recession, which worsened over the next few months and successfully curtailed demand for bank credit, the Fed's objective.

Was this drastic monetarism welcomed by the White House? Apparently, as long as there were no electoral setbacks. During the first half of 1981, the president reaffirmed several times "his profound respect for the Federal Reserve Board's independence," adding that the high interest rates "were a consequence rather than a cause of inflation," and that the Fed should continue to watch out for the expansion of the money supply. In June the Treasury Secretary stressed "there is no divergence between the White House and the Fed on the fundamental objective of reducing inflation by decelerating the growth in the money supply."

Even when Congress, anxious about the deteriorating economic situation, denounced the "literally murderous" high interest rates and some Congressmen and women accused the Fed of "legalizing usury" and "destroying small companies, the American middle class," Reagan continued to support Volcker. Toward the end of the year even Reagan appeared worried by the extent of the recession and made a few criticisms of the Fed's policies, which had been "unable to maintain the money supply within fixed limits" (too low in his opinion), "and did not take into account Wall Street's reactions."

Apart from these revelations, the president publicly stated he could not dictate policy to Volcker, who had the last word when he told Congress imperturbably "Do you have a better way to fight inflation?" The reply was obvious: in a country where the legislature and the executive abhor using price controls, wage freezes, or credit controls, only the monetary authorities could intervene, whatever their effectiveness and the consequences on the economy.

A SEVERE PURGE

In 1981 the United States had its eighth recession since World War II. A recession precipitated by its monetary policy: the high interest rates discouraged purchases on credit and investments. In an attempt to curb inflation, the Fed forced the country, for the second time in two years, to slow down economically. Before Christmas, Reagan took the credit for reducing interest rates and inflation. The prime rate had dropped from 21.5 percent in January to 15.5 percent in December. Retail price increases had been under 10 percent in 1981 as opposed to 12.4 percent in 1980 and 13.3 percent in 1979. However borrowing money remained very expensive until fall and inflation had not diminished enough to stimulate an economic recovery.

Two sectors got the full force of the recession: cars and house building. The rot soon spread to other industries, such as iron and steel and machine tools. The world figures would have been even worse if the advanced technology industry (electronics, aeronautics, energy) had not been able to withstand the pressure. In November American factories were only using 74.9 percent of their capacity, that is 4.4 percent less than in November 1980.

Unemployment hit 9.5 million, that is 8.9 percent of the working population — the worst result for six years. This rate was twice as high among the ethnic minorities among whom there was 17.4 percent unemployment. The Reagan administration and employers wanted to use the recession to reduce wage demands. The monetary policy strengthened the dollar so it was more difficult to export. The American people suffered more from the recession because the government would not increase its assistance programs or create jobs.

A GLOOMY HORIZON
FEEBLE GROWTH

Economic growth was feeble in 1981, as it had been in 1980: in the OECD countries GNP did not grow by more than 1.2 percent. Industrial output stagnated (0.7 percent increase after a drop of 0.8 in 1980) and lay behind the mediocre result, which could be explained by the second oil shock and the rise in the dollar. Successive increases in the price of oil pushed the average price of a barrel of oil from $13 at the end of 1978 to $35 at the beginning of 1981. The oil bill for the industrialized countries was on average 4 percent of their GNP at the beginning of 1981. The effects of the second oil shock were aggravated by the sustained rise of the dollar until the summer of 1981, which increased the price of oil and further depressed the industrialized economies. These were exacerbated by the policy of high interest rates from June to November 1980 followed by the monetary authorities. It was in these unfavorable circumstances that the American economy went into recession in the second quarter of 1981. Gross Domestic Product (GDP), however, increased by an average of 1.8 percent in 1981 thanks to the strong economic performance of the first few months.

Japan's growth rate was equally lackluster: 3.7 percent after 4.2 percent in 1980. The Japanese economy's success in 1981 was to get back on an even keel. This was also the case in West Germany whose GDP dropped by 1 percent in 1981 because of lack of household demand (down 1.7 percent) and a drop in investments (down 4.5 percent). Inflation dropped marginally throughout the world in 1981. In 1980 prices had risen by 12.9 percent but in 1981 this fell to 10 percent. According to the OECD by the end of the year there were more than 25.72 billion unemployed (as opposed to 23 million in 1980, that is 12 percent more), that was more than Canada's population.

INTERNATIONAL TRADE:
ONE STEP BACK TO CORRECT DISTORTIONS

World trade dropped in volume in 1981 compared with 1980, whose results were only slightly superior to those of 1979 (1.5 percent up). They fell below the $2,000 billion of 1980. These figures hid a big reduction in world trade at the beginning of the year and continual, slow buildup thereafter. The dip in economic activity produced a drop in trade in oil, aggravated by a drop in real prices and the reduction of oil stocks. The year was also notable for correcting distortions: a fall in the OPEC trade surplus; reduction of two-thirds of the OECD deficit.

8. 1982 — Cracks

THE YEAR OF LIVING DANGEROUSLY

THE RECOVERY GOES MISSING

The expected worldwide economic recovery did not happen. While the GNP (industry, agriculture, services) of the G7 countries (the United States, Japan, West Germany, France, Great Britain, Italy, Canada) had grown by 1.3 percent in 1981, in 1982 it fell by 0.5, industrial output dropped by even more (by 5 percent). The Eastern Bloc countries, apart from Bulgaria, also had a depressing year resulting in a business slowdown and serious financial difficulties for some: Poland and Romania. Even East Germany and Hungary were affected by the crisis which hit Third World countries, and all producers of raw materials. This was a drop in business due to the recession and in agriculture, due to superabundant harvests.

Anti-inflationary policies pursued by most of the large industrialized countries lay behind the general downturn and in the OECD countries price inflation, which had stood at 10 percent at the end of 1981 fell back to 7.2 percent at the end of 1982, its lowest level since 1973. Great Britain and the United States were particularly effective in this domain. During the first half of the year the Fed continued, more or less successfully, to rein in the expansion of the money supply, provoking constant tension between American interest rates and a strong rise in the dollar.

MEXICAN BAIL OUT AND FINANCIAL CRISIS

Mexico let it be known that it could not repay its debts. This was a symbolic and worrying failure of a developing country, producing and exporting oil, to whom banks had lent huge sums of money — to their profit. This came as a shock to the financial wizards on the international scene. However it was only the beginning. After Mexico, came Argentina and later on Brazil, equally burdened with debts, which also announced they were unable to fulfil their repayment terms.

The doom merchants had long denounced the excessive growth of debt, which for the developing countries alone had risen by $96 billion to reach at the end of 1982 $626 billion — the debt service had gone in one year from $109 to $131 billion. They now saw their worst fears realized: a major financial crisis. Thanks to the international bodies — the World Bank and the International Monetary Fund (IMF) — which, facing up to the catastrophe, averted the crisis by introducing a plan which rescheduled the debts and granted new credits at the end of the year.... This was a story which would run and run.

This red alert led to a buildup in the IMF's resources, notably by increasing national contributions which totaled about $100 billion. The increasing power of the IMF — already a major force in Africa — enabled it to take on the role of "pompier volant" — flying firefighter — as Jacques Delors put it. These financial cracks added more gloom to an already dark picture.

BANKRUPTCIES AND AUSTERITY

American policy aggravated the world economic problems. The two motors of consumption and investment had slowed down because of the pressure on wages of companies coping with massive debts. It was not surprising that there were a record number of unemployed and bankruptcies during 1982. At the end of the year there were more than 32 million unemployed in the industrialized countries (an average of 9 percent of the working population in the OECD countries, sometimes as high as 10 percent). The unemployment rate showed no signs of slowing down, in fact it accelerated: in Canada up 50 percent between January and December; the United States up 30 percent; and West Germany also up 30 percent. In the Third World the picture was much bleaker and there were over 500 million without jobs or fixed incomes.

The protective wall of social security, built during the boom years, could not cope with this massive influx. Everywhere there were reductions in benefits, cutbacks on help to the poor, including the unemployed, increases in social contributions. At the European Council conference at Madrid in September 1982 the ministers of social affairs admitted that benefits for all could not be maintained. The European Commission invited the EEC members (ten) in November to a global review of the social security system, which no longer worked, and whose financing called for a new deal between the state and citizens.

At the same time, protectionism spread ominously. There was a spectacular showdown between the EEC and the United States over European steel exports and the Common Agricultural Policy (CAP). Contrary to international trade rules, there was a proliferation of sectoral and bilateral agreements. In November the representatives of the 88 GATT members met for the first time since 1973 in Geneva. The meeting proved fruitless and showed how withdrawal into isolationism threatened international trade.

France experienced a change within a change in 1982. At first the government followed a policy aimed at stimulating recovery and redistributing wealth but there was a brutal about turn and an austerity program following a second devaluation in June was launched. This was accompanied by a price and wage freeze up to November to stifle inflation. The government had to cut back on social spending, use a prices and incomes policy to fight inflation, renew industrial plant, reduce companies' charges by transferring the financing of family allowances, and declare a moratorium on debt payments for those companies most badly in debt. There was a notable success in reducing the increase in unemployment but there was still the trade deficit which had led to massive borrowing abroad.

France was not the only country to change tack. The United States had to dilute its monetarism, which provoked a drop in interest rates and a decline in the dollar's value. Would these measures be enough to get the world economy out of its rut? This was unlikely given the world recession was not cyclical but the result of technological changes, which had completely upturned industry and left it with huge debts and a deregulated international financial system. In order to face these problems and prevent deflation, harsh measures were called for. Would the industrialized countries be able to take on these responsibilities?

THREE EXPLANATIONS FOR THE FAILURE TO RECOVER

When the 1975-76 recovery petered out in 1979-80 with the second oil shock, most experts predicted a rapid recovery. But this no more happened in 1982 than it had in 1981. The reasons behind the failure to recover appear obvious with hindsight but they baffled the experts at the time.

1) Firstly, demand dropped from OPEC countries, which suffered from the world recession leading to a drop in oil consumption (down 5 percent in volume in 1982 after a 15 percent drop during 1980-81). The OPEC trade surplus disappeared, after having stood at $65 billion in 1981. As a consequence demand from oil-producing countries to the industrialized countries dropped by 8 percent between the end of 1981 and the end of 1982. Non-oil producing developing countries experienced the same lack of demand. They sold their raw materials with difficulty for lower prices and were unable to make up the difference easily with credits as before, because the Western banks had had their fingers burned by Mexico. In 1982 world trade contracted by 2 percent.

2) Secondly, the very high real interest rates depressed investments in industry but also construction. The high cost of borrowing money had an even greater impact because the rate of usage of industrial capacity had fallen to an all-time low (in the United States it fell to 40 percent in iron and steel and by the end of the year to 68.4 percent in industry as a whole, something which had not happened since 1948).

3) Thirdly, most industrialized countries decided the way out of recession was to alter the share out of wages and profits to the companies' advantage to allow them to reinvest and take on more staff. This action adversely affected consumption (this called into question the practice of linking wage rises to price increases) and business. The Netherlands, Italy (a little), Belgium (a lot), all embarked on this course in 1982. Great Britain, Japan, and West Germany continued to follow this line of action. The effects on business of this attempt to restore companies' profitability were amplified by the parallel efforts of states to reduce their budget and social deficits. Most industrialized countries — like France — adopted strict budget controls in 1982.

RECOURSE TO EXPEDIENCY

The house of cards began to tumble. From August 1982 the international financial community worked on a rescue package for those countries most in debt, unable to meet the terms of their payments, the servicing of their foreign debt accounted for up to 50 percent of their export receipts. Simultaneously, the most important industrialized countries, particularly the United States, realized the seriousness of the situation: they urgently needed a plan to provide the international institutions, starting with the IMF, with the necessary funds for the months and years ahead. As things stood, these institutions did not have the means at their disposal.

It has to be said that the banks had been irresponsible. In early 1982 they were still lending to Mexico and Brazil. There was no shortage of warning signs. The quality of loans was deteriorating. From 1981, the Eastern European countries, Brazil, Argentina, Mexico, were no longer able to make long-term (seven-year) loans. These countries had to make short-term loans. The borrowing countries had to fall back on expediency, at which Eastern Europe and Brazil to name a few, were past masters. Thus these countries were asking the banks to finance not only imports of capital goods but also local, large-scale expenses with money credits.

THE FIRST EMERGENCY RESCUES

The reaction of the banks to the principal debtor countries was brutal: from one extreme to another, imprudence in the spring and early summer was followed by a refusal to accommodate countries in difficulty, which merely rendered the situation more intractable. The June devaluation of the peso sounded the alarm. From the summer, Mexico announced it was incapable of meeting any interest payments, let alone paying back the debt principal. Mexico had launched itself on a vast capital expansion program on the assumption that oil prices would continue to rise.

From August, the first emergency measures were in place: two American loans of $1 billion each, a moratorium on payments of three months, discussions with the IMF. Shortly afterward Argentina announced it was unable to repay its debt, while in November it was Brazil's turn to ask the IMF for help, which up till that point it had steadfastly refused. Those were not the only countries in difficulty. Very few countries were able to borrow money on the international market under normal terms. All of Central America was in trouble, and Africa was in no better shape. Only the Southeast Asian countries kept their credit rating. The Third World countries were not the only ones getting further into debt. Several industrialized countries, including Canada, France, Spain, Italy, continued to borrow massively. In 1982 France's foreign debt went from $30 billion to $50 billion.

RUNNING INTO DEBT:
AN ACCUMULATION OF MISTAKES

The medium and long term foreign debt (that is, repayable after more than a year) of all the developing countries hit $626 billion by the end of 1982, of which $520 billion came from non-OPEC countries. The weight of this debt (growing by $96 billion a year) and its servicing — that is $131 billion ($60 billion in interest payments and $71 billion to repay the capital) out of which $98 billion was for non-oil producers — became even heavier in the early 1980s, with the increase in real interest rates, the weakening of world trade, and the drop in the commodities' markets. By contrast, during the 1970s inflation had reduced the debt.

Also, it seemed, according to a study published at the end of the year by the OECD, that some developing countries had borrowed "most injudiciously... to finance consumption, as well as dubious investments, instead of improving their productive potential." Similarly the banks "by making loans too easy, sometimes allowed countries to put off necessary adjustments."

In fact, concluded the OECD, "there was no problem of debt" but problems concentrated on two types of developing countries: a small number of very impoverished nations and some "advanced" countries, which had increased their borrowings at variable, high rates of interest. Thus private banks — whose credits to the Third World represented a third of their loans to the international community (6 percent of the combined total of their home and foreign loans as opposed to 2 percent in 1977) — mainly lent to four countries: Argentina, Brazil, Mexico, and South Korea, a total of $40 billion by the end of 1982. These four countries accounted for more than half the outstanding loans made by private banks to non-oil producing Third World countries (85 percent of this debt at variable interest rates).

A GENERAL AND QUALITATIVE WORSENING OF UNEMPLOYMENT

Most OECD countries experienced an acceleration in the rise of unemployment. The number seeking work rose by about six million, an increase of 23 percent on 1981 (between 1980 and 1981 the rise was 12 percent). By the end of 1982, unemployment had hit 32 million, that is 9 percent of the OECD's working population. Employment deteriorated in almost all OECD countries, but some countries suffered particularly.

In the United States, the unemployment rate passed the 10 percent mark, for the first time since the Great Depression of the 1930s. By the end of the year the country had more than 12 million unemployed (10.8 percent of the working population in

December 1982), which was a 30 percent increase compared with 1981. Unemployment was worst in the industrial northeast; but areas like Texas, which usually were unaffected, also suffered. The ethnic minorities were the main victims of the recession, representing 10 percent of the total population, but 20 percent of unemployed. Blue collar workers and young people were the worst affected, with unemployment rates of 16 and 24 percent respectively.

The deteriorating unemployment situation produced a qualitative change. In many countries increased unemployment hit male wage earners (between 25 and 45 years old), showing the length and depth of the recession. The number of long-term unemployed also grew: in Great Britain in July 1982 55 percent of jobless had been seeking a job for more than six months compared with 46 percent in July 1981. In the United States more than two million had given up hope of finding a job. Young people were the perennial losers on the labor market: 20 percent of unemployed in France, 30 percent in Spain and Italy.

There were two reasons for the decline in employment in Europe: a drop in GDP and employers' attempts to rationalize. The surprising vigor of European labor productivity faced with a decline in the GDP probably corresponded to a delayed adjustment of employment to much lower than predicted production levels. The intensification of both national and international competition made it difficult to pass increased costs onto prices and also led to more layoffs.

9. 1983 — Westerly Winds

THE GIANT AWAKENED

WASHINGTON TOOK THE LEAD

The year 1983 was undoubtedly that in which the United States took the lead. The West had the winds in its sails. Inflation was being held in check, and most Western countries made industrial modernization their top priority. Companies had to have the will to invest as well as the financial means. To provide finances, at first, profits had to be maximized at the expense of wages. The problem was how to restore sufficient profit margins without denting household demand, which would have a knock-on effect on investments in some sectors. How could growth be sustained without a too heavy burden on public spending. This were the parameters within which the managers of the leading industrialized countries had to operate.

It is with these questions in mind, that the American recovery must be analyzed. This was the leading event of the year: the recovery had finally arrived. GNP, industrial output, went up, unemployment went down, both unmistakable signs of recovery. Some interpreted this as proof of "hardline" capitalism, which made sure wage earners paid for some of the costs which up till then had charged to companies. A capitalism which had managed to reinvigorate a slumbering economy weakened by years of inflationary expansion.

Is what is good for the United States good for the others? Without doubt the awakening of a giant — the United States represents a quarter of world output — had a knock-on effect. In response to this question, US leaders always pointed out that in

1983 the trade deficit was $70 billion, proof that their economic recovery benefited others.

However many were curious about the effects of the White House's and Fed's budgetary and monetary policies. European countries and others had difficulty accepting the uncontrolled rise in the deficit, which touched a record $200 billion. How long can they put up with the fact that part of the deficit is funded by foreign capital attracted by the high interest rates, which explain the continual rise of the dollar against all other currencies, except the Japanese yen.

Even an ally as faithful to the United States as Margaret Thatcher had to reply negatively. The British prime minister spoke of the "enormous prejudices" that this exodus of capital had caused Great Britain and its European partners. The old world had taken its time renovating its industrial plant and could not reap the benefits of its austerity programs (budgetary, social, in wages). The success against inflation did not compensate for the persistent unemployment, a consequence of the industrial modernization, which job creation schemes cannot dent.

PROFITS SURGED

In many areas the US economy led the field, as well as defying economic logic. The rising dollar, which many thought overvalued, made life very difficult for US producers, who face stiff competition at home from Japanese and European exporters. However the United States has the highest profits.

The dollar continued to rise even though the balance of payments and the balance of trade both showed record deficits (more than $40 billion for the former and more than $10 billion for the latter in 1983). Interest rates remained high in relation to the slowdown in the rise in prices (a bit more than 3 percent for the year) and proved no more than the overvaluation of the dollar an obstacle to a recovery, which since November 1982 was surprisingly vigorous.

In some ways, the rise in the dollar is more like a long fever than a show of strength. Constrained and forced by the aftershock of previous excesses, mainly in credits, the world economy, of which the United States was one of the leading components, was involved in an enormous process of readjustment. Few governments were capable of cushioning the cost to their people. The United States had taken a massive lead in this process.

BUDGETARY CHAOS
AND EXCESSIVE PUBLIC SPENDING

During the presidential campaign, Reagan had promised that by 1984 the budget would be balanced. Following the measures taken during his first term of office up to 30 September 1983, the deficit was higher than ever: $196 billion almost double the level predicted by official experts a few months previously. Worse still: Reagan was up in arms against state intervention and the proliferation of public spending. Since his arrival in the White House, the taxation bill (taxes to fund the budget, social security and pensions) had increased enormously. From 23 percent in 1980, the percentage would pass the 25 percent mark in 1984, according to the forecast.

GROWTH UP

The American president had promised a return to economic prosperity and price stability and in these areas he was more fortunate. He almost kept his promise. The growth rate was higher than it would normally have been at this stage of the recovery: the takeoff was slow (2.5 percent growth in the first quarter) but in the second quarter the growth rate approached 10 percent. Was this a leap in the dark? Many economists were afraid of this, mindful of the failed recovery of spring and summer 1980.

During the third quarter Americans began to believe in the recovery: the growth rate was assessed at an annual rate of 7.6 percent. During the fourth quarter the growth rate was maintained but at a slightly reduced rate of 5 percent. Both the automotive industry and construction took off, having shaken off the preceding years' effects of the spiraling interest rates. They were important in employment terms as well as sales figures.

A WORLD OF CONTRASTS

Strong in North America, uncertain in Europe, the 1983 recovery occurred for many reasons and had varying effects. Industrial output, which had dropped on average by 5 percent in 1982, rose by 3.5 percent in the seven most important industrialized countries of the OECD (the United States, Japan, West Germany, France, Great Britain, Italy, Canada). This global improvement hid great disparities because the US 6 percent growth rate is balanced by a contraction of 4.6 percent in Italy.

* Only the motor of the world recovery, the United States ended the year strongly. The forward impulse came from household spending, helped along by improved employment conditions, and a drop in savings rate. This was the opposite of what happened in Japan, where demand at home petered out but was more than compensated for by increasing sales abroad, which allowed industrial output to grow monthly. To get back on a even keel, and sustain demand at home, Tokyo announced various budgetary measures (financing of housing, public works) on 21 October.

* On the contrary in West Germany and Great Britain increasing private consumption led to a business boom. In West Germany, this went up for the first time in three years, despite a drop in salaries and wages and a stagnation in social spending (notably welfare payments). The quasi-stability of prices in relation to consumption in the first months of the year led to a small increase in the real income of households; but, more importantly, there was a severe drop in the savings rate. Kept up during the first quarter, demand at home dropped off at the end of the year, the balance was maintained by the recovery of other markets in foreign trade.

EMPLOYMENT: A SIGN OF STRENGTH
IN THE UNITED STATES, WEAKNESS IN OTHERS

The year was notable for the sudden deceleration in unemployment in the United States during the fourth quarter, which confirmed the beneficial effects of the recovery on employment. In December 1982 unemployment had hit a record level since World War II of 10.8 percent of the working population and 12 million people were out of work.

Since then the decline had begun slowly with a drop of 0.1 percent during the first quarter, then it had accelerated after July. There was the extraordinary phenomenon of the levels of manpower rising and the number of unemployed regressing; in August 9.5 percent of the working population is unemployed and there are 10.7 million unemployed, but in October 8.8 percent of the working population and 9.9 million unemployed, partially explained by the number of young people going back to school. By the end of November there were 9.4 million unemployed and at 8.4 percent of the working population, it had hit the lowest level since November 1981.

With the exception of Canada, whose economy was strongly bound up with the United States, unemployment worsened the world over. According to the OECD the 32 million unemployed registered in 1982 in the 24 countries of the organization, rose to nearly 33 million in 1983. At the end of the first half, 9.1 percent of the working population was affected, as opposed to 8.4 percent in 1982, since the OECD estimated there were 328 million in work. No country was spared, not even Japan, which was still performing strongly. As far as the OECD was concerned, Europe had the most severe problems with unemployment going from 16 to 18 million, that is 9.5 to 10.5 percent of the working population.

Except for France, where the stability of the employment figure was due to its social handling over several months, all other European countries had a more or less rapid increase in unemployment.

WORLD TRADE SEIZED UP

In 1983 world trade grew feebly, after having weakened in 1982. In monetary terms trade was upheld by an increase in the dollar's value but still represented $1,850 billion, that is 6 percent less than in 1981. For GATT, the recovery of world trade, which accompanied the slight international economic takeoff, risked running off the rails because of problems in the commercial and financial system: many developing countries were deeply in debt, many Western countries were in dire straits trying to fund their budget deficits. GATT also criticized protectionist policies.

Nonetheless, according to the UN's Economic Commission for Europe, world trade could increase by 4 percent in 1984 to reach $1,940 billion, while the price of trade relations could rise by 4 percent.

The Industrialized Countries' Thaw

The thaw in world trade was attributable to trade between industrialized countries — led by the American recovery — which according to the OECD experts, increased by 5 percent (it had stood still in 1982). The 24 OECD countries exports grew by 2 percent (by 4 percent for manufactured goods), while sales of OECD goods to the rest of the world shrank by 2.5 percent (in 1982 it shrank by 5 percent).

By contrast, the rest of the world's exports diminished by 2 percent (for OPEC countries the drop was of 8 percent, for developing countries there was a rise of 4 percent, for other countries exports stood still). In 1982 exports had decreased by 8.5 percent. Imports also dropped by 3 percent (a drop of 8 percent for OPEC countries, 1 percent for developing countries, and 3 percent for others). Imports in 1982 had also dropped by 3 percent.

World trade seized up: from 1963 to 1973 world trade had increase by an average of 9 percent annually, more quickly than international output (which grew by 6 percent). This gap was reduced until it disappeared in 1982, output had also dropped by 2 percent that year. Trade was no longer on an upward curve.

10. 1984 — Drifting

SUCCESS IN NORTH AMERICA,
UNEASE IN EUROPE

THE UNITED STATES SET THE PACE

It was the United States that led the recovery, even more than in the previous year. It enjoyed a growth rate of 6.7 percent, reduced inflation, increased industrial output, as well as more ominously a huge budget and trade deficits, the high unit costs of wages, and 35 million living in poverty. It did not matter that Reagan's conservatism had been transformed into Keynesianism, with a consumer-led recovery — mainly in cars and housing — financed by deficits and stimulated by the deceleration of prices and a tax-cutting program since 1981. There was real growth. With the increasing profitability of companies, the United States was again a safe haven. These factors helped the external financing of the economy and the vigor of the dollar.

In two years six million jobs were created, mainly in the service sector. Despite reservations about these jobs, which were often part-time and unskilled, causing the unemployment rate to drop to 7.2 percent of the working population, comparisons with the old world did not reflect well on the latter. Europe lagged behind in employment, lacking flexibility — the in word in 1984. In spite of costly and ambitious policies, all European countries, except West Germany and Luxembourg, had more than 10 percent unemployed.

Pulled along by the United States, the recovery was marked by rapid expansion, the strongest since 1976 (an average of 4.9

percent growth in OECD countries), almost without inflation, and a net increase in world trade. Nonetheless the increase in US imports benefited Japan and Southeast Asia more than Europe and the Third World. Japan (5 percent growth) and the newly industrialized countries of Asia — from South Korea to Singapore — with enviable growth rates (of the order of 8 percent), enjoyed the benefits of their lower wage costs, which increased their competitive edge.

By contrast, the rest of the world was getting bogged down: Europe enjoyed feeble growth (2.2 percent in the EEC); Latin America had $350 billion in debts and was constrained by IMF rules; while Africa suffered from massive population increases, industrial stagnation, and an unprecedented drought.

TECHNOLOGICAL BACKWARDNESS?

It was not the first time the Europeans had the feeling of being left behind by their American, or more recently Japanese, competitors. Europe's backwardness was blamed for allowing a gap to develop with the supposedly superior industrial and technological capabilities of the United States and Japan. At the end of the 1960s the theory of a gap had been brought up, but it was followed by a new phase in economic history, characterized by the relative decline in American power in terms of industry, money (continual devaluations of the dollar, then downward floating), politics (Vietnam, Watergate and their consequences), and even technology (in comparison with the Soviet Union in armaments and with Japan in consumer goods). The argument did not hold water especially since technicians and academics had not analyzed this rather vague concept of technological backwardness.

Any explanation lay in the realm of economics and finances. Since 1982 the United States had definitely forged ahead compared to the Western European countries, whose growth had been two to three times slower, and Japan, whose progress had been 5 percent in 1984 (about 6.7 percent in the United States), almost half that of the years before the 1974-75 recession. Hi-tech was very risky and American financial structures seemed the best adapted to nurture it, rather than those of countries with huge public sectors, where hard times meant the meager resources were spent bailing out companies in difficulty.

THE 1980S WERE THE OPPOSITE OF THE 1970S

In many respects this was the case. If one had to highlight two dates to show this, the first would be October 1979 showing the United States' great importance: the new president of Federal Reserve System reversed the easy money policy by raising interest rates to the level dictated by national and international demand for credit. The other would be August 1982, when Mexico announced it could not meet its debt repayments. Since that time banks stopped looking for other clients and were mainly concerned with increasing their assets.

Some banks which had been heavily engaged in loss-making activities (for example, oil) became the victims of the sudden massive withdrawal of money by the depositors. No one had anticipated that this would happen in this day and age. The Continental Illinois of Chicago was the most spectacular of these bankruptcies, which involved a massive rescue operation by the federal authorities as large as the one necessary to save Brazil or Mexico. As for the numerous debtors, they tried to improve their balance sheets, which led many companies to postpone investments and lay off part of their workforce. Even in the prosperous United States, the level of bankruptcies was well above average.

Disinflation was the more or less inevitable outcome of the accumulation of debt from the previous decade. This did not prevent some debtors, such as the richest countries, from borrowing enormous sums. Great importance was attached to the financing of the considerable American budget and balance of payments deficits. The conditions in which they operated had completely changed and their effects were likewise opposite.

In the 1960s, the dollar was already overvalued (this allowed Americans to buy up European companies) and the US balance of payments was in deficit, but the central banks of West Germany, France, Great Britain, the Netherlands, Switzerland, and Japan supported the American currency by buying back from commercial banks huge numbers of dollars, which were accumulated as reserves. This buying back gave the commercial banks great liquidity which they used to extend credit, a highly inflationary process, since it emanated from paying off the American deficit by the European and Japanese banks of issue, or the creation of money from nothing.

THE DISAPPEARANCE OF SAVINGS

Today only private investors — institutional or individual — buy shares (or bonds) in the American National debt, something the American Treasury almost made official when in fall it organized a bond auction for non-residents. The system stopped contributing to inflation, because the deficit was financed by a massive influx of American and foreign savings, but it was deflationary for the rest of world which lost capital. In 1984 almost $90 billion flooded into the United States, which did not escape the inflationary consequences. The dollar was overvalued (imports were relatively cheap) so there was a trade imbalance. Yet again, but in very different circumstances, the results of this process were perverse, because one day investors would lose confidence in a manifestly overvalued dollar.

There were other harmful consequences: the overvaluation of the dollar exacerbated protectionist tendencies in the United States on several occasions in 1984, without providing any relief to the countries whose currency was undervalued (Europe, Japan), given the more or less powerful deflationary pressures operating there.

As well as the malfunctioning of the new monetary and financial system, there were structural differences which operated to Europe's disadvantage. The American economy was more supple and adaptable, which helped employment (fewer rules and regulations, wages more in tune with economic cycles, except in the very large companies) as well as hi-tech industry. It was up to the European countries to change. American flexibility had existed before Reagan came to power, but his deregulationary policies heightened it or reintroduced it to areas where it was lacking.

UPWARD MOVEMENTS

The United States' growth spurt in the fist half of the year had a widespread influence on the rest of the world. The American Gross National Product (GNP) increased in volume by 8.3 percent in the first quarter and 3.7 percent in the second. This spurt — 6.8 percent in all — boosted the 24 OECD countries' growth rate to 4.7 percent, compared with 2.7 percent the previous year (a drop of 0.3 percent in 1982), the biggest increase for eight years (in 1976 there had been a 4.8 percent rise). The industrialized countries could only benefit from the American surge. It is thought that the European Economic Community (EEC) countries' GNP rose by 0.7 percent thanks to American vitality. Between the second quarter of 1983 and the first quarter of 1984, American imports from the EEC rose by 32 percent.

THE DOLLAR'S RISING STAR

In 1984, as it had done in 1983, 1982, and 1981, the dollar was the darling of the foreign exchange markets. In Paris and Frankfurt, it rose by 14 percent, in London by 12 percent, and in Tokyo by 7 percent. At first the promise of greater returns on the dollar helped its rise. During the first quarter of 1984 interest rates rose in the United States, going from 10 to nearly 13 percent on the Eurodollar in six months, the reference point for Eurocredits, and from 11 to 13 percent on the American banks' base rate.

But in a marked change from previous years, the "rate effect" could no longer be the only explanation for the dollar's rise, which persisted even when American rates began to drop. Other factors were keeping the dollar high. The first explanation was the multinationals' demand for currency for their international business. This demand had always been strong and it increased regularly. Another explanation was the American Treasury's loans to finance the budget deficit. These loans were heavily subscribed (up to $90 billion so they say) by foreign holders of capital, who had to buy dollars. This was particularly true of Latin America, which had to buy massive holdings in dollars to pay off interest, since it could not pay off any of the capital.

Also, as Emile Van Lennep, the secretary general of the OECD until the end of 1984, pointed out, the dollar was strong because it made sense to invest in a highly profitable economy. As long as the market thought there was more money to be made in the United States than in Europe or Japan, people would buy dollars to invest there. However the prospect of a fall in the dollar was a specter at the feast all year long.

WORLD TRADE WAS STIMULATED

There was a strong showing in international trade: GATT experts thought it grew by at least 8 percent in 1984. World trade had grown by 2 percent in 1983, after having dropped by 3 percent in 1982, and stagnated in 1981. To find a higher increase, you have to go back to the 11 percent rise in 1976. From January to September 1984, according to the latest figures from GATT, world trade enjoyed an 8.5 percent increase at constant prices, compared with the same period in 1983. According to the authorities in Geneva, "the vigorous recovery in the United States was the principal, if only, driving force." Thus in the first nine months of the year the value of American imports exceeded by a third that of the same period in 1983. It was the biggest growth rate the United States had recorded for 30 years. Taking into account the United States' pull as well as greater demand in West Germany and Japan, the industrialized countries' imports rose by 11 percent between January and September 1984, according to the IMF.

CONFIRMED DISINFLATION

The industrialized countries were keen on disinflation just as they had been on price increases in the 1970s. The leading countries (the United States, Japan, West Germany, France, Great Britain, Italy, and Canada), which between them accounted for 85 percent of OECD output, saw inflation drop from 10 percent in 1981 to 4.6 percent in 1983. From September 1983 to September 1984, the seven countries recorded a 4.3 percent increase in prices.

It was possible they might fall back to the 1960s levels, when the average rate was 3.2 percent (1961-70).

All the disinflation elements were in place: the commodities' markets were depressed, and the oil market was heading downward in the last days of 1984. The OPEC countries met at Geneva, near Christmas, and failed to find a way to stop the decline of the oil prices on the open market. The OECD experts based all their projections on the hypothesis that oil prices, in dollars, would remain unchanged until 1986. Of course the different exchange rates from country to country might modify this. Also, apart from the United States, most countries had managed to balance their budget deficits within the limits they had set themselves. Disinflationary policies required the tightening up of finances.

THE WAGE-PRICE SPIRAL WAS BROKEN

The determining elements were still wages and the unit costs of production. In the G7 countries the unit costs of production had dropped markedly in 1982, and had barely moved in 1984 (up 0.25 percent). The OECD noted "You have to go back to 1959 before finding a period of such stability." Increases in hourly rates in industry remained at a low level, and in fact were not as high as in 1983 (7.1 percent in that year compared with an average of 6.4 percent in 1984). The growth in output and productivity led to a quasi-stability in unit costs of workers in the manufacturing industries and allowed companies to adjust their accounts and not to increase their production prices too much.

Finally, fear of unemployment made it more difficult to make excessive wage demands. Since 1980, the "Phillips law" has been in force: wage increases decrease in relation to the increase in unemployment. By the end of 1984, this was still valid. Yet the OECD reported "On the other hand any new drop in inflation risks being slowed down if the effects of high levels of unemployment on wages were neutralized by a growing segmentation of the labor market or an increase in profits." This did not happen in 1984, when wage demands continued to be restrained. Trade unions adapted their thinking and strategy to the situation. In the United

States automotive workers preferred security of employment and better training facilities to nominally high increases in wages.

UNEMPLOYMENT: OPINIONS CHANGED

* Employment: the European paradox. The relation between employment and production showed the specificity of European developments, which deteriorated despite the various economic policies followed. In fact on the whole they were similar and either made employment a secondary priority or the result of reforms in other areas. According to the OECD "as the working population continued to grow in Europe, unemployment also increased, reaching a record high of 10.9 percent (18.7 million) during the first quarter of 1984." The increase in the number of jobs remained the same despite increases in production and of "a new drop in the real costs of labor in relation to productivity."

Europe continued its forced march into renewed competitiveness through industrial restructuring and plant modernization. It slowly moved to the point where it could compete with other continents. However, its backwardness was such that it has an "atypical profile" in that increases in productivity were "exceptionally well maintained given the weak growth in production" which led to more redundancies and improved profit margins. As long as the economic recovery was weak, unemployment could only get worse. Especially if, as was the case, investments were aimed "at acquiring capital rather than creating jobs."

* Employment: the fascinating American model. In the OECD countries unemployment fell from 32.4 million in 1983 to 31.2 million, that is 9 percent of the working population to 8.5 percent. But there were many discrepancies: the United States made the most difference by reducing its unemployment rate in November 1984 to 7.2 percent, while Japan's rate stagnated, and Europe's declined. This accounted for the fascination exercised by the American model and the sudden conversion to conservatism in many countries: the rediscovery of the need for flexibility supplanted the older idea of a reduction in working hours in many people's minds.

Unemployment had hit 10.7 percent of the American people in November 1982, at the lowest point in the recession, so the recovery in 1983 breathed new life in the labor market, which continued in 1984 though to a lesser extent. Observers almost failed to notice that the downward trend had petered out and that the number of unemployed had not returned to the traditional American rates of 5 or 6 percent.

The number of jobs created in such a short period of time was awe-inspiring. In its annual report on Perspectives on Employment, the OECD noted that, referring to its 1983 predictions that member countries had to create 20,000 new jobs every day for five years (1984-89) in order to get back to the 1979 position, that is 19 million unemployed, only the United States had improved on this rate, Japan had only just managed it, and Europe had fallen well short. The United States had created nearly six million new jobs in 18 months. In December 1982 there were 88.7 million working in the non-agricultural sector compared with 94.5 million in August 1984; but then 91.5 million had had jobs in July 1981. Supple, mobile, able to adapt, the American economy had changed since more than half the new jobs were in services. This led some commentators to say that the healthy job market was the result of addiction to fast food and the need for security and janitors (there would be 900,000 more from now until 1990).

The manufacturing sector had lost more jobs than it created and had been gradually losing its importance. In 1983 it had made up 21 percent of jobs, as opposed to 24 percent in 1975 and 30 percent in 1960. The industrial restructuring had seen to that: but this did not prevent the American economy from improving its productivity in the private non-agricultural sector by 3.5 percent, at a slightly lower level than in 1975 (5.2 percent) and 1961 (5.4 percent). The growing importance of the services sector was behind this, as well as reduced working hours because of the increasing number of part-time jobs.

Some Americans would act as a safety valve, allowing industry to hire and fire according to the economic climate. Many Americans would not be affected by these ups and downs, according to the OECD which stated, that most wage earners in the

United States had been in their jobs for 14 years as opposed to 17 years in Europe and 21 years in Japan. The number of those living below the poverty line had also grown, to the point, that a few weeks before the presidential elections, the US episcopate made an urgent claim on behalf of the 35 million poor people living in the country.

11. 1985 — The Interval

THE RECOVERY SET IN AND NEW STABILITY

THE ECONOMIES CONVERGED

Did the Western countries' economic recovery set in as most international experts predicted? In 1985, for the third consecutive year, the 24 OECD countries enjoyed an increase in their Gross National Products (GNPs). Also, in contrast to the preceding period of growth (1976-81), this was accompanied — even preceded by since 1981 — a slowdown in inflation. The difference between European and the US performance indicators had more or less disappeared. On both sides of the Atlantic GNP had increased by about 2.5 percent, while Japan only slowed down marginally.

The convergence of the Western economies, beneficial in that it can reduce monetary tension and trade imbalances, came at the lower end of the scale. On average growth rates went from 4.7 in 1984 to 3 percent in 1985 — the total GNP had increased by 2.7 percent in 1983, after having diminished by 0.3 percent in 1982. The slowdown in the American economy from 6.8 percent to 2.4 percent accounted for the slight decrease in growth rate. After the spurt in 1984, the best year on record since 1973 (6.1 percent growth), there was a breathing space. According to the OECD economists "it is possible that more prudent policies have allowed a `soft landing' after a period of rapid recovery, easing the way for more balanced and lasting growth."

After the two oil shocks in 1973 and 1979, the need for adjustment became increasingly necessary. The European economies were trying to become more flexible, while individual behavior had also changed, putting greater value on suppleness. There was a bit of a thaw, accompanied by a wind of conservatism.

Thus Europe recovered its strength. The old world, which in 1984 seemed to be floundering before a triumphant United States and a dazzling Japan, had in some ways got a grip on itself. Aware of the technological backwardness, especially in hi-tech, the Europeans launched, at France's instigation, the Eureka project for technological cooperation. In November its charter was drawn up and several projects approved.

THREE IMPORTANT DECISIONS FOR THE FUTURE

Three decisions, taken at the end of 1985, would be important in 1986. On 22 September the finance ministers of the five leading industrialized countries (the United States, Japan, West Germany, France, and Great Britain), met in New York and decided to lower the dollar's value, using their central banks. The dollar, which had hit 10.61 francs at the end of February, fell back to 7.56 at the end of December.

On 11 October, at Seoul, at the IMF and the World Bank general assembly the American Treasury Secretary James Baker put forward a plan. He advocated an increase in the commercial banks' loans to 15 countries, whose default on payments would particularly endanger the world financial system, as well as an increase in the level of the IMF's and World Bank's operations. In exchange for this infusion of capital, which would allow debtor countries to expand, they had to agree to austerity policies.

The US budget deficit continued to be Congress' preoccupation and on 11 December it voted for the Gramm-Rudman law, which stated the budget had to be balanced by 1991. Since the United States imported more than $50 billion of oil, a drop in oil prices would reduce that bill, as well as contributing to the downward movement of prices. Thus, twice within the space of a month, the Americans had set aside the virtues of market forces as a way of solving economic imbalances and rediscovered the pragmatism of intervention. In any case, for the first time in ten years, the leading currencies were no longer completely at the mercy of the money market or speculation. This was a step in the right direction.

So was the Baker plan, even if did not lay down rules on the Third World's massive debt problem and left some people skeptical. It had been introduced after a new Mexican panic, a Nigerian one, and several cases of arguments between the IMF and debtor countries, like Argentina. A new drop in oil or commodity prices, a gift of some $70 billion from poor to rich countries, threatened to worsen the situation for several countries.

THE DOLLAR: A CONTROLLED FALL

After four years at the top, in perpetual ascent, king dollar if not actually dethroned was at least strongly challenged and shook up in 1985. It fell by almost 20 percent in relation to all the other currencies, whereas in the previous year it had risen by 14 percent in Paris and Frankfurt, 12 percent in London, and 7 percent in Tokyo. The factors behind this movement included the slowdown in growth and the drop in US interest rates which made it a less attractive prospect to foreign capital seeking lucrative and reliable investments, such as, American treasury loans destined to cover the budget deficit. There was also the persistence of that deficit as well as the growing negative balance of payments and trade balance. Moreover, at the beginning of fall, the five most industrialized countries' (United States, West Germany, France, Great Britain, and Japan) concerted action to bring the dollar down was highly effective: in three months it fell by 12 percent.

THE TURNING POINT ON DEBT

The fact that the two most important Third World countries, Mexico and Brazil, were unable in 1985 to effect the austerity programs dictated by the IMF had the most profound implications on the crisis. The Mexican failure had the most impact, because during the previous two years, against all expectations, Mexico had been heralded by the international financial organizations and the

United States as a model debtor, an inspiration for the other debtor nations.

Many other countries (Peru, Zaire, Ghana, etc.) were a source of disappointment. The growing skepticism aroused by the IMF's tactics was reinforced rather than diminished by the first, spectacular results achieved in Argentina by President Raul Alfonsin and his brilliant team of economists, who introduced on June 14 wide-ranging monetary reforms. This policy was a frontal attack on inflation (which stood at a 3,000 percent annual rate) and went against the gradualist approach recommended by the experts. Juan Sourrouille, the minister of economics, was the plan's architect, and he had to convince the IMF of its merits. Argentina needed the IMF's signature to get the banks' agreement to reschedule $14 billion of foreign debt out of a total of $50 billion and to obtain a credit of a further $42 billion. The announcement of these new credits, a sign of confidence from the international financial community, was necessary to ease the launch of the reforms (which involved the substitution of the austral for the peso).

It was a combination of circumstances the led Reagan's government to change tactics during his first term. The president and his team seemed to be guided in their Third World policy by the adage "help yourself and God will help you." James Baker presented a plan to the general assembly of the IMF and World Bank, which would bear his name. The plan was a declaration of intent and contained: firstly, an appeal to commercial banks to increase during the next three years by $20 billion help to 15 particularly hard hit countries (ten Latin American countries, the Philippines, Nigeria, Morocco, Yugoslavia, and the Ivory Coast); secondly, an increase of 50 percent (from $6 to 9 billion) during the same period of loans agreed to by the World Bank and by other specialized institutions (the Inter-American Bank for Development, etc.) as long-term credits; thirdly, the exhortation to the recipient countries that they put their house in order to stop the flight of capital.

At the same time, Baker let it be understood that the United States would lift its opposition to any substantial increase in the World Bank's capital in the year to come. This made for a better atmosphere. The treasury secretary imposed one condition: Washington would only agree if the World Bank maintained the quality of its balance sheet in between time — a rather difficult task.

WORLD TRADE SLOWED DOWN

There was a sudden about turn: after having grown by 9.5 percent in volume in 1984, world trade grew by well under 3 percent, according to the experts in the GATT secretariat. This was a similar rate to that recorded in 1983. Since World War II international trade has dropped three times: in 1982 (down 3 percent), in 1975 (also down 3 percent), and in 1958 (down 1 percent). However there was record growth in 1976 (up 11 percent). Generally the rise in trade accompanied and stimulated — or even preceded — an expansion in production. Thus from 1963 to 1973 world exports had risen by an annual average of 9 percent, while total production had only risen by 6 percent. Trade pulled growth along. During the decade the gap between the two dropped to the point of disappearing: from 1973 to 1983 both trade and production increased by an average of 3 percent annually.

THE MULTIPLIER DIPPED

The capacity of trade to react to the growth of world income dropped. Between 1950 and 1973 any upward movement of 1 percent in income was accompanied by an average growth of 1.6 percent in trade; from 1973 to 1984 the latter rate had dropped a third to 1.1 percent. There was a tendency for trade in a growing number of products (steel, automobiles, household electronic goods, agricultural) to be administered bilaterally.

In any case the 1984 rebound had been pulled along by the United States (business and a strong dollar attracted imports to the United States from the rest of the world), while total production had risen by 5.5 percent. The slowdown in 1985 mainly affected energy — where trade dropped —, but also raw materials. Therefore it hit the OPEC countries and developing countries, which saw a big downturn in the commodity trade.

Trade in manufactured goods also suffered. According to the OECD experts, its members' exports in this area rose by 5.5 percent in 1985, compared with 10 percent in 1984, while their imports grew by 7.5 percent instead of 15 percent. Globally trade in manufactured goods rose by 5.5 as opposed to 11 percent.

UNEMPLOYMENT SEEMED INCOMPRESSIBLE

In 1985 economic policies seemed to have reached their limit in the fight against unemployment. No country achieved any significant results or could serve as a model. Even Reagan's United States, which had seen spectacular successes the previous year, was unable to repeat that performance. It seemed that all the developed countries were suffering to a greater or lesser extent from the same sort of symptoms, if not identical ones. The labor market had split into several distinct categories. On the one hand there were jobs within competing industries, and on the other jobs for the home market.

In the important industrialized countries, budget policies were still on a tight rein, because there were notable imbalances and also because of the general move away from state intervention. However it was difficult for governments to maintain their austerity plans. On the spending front, the first wave of cuts had been favorably received by public opinion because it hit government expenditure and was aimed at slowing down increases in welfare payments. However in 1985 several subsidized sectors and the foundations of social protection were under threat. In terms of revenue, conservative dogma required a lightening of the tax burden and of social charges to stimulate investments and job creation. But the slowdown in growth since the beginning of 1985, especially in the United States and Japan, hit taxation and led to increased spending. There was also the temptation to relax restraints to help business. Forthcoming elections in the West Germany and Great Britain produced some relaxation. In the United States, and even more so in Italy, there was a degree of laxness. Only Japan persisted in trying to improve its public accounts, despite the policies pursued by its partners.

DISINFLATION AND DEINDEXATION

Economic historians will probably point to the 1980s as a time of disinflation. After having suffered large price increases almost to the point of making them part of their development, the industrialized countries decided to change tack because inflation led to massive imbalances

THE FIRST CRISIS LED TO LAXNESS, THE SECOND TO AUSTERITY

Most countries responded to the second oil shock of 1979, having learned the lessons of their prior laxness following the first oil shock of 1973. In 1974, the price increases had hit 24.5 percent in Japan, 11 percent in the United States, 7 percent in West Germany, 13.7 percent in France, 16 percent in Great Britain, and 19 percent in Italy. The seven leading OECD countries (the United States, Canada, Japan, West Germany, France, Great Britain, and Italy), which produced 80 percent of the OECD total GNP, the price index had risen by 13.3 percent, to drop back to 9.3 percent in 1979. The oil price had gone from $13 per barrel in early 1979 to nearly $34 in early 1983 and it seemed the mistakes of 1974 would be repeated. This did not happen. The inflation rate, which for these same countries had risen to 12.2 percent in 1980, dropped back to 4.6 percent three years later (3.9 percent in 1984 and 3.5 percent in 1985. This general slowdown, which was staggered in different countries, was greatly helped by a marked drop in raw materials' prices (apart from oil), as well as a slowdown in the nominal wage rises which sometimes led to reduced purchasing power.

In 1985 the OECD noted that wages moderation had led to the lasting modification of wage bargaining "particularly over indexation clauses and attitudes to traditional differentials in wages." The OECD cites the United States as an example, where wage rises, agreed by the unions in 1984, were the smallest for 17 years. Almost a quarter of US wage earners accepted a reduction in wages or a freeze. The ever-present fear of unemployment, which continued to be high, mainly in Europe, meant wage demands were moderate. Most governments made the most of this and put in place mechanisms designed to destroy the wages-prices inflationary spiral. The principles of indexation in determining wages were questioned.

It was unlikely that economic growth would ever occur again alongside the anarchic leaps in prices and wages of the 1970s. But this possibility has not been eliminated either. The industrialized countries had to do something about unemployment and diminish the effects of recession. Would they be able to prevent the overbidding for wages, when employment began to improve and purchasing power started to rise again? In 1985 it seemed that very little was required to unleash wage demands, which would rise up at the earliest opportunity.

12. 1986 — Counterattack

ANXIETIES AND IMBALANCES

DOLLAR AND OIL DROPPED

The slowdown in growth in 1986 awakened people's fears of a recession. There were enough imbalances to make one anxious: the American budget and trade deficits, the Japanese and German surpluses, and the massive indebtedness of the United States and many Third World countries. Nonetheless Finance Ministers still saw inflation as the number one enemy, while the rise of prices compared with consumption fell to 2 percent in the G7 countries, its lowest level for 21 years. Unable to coordinate their policies, they refused to stimulate growth and chose the wrong war. The monetary and oil "counterattacks" did not have the anticipated effects. The year 1986 had started rather well. The September 22, 1985 agreement signed at the Plaza Hotel in New York by the finance ministers of the United States, Japan, West Germany, France, and Great Britain had opened the way for the dollar's "soft landing," and reductions in imbalances.

According to the world's economics institutions, the drop in oil prices should have helped reduce inflation and stimulate growth in the industrialized countries. By offering new credits to the most indebted countries as long as they effected austerity programs, the Baker plan offered the hope of a solution to the world debt problem, which threatened the financial system. However it did not lead to the expected outcome. The dollar dropped in value, losing a further 10 percent against the leading currencies to reach a level 35 percent lower than that of February-March 1985. But the volume of American exports remained unchanged, while imports continued to rise. The US trade balance hit an all-time high with a $170 billion deficit. There were strong protectionist pressures resulting from the West German and Japanese record surpluses. These pressures were not allayed by the new round of talks on the removal of trade barriers, especially in services, held at Punta del Este in Uruguay.

The drop in oil prices, the result of OPEC's attempts to regain its market share (a strategy whose immediate failure cost Sheikh Yamani his job), was more dramatic than predicted. The price of a barrel had stood at $30 but fell to $10, before ending the year at $17. But the savings the oil-importing countries made on their oil bills, at the time called a bonanza, which was supposed to stimulate economic activity, proved volatile. The oil-producing countries adjusted their spending to well within their income and cut back on their imports of manufactured goods. Other Third World countries followed suit since they were also affected by falling demand for commodities.

A TIME BOMB

One of the consequences was that developing countries saw a 3 percent drop in their global GNP because of the worsening terms of trade, and they could not avail themselves of the private sources of finance of the Baker plan. Thus Mexico, which had been the first to shake up the international financial system in 1982, found itself facing disaster again in 1986. Accumulated during a time of inflation, the debt time bomb threatened the world economy, ready to be detonated by a recession. Many economists predicted that only a real recession would rectify the American trade balance....

So there was no upturn in demand, one of the supposed results of the drop in oil prices and the drop in interest rates, started at the beginning of the year but only kept up by the United States. Individuals preferred to save and companies preferred to remain in debt rather than invest. The optimists maintained that growth was holding up, for the 50th consecutive month in the United States, that is the longest period since the war, but it was low: 2.5 percent against an average of 3 percent in the OECD in 1985 and 4.7 percent in 1984.

In any case it did not allow Europe to solve the painful problem of unemployment. In global terms the old world had created one and a half million new jobs but this was more than matched by the growing population, so the unemployment rate remained the same. The only good news was that the proportion of unemployed under the age of 25 was declining, except in Japan.

"RAIDERS" AND FINANCIERS: THE NEW WINNERS

Against this backdrop of economic and social depression, finance was prospering. Especially in the Latin countries: in Madrid the stock market rose by 105 percent, in Paris 57 percent, in Milan 55 percent; but also in Tokyo 51.5 percent, even Wall Street 24 percent, where Dow Jones recorded its highest mark and single biggest fall on the same day, Thursday September 11. There were also unlikely takeover bids, the deregulation of the markets, the "Big Bang" deregulation in the City of London, and the large fines on "insider dealing" by Ivan Boesky and David Levine. This feverish activity seemed worrying.

In truth companies preferred to use their liquidity to their advantage rather than invest. There were raids on Goodyear, which profited a few financiers, but harmed the industry. The idea gained ground that finance no longer maintained the real economy, the manufacturing of goods, but acted against it. This was a new threat to the financial system.

OPEC CAME TO GRIEF

OPEC had managed to keep oil prices stable for four years but now it came to grief, unleashing a cataclysm which was part and parcel of oil history. Within a few months oil prices dropped by more than half to stabilize at about $15 a barrel, almost 45 percent less than in 1985. Oil prices were back to where they had been in 1974 in real terms.

For four years it had been obvious that prices would have to fall. OPEC, caught between falling consumption and increasing oil production, had been forced to cut back production by a third since 1981 to maintain the market which was under threat of world overproduction. Nonetheless the collapse in oil prices was surprisingly sudden. No one had thought before the historic December 1985 conference that OPEC would do an about turn and abandon all constraints on production unleashing a price war without precedent.

OIL PRICES FROM 1973 TO 1986
A CAUTIOUS DOLLAR AFTER THE PLAZA AGREEMENT

After a four-year reign, king dollar further declined in 1986, losing 21 percent to the Deutschmark, which was back to its 1980 level, and losing 21 percent to the yen which continued to beat all records as it rose. The dollar's decline against the franc was diminished by the franc's devaluation against the Deutschmark and ended as a 16 percent drop. As in the previous year, the dollar's fall was in accordance with the terms of the Plaza agreement, signed in New York, on September 22, 1985 between the world's five most industrialized countries. This agreement included the exceptional decision by the United States to give up "benign neglect" and join forces to bring the dollar down. This policy had been forced on it by the damage inflicted on its industry of four years' uninterrupted rise in the dollar's value, which made imports cheap.

Such a change was decisive and allowed the dollar to fall gradually during the last quarter of 1985, a process which continued in 1986, slowing down in August but increasing after September. From the end of July, in fact, the dollar's fall against the yen ended at the historic rate of 150 yens. In October there followed a rise which was firmed up by an agreement, signed October 31, which stated that both countries thought the dollar and yen had reached "a level compatible with the evolution of fundamental economic parameters." This meant the dollar fall in Tokyo had ended, which was immediately translated into a slight increase in the US currency to 160-165 yens, a level it maintained until the end of 1986.

WEAK WORLD GROWTH

Promises were not kept. After waiting for the favorable effects of the oil price drop, the drop in the dollar, and interest rates, economists had to acknowledge that they were more than offset by the deflationary downward trends of the increasing yen, the economic setback in the United States, the problems of oil-exporting countries, and the persistent difficulties of indebted nations.

The fourth year of world growth proved mediocre, 2.5 percent in the OECD as opposed to 3 percent in 1985, postponing again any improvement in unemployment which still affected 31 million people at the end of 1986 in the Western industrialized countries. This result came at a time of quasi-general budget austerity. The drop in the price of a barrel of oil backed up the previous year's progress and stifled inflationary tensions: 4.5 percent inflation rate for OECD countries, price rises fell to 2.7 percent in 1986. Even if the effects were very slow a coming, the anticipated kickstart from the drop in oil prices began to reverberate and persisted for several months.

In early 1986 economists misjudged governments' as well as companies' reactions. The former sometimes chose to use the drop in oil prices to cut their budget deficit. The latter remained cautious, preferring to gather in the profits rather than invest. Some of this was not new. The industrialized countries knew the fundamental reasons behind the surprisingly fast and widespread cutback in imports by oil-exporting countries, as well as indebted developing countries. The fact that the world had proved unable to manage the debt of more than $1,000 billion, which hung over the Third World and threatened growth, was a potential source of problems.

WORLD TRADE: RELATIVELY DULL

International trade was lackluster. It no longer dragged along at the average annual rate of 0.5 percent, as it had during the 1980-83 period. But the forward leap of 9.5 percent, recorded in 1984, was exceptional. The results for 1986 of 4 percent were a marginal improvement on 1985 with 3.5 percent but according to the OECD experts they lacked vigor. How could it be otherwise, when the world economy underwent such brutal changes as the fall in oil prices and the drop in the dollar.

The gap between the 2 percent rise in OECD exports and the 7.5 percent increase in OECD imports afforded some illumination. All the experts had anticipated a slowdown in industrialized countries' sales to oil-exporting countries, forced to adopt austerity in the face of declining oil receipts. None had anticipated a similar response from the other developing countries. This was what happened: China suddenly tightened up on imports to limit its deficit, while Third World countries, whose indebtedness was aggravated by the drop in demand for raw materials, made few foreign purchases.

MORE ACTIVE ECONOMIC POLICIES

The year 1986 was a turning point in revitalizing budget policies. The neo-conservative doctrine had stressed the virtues of laissez faire and balancing public spending, even if in practice only Switzerland had achieved this. The main threat to the industrialized economies was no longer inflation, but a weakening of growth, deterioration in unemployment, and the inability of developing countries to meet their debts.

Following the most recent drop in interest rates, monetary policies could no longer stimulate growth. Any substantial drop in the central banks' loan conditions in 1987 would dent their credibility and encourage financial speculation. It seemed an opportune moment to loosen budget constraints. This was begun with great caution. Enjoying healthy accounts, West Germany and Japan were best placed to cope with a measured increase in public spending. The United States and Italy, faced with heavy structural deficits, decided to live with their pain rather than risk dangerous surgery.... Only Great Britain seemed attracted by the idea of loosening restraints.

Governments preferred to lighten the tax burden rather than increase public spending, whose immediacy nonetheless appealed to the British cabinet. The almost universal reduction in direct taxation had the merits of being conservative and seem like a recompense for previous sacrifices. Selling off public assets was used to cushion the budget: rather unorthodox, but welcome to hide the break in monetary rigor.

13. 1987 — Crash

A BRUTAL FINANCIAL SHAKEUP

A HISTORIC YEAR WITH $2,000 BILLION LOSSES

The year 1987 was one for the history books. Characterized by the worst slump since the beginning of the century, it was bad in every respect. The stock market crash affected every stock market. After hitting New York, the aftershocks spread at lightning speed, demonstrating the interconnectedness of the world markets. Globally world stock market capitalization shrank by $2,000 billion, half of this on Wall Street.

THE TRIGGER

There was no doubt about what set off the crash: the increase in West Germany's Bundesbank's interest rates and the announcement of a US monthly trade deficit, which was much worse than predicted. These were two well-chosen indicators, since the high cost of borrowing money had been a running sore during the previous months and the US deficit was the weak point of the international economy. The effect was radical: the Dow Jones index lost 508 points (22.8 percent) in one day.

The disaster's causes lay in the massive structural imbalances — commercial and financial — in the industrialized countries. The US record trade deficit in August was not merely a pretext. It was the detonator of a crisis that had been waiting to go off and that computerization aggravated. The rise in US interest rates and

Treasury Secretary James Baker's threat to let the dollar fall did the rest. There were also aggravating factors.

The interdependence of the markets was an asset during good times but at this point it acted like an echo chamber. The sophisticated financial systems and new computers accelerated the fall which the drop in the dollar's value and Baker's ill-timed remarks had already unleashed. The crash was the product of a combination of unusual circumstances, which were numerous and diverse. The resulting cyclone was so overwhelming that most governments dared not intervene. Only the Hong Kong authorities decided to close down the stock market for a week — a radical but ineffective solution. Experience also proved that the free circulation of capital was not pain-free, another consequence of deregulation. New York registered a strong depression.

A PRECIPITATE RETREAT

In many cases to pay off their astronomic debts, US investors clawed back their investments from the European and Asian markets, where they were still ahead, but this literally dried them up. The result of this precipitate retreat was that the old world's stock exchanges were often relatively small, insufficiently prepared and suffered the consequences. The full impact was felt by Frankfurt (down 37 percent in one year), Amsterdam (down 33 percent), Zurich and Milan (down 31 percent), and Paris (down 29.5 percent). However the English-speaking stock markets were so huge they escaped the worst: New York ended the year up 1 percent and London up 10 percent. Thanks to its traditional structures and a sense of national duty, Tokyo emerged unbowed, and it would have been safe to say that without foreign sales, the Japanese stock exchange would have emerged with its best set of results ever.

Looking beyond the year's results, it was clear that the crash and its attendant slump meant the end of an era. After five glorious years, the stock exchange bonanza was over. It was a time of financial engineering. The yuppies (young urban professionals) had become the puppies (poor urban professionals). The golden boys had been replaced by the rocket scientists, the so-called Ivy League graduates who made sound and canny investments.

This new era arrived at the same time as most of the bigger markets were going through upheavals. London had its "big bang," Paris was undergoing more modest reforms, Frankfurt was trying to catch up with modernization. After all in five years' time the 12 European Community countries would be part of a single market. The financial crisis which shook the world had some positive aspects: by stopping the almost suicidal upward movement and imposing a dramatic readjustment, the stock exchanges of the old continent had the opportunity to reorganize itself for the European super-market. In any case there was no longer much choice about which road to follow. In the year 2000 only the fittest would survive in dealings in stocks and shares. The drop in market capitalization would favor transfers and help large predators, who had massive liquidity and intended to use it.

THE DOLLAR DROPPED AGAIN

The year 1987 was marked by a new weakening of the dollar, which occurred in two phases, one at the beginning of the year and one at the end. In between there was a period of relative calm thanks to the Louvre Agreements, signed in February with the aim of securing stability. As in 1986, the US currency dropped in total by 20 percent (21 percent against the yen, and 19 percent against the Deutschmark). In the early part of the year the problem facing the five leading industrialized countries (West Germany, the United States, France, Great Britain, and Japan), seven if you included Canada and Italy, was how to stop the dollar's decline, which had been decided on in the Plaza agreements, and was becoming dangerous.

In January and February 1987, in fact, this drop had accelerated because of dreadful US balance of trade results, the deficit remained considerable despite a 40 percent devaluation in the dollar. After long negotiations the Five signed an agreement on February 22 at the Louvre in Paris, which would put an end to the fall of the dollar, whose fluctuations would be contained within the day's parities, that was, 6.10 francs, 1.82 Deutschmark, and 153 yens. This was in fact a calculated gamble on a drop in the US balance of trade deficit. The United States' partners expected it to reduce its enormous budget deficit.

The agreement worked fairly well thanks to the central banks' intervention, which used $90 billion to stabilize the currency markets, mainly in Tokyo. However, the US currency was under attack from the Japanese themselves, who were frightened by US threats and posturing, and retaliated with customs duties. In the spring, the dollar fell heavily vis-à-vis the yen, beating the 137 yen record drop to climb back. During the summer of 1987, the dollar even managed a spectacular rise on all the markets, fed by fears of further wars in the Persian Gulf and a rise in oil prices. This was short-lived. After September the dollar dropped again. At the end of October this had accelerated following some ill-timed remarks by Baker, who threatened to go back on the Louvre agreement if West Germany continued to increase its interest rates, and then later said he preferred a drop in the dollar to a recession triggered by high interest rates. In the middle of October and December (mid-November was not so bad), there were very poor US foreign trade figures, which had a depressing effect on the dollar, which lost a further 1 or 2 percentage points with every bad result. By the end of the year the dollar had broken all downward records to stand at 1.57 Deutschmarks and 121 yens. Nonetheless in early 1988 there was an upward movement due to the central banks' intervention and the hope of a reduction in the US balance of trade deficit.

MONEY WAS STILL VERY EXPENSIVE

Worldwide interest rates underwent a pendulum swing, in the hope of remedying the trade imbalances and slowing down the drop in the dollar. Thus the United States raised its minimum lending rate for the first time since 1984. Leaving out inflation, real interest rates on the whole reached historic levels worldwide between 4 and 7 percent, the nominal rates remained high even though disinflation continued apace. This seemed worrying to many economists, who feared its depressing effect on investments.

It was true that this period of high interest rates, producing positive results, had followed a long period when rates were lower than inflation and therefore negative, destroying savings.

FRACTURED WORLD TRADE

Within a more and more fractured system where protectionism and bilateral agreements were gaining ground, world trade fared relatively well in 1987 (it grew by 5.7 percent). Exports from the United States and the newly industrialized Asian countries during the first three quarters of the year performed well and helped sustain the level of world trade. This phenomenon partially compensated for the poor performance of oil-exporting countries. The year 1987 confirmed that the system was dangerously fractured. The European Economic Community was the only commercially integrated world organization.

PERSISTENT GROWTH

At the start there had been signs of disillusion, but the year 1987 ended very uncertainly. After a fifth year of weak growth (2.75 percent in 1987, almost the same as in 1986), the OECD countries could expect, barring any major accidents, another grey year in 1988. This outlook meant there was little prospect of any drop in unemployment in the industrialized countries, or that developing countries would find new outlets or an increase in demand for raw materials. This showed that there were still deep imbalances, of which the stock market crash and the fall monetary crisis were merely symptoms.

The stock market losses from the crash would probably lead to a slowdown in growth in 1988: many households and companies would hold back consumption and investments; but even if this was the case, growth could still hold up during most of 1988. At the end of 1987 exports and investments in most industrialized countries helped push consumption along as a motor of demand. So there were glimmers of hope.

HOPE DESPITE THE CRASH

Globally the year 1987 saw unemployment decrease. The most remarkable performances were in the United States and Great Britain. In the United States the unemployment rate dropped to 6 percent. In Great Britain, Margaret Thatcher's conservative policies, which often had drastic social effects, reduced the number of unemployed by 400,000. The iron lady had passed a few hurdles: unemployment was under 3 million, and under the symbolic 10 percent of the working population. There was a negative side to these victories: although the number of unemployed had dropped by more than a million in one year, the jobs available were often unskilled and precarious, mainly in the services sector.

One year was not enough to gauge the magnitude of the changes provoked by the economic crisis and the restructuring of employment in most industrialized countries. The classic model of male, industrial, full-time, secure employment lost further ground amid enormous redistribution of labor. Not surprisingly governments encouraged more and more "small jobs," often temporary and with less security.

The year 1987 allowed most governments, faced with ever-increasing welfare expenditure, to draw up new laws to cut back on their commitments. However it was significant that no state embarked on the wholesale dismantling of social security. In West Germany, the Christian-Democratic government cut back on healthcare benefits by refunding the cost of medicines, but the cheapest ones had to be prescribed. In Canada the government reined in retirement costs by allowing people to retire between 60 and 70. Would other countries follow this example?

Many states made more convincing — even spectacular — attempts to reduce their budget deficits, in line with the Louvre agreement. The United States brought its deficit down to $148 billion, compared with $221 billion in 1986. But since this improvement was due to increased, and in many ways exceptional, receipts, it could prove transitory. With all the industrialized countries facing a budget deficit, the role of the welfare state was under attack. Even the most conservative politicians in power had to hold back on deregulation and could not abandon intervention, even social. This trend went with a drop in union membership, which only spared the Scandinavian countries. The decreasing union influence was accompanied by fewer industrial disputes. However, in 1987, there were many "wildcat" strikes organized by unofficial committees, intent on showing up the traditional unions' torpor.

Wage demands in 1987 were fed by increasing inflation, which rose by an average of 3.5 percent, compared with 2.5 percent in 1986. Everywhere the average wage's purchasing power increased, or, at worst, remained the same. However in the United States wage earners lost purchasing power at the end of the year. Suffice it to say that companies remained cautious and governmental policies continued to be restrained.

14. 1988 — Rebound

FROM ANXIETY TO ELATION

From the uncertainties of the stock market crash, the year ended in elation. In the first days of the year, no one would have predicted 1988 would be special. The most pessimistic conjured up pictures of 1929. The most optimistic, having discovered late in the day that 1987 was quite a good year, thought 1988 would end in decline. This vision led international organizations to produce their forecasts, allowing the industrialized countries only feeble growth potential: no more than 2.5 percent.... We now know that 1988 was one of most prosperous years in terms of business, trade, investments, and even employment that the world had seen for a long time.

ANTI-CRISIS ECONOMIC POLICIES

While the crash had absolutely no impact on household and company demand, it forced the richer countries to draw closer together. Especially in the realm of exchange and interest rates, which was enough to rebuild confidence — both that of company directors as well as individuals. This was followed by a surge in investments, a decisive factor of the year. Another was the resurgence in industry, which in some ways took its revenge on the financial speculators.

There were areas where there was no international solidarity. The halfway session in the Uruguay Round, held at the end of the year in Montreal, ended in failure, yet again proving the strength of national self-interest and the risk of protectionism. During the last days the deadlock between the United States and the European Community over beef treated with hormones was another example of this.

The central banks were able to work together in a common strategy: they coordinated massive injections of liquidity after the stock market crash as well as adjusting interest rates throughout the year. This positive attitude pacified the financial markets, then took them to greater heights, allowing the governments to encourage savings.

WHY THE REBOUND?

There were many reasons behind the rebound. Since the second half of 1987, there were favorable signs: the drop in oil prices, the moderate level of wage demands, renewed profit margins, and also increased productive investment. Alongside this, the central banks' injection of liquidity, following the stock market crash, to prevent the total collapse of the financial markets stimulated economic activity. The bursting of the "speculators' bubble" encouraged the return to productive rather than speculative investments. For most of the OECD countries, spending on new units of production or on modernizing plant increased by 10 percent. This new drive on investments was supplemented by rapid growth in international trade, from 5.7 percent in 1987 up by 9 percent in 1988. The euphoria which came at the end of 1988 was strengthened by the absence of inflation. Price rises averaged 4 percent a year in the OECD countries.

COMPANY STRENGTH

The calming down of the markets helped achieve relative stability for the leading currencies, leaving aside the difficulties of the dollar, which was threatened by budget and trade imbalances in spite of a dynamic economy. Fear of uncontrolled price rises meant all governments mounted a strenuous operation to safeguard against inflation. The relative moderation of wage costs and the drop in oil prices compensated for the increase in raw materials' prices in 1988. However the disinflation which began with the decade ended and there were many pressures on prices. From 2.5 percent in 1986, the lowest rise for many years, the inflation rate went up in the OECD countries to 3.5 percent in 1988. In the background there was always the possibility of recovery in the oil market and demand for raw materials forcing prices up.

The fact that the Western economies were able to withstand the threat of inflation was due to the strong position of many companies, which had for the last eight years adapted to the changes forced on them by the oil shocks. This was evident in the new methods of stock control and hiring labor, in increases in productivity which accelerated in industry, allowing an improvement in real wages without increasing prices. This did not apply to Great Britain, whose performance did not conform to the norm.

THE RETURN OF INVESTMENT

Productive investment — particularly industrial investment — was the principal motor of 1988's strong economic growth. There had not been such a strong and uninflationary upturn for a long time, and since many new plants were now well-placed to satisfy growing demand 1988 was special. Many countries were able to make up for lost time. Between 1980 and 1983 many companies had lost out because of the second oil shock and had lost confidence in the future, so they made few investments. For only 1981 and 1982, the bottom of the recession, the seven leading industrialized countries saw spending on new plant drop by almost 5 percent in volume. In the United States this drop in 1982 and 1983 had reached 10 percent.

This was a time of stagnation for productive capital, but also its reduction in volume and effectiveness. Every year many of the machines brought into service ten or fifteen years before were declared obsolete or should have been. In France the drop in investments lasted for four years (1981-84). From 1984 there was a recovery in investments. In four countries there was a significant upturn (the United States, Japan, Great Britain, and Italy), and though it stopped in 1986, later it spread little by little all over the world to culminate in 1988 in an increase of about 10 percent.

This was the result of two factors: one was national policies, the other the strategic-political vagaries of the market. The former took the form of a significant enrichment of companies in the 1980s. All "capitalist" governments had — after having held profits back between 1974 and 1978 — maximized them at the expense of wages. This was achieved by fiscal and budget policies, and indirectly by allowing companies the freedom to set their own prices and wages.

A VIRTUOUS CYCLE

Some very good financial results led entrepreneurs — after being tempted by all kinds of speculations and investments — to speed up their investments. This was all the more important because of the drop in oil prices in 1986: the industrialized countries' "purchasing power" increased suddenly in relation to the drop in energy costs. This meant consumers paid less for gasoline, domestic fuel, but also indirectly for many oil-based manufactured products. From 1987 the delayed effects of oil counterattack played a very strong part, as shown in the OECD studies. Household demand grew, giving companies solid reasons to invest.

This led to the virtuous cycle. In 1988 in almost all the industrialized countries factories operated at more than 80 percent of their productive capacity, which was very high. In some ways 1988 saw the revenge of industry on services: it was the former which led the way in the boom in investments — contrary to previous years. These investments were not aimed at rationalizing or at saving on labor costs, but increasing the quantities of goods produced. There were many large-scale industrial plans: in paper, glass, aluminum, steel. Ten years before, industry had been closing down but now business had turned around.

The strong growth in 1988 resulted in solid job creation in the industrialized world and a drop in unemployment. The experts had failed to predict this and now they tried to discover why it had happened. In five years almost 6 million jobs had been created in

Europe. The OECD underlined the importance of part-time work in the services sector, mainly for women. But the international experts also noted the growth in industrial employment which "led to an increase in full-time jobs for men." If this persisted 1989 would be another good year.

INDEBTEDNESS AND FINANCIAL MANEUVERS

There was a cloud overhead: the increase in household debt, even in countries where there was a savings tradition like France. Companies also succumbed, through leverage buy-outs, financing successful bids by borrowing; some of these were so precarious (such as the very risky junk bonds) that the leverage buy-out became suspect. Some of these maneuvers were confusing. By devaluing the price of shares listed on the stock market, the 1987 Crash set the scene for several takeovers, including Carlo Benedetti's attempt on the General of Belgium in January. In the end Suez bought it, but at a cost (12.7 billion francs). However this was nothing compared with what followed. In the United States and Europe there were more than 20 gigantic takeovers (including RJR-Nabisco). Most were spurred on by the same thought: to improve the companies' standing in the forthcoming market struggles between the three blocs: American, European, and Asian spearheaded by Japan. On the old continent mergers, buyouts, and amalgamations showed the industrialists', insurers', and bankers' concern to attain the critical size for the single market of 1993. They were all worried about how to make the most of this immense market... and not suffer.

INTERNATIONAL TRADE:
THE THREAT OF REGIONALISM

The new vigor in trade showed the world economy's ability to bounce back. In volume, trade rose by 9 percent in 1988, as opposed to 5.7 the previous year, according to the OECD. Even though since 1987 manufactured goods had been the motor of world trade and lay behind the strong demand in the industrialized countries, and there was a healthy and encouraging growth in productive investments, there were still pressures on the economic upturn. One of these was the slowdown in the rebalancing of the American deficits and West German, Japanese, and the newly industrialized countries' surpluses. What was at stake was confirmed by the breakdown of talks at Montreal where a ministerial GATT session, from December 5 to 9, was supposed to draw up a midway statement on the multilateral trade negotiations of the Uruguay Round.

The United States and the European Community (EC) clashed bitterly over agriculture. However the political dimension was greater than the economic reality. Agriculture represented only 3 percent of the industrialized countries' income, while it represented 20 percent of the Third World's income. Agricultural products had declined in world trade from 46 percent in 1950 to 13 percent in 1987. The clash between Washington and Brussels at Montreal had the hallmarks of a violent rearguard action. It risked jeopardizing world trade relations, even if the EC intended to take it on board and accelerate the community's agricultural reforms. While the United States' partners waited for the arrival at the White House of President George Bush on January 20, 1989, there were many other sources of anxiety. The new American law, the Trade Bill signed on August 23, 1988 by President Reagan, contained an arsenal of retaliatory measures. Although claiming to be opposed to protectionism and in favor of multilateralism, Bush had at his disposal several ways of bringing in line the Europeans, the Japanese, also the four Asian dragons (South Korea, Taiwan, Hong Kong, and Singapore) which were excluded from the system of preferential duties by the Reagan administration, and states like Brazil, India, and Mexico, trying to protect their services or newer industries.

The unilateral adoption of free trade became more and more important in 1988. Brian Mulroney's victory in the Canadian elections paved the way for a free trade treaty, signed in Washington on January 1, 1988, and taking effect a year later. The United States looked at strengthening their commercial relations with Mexico and contemplated a US-Japanese pact. The EC's single market of 1993 was part of this renewed regionalism, even

Tokyo did not preclude the creation of a Asian-Pacific commercial zone. If these tendencies persisted, this criss-cross of alliances could mark the end of multinationalism, which had been the dominant theme since the end of World War II and which GATT had tried to maintain. Already many Third World countries were being marginalized.

Despite the boost of the adjustment of raw materials' prices in dollars, the developing countries' share of world trade diminished to 19.2 percent. However, apart from energy, this phenomenon was reversed thanks to constant efforts to diversify sales abroad. But the Third World was still vulnerable because of its foreign debt and its overdependence on exports of basic commodities, while demography made it a prime market for the industrialized countries.

The Eastern Bloc countries' trade increased at a much slower rate than the world average in 1987. Their imports dropped to compensate for the lack of an increase in energy prices and to prevent the growth of deficits. Even though they only represented 9.5 percent of world trade, these countries confirmed that they wanted to take a greater part in the international system. The Soviet Union underwent a spectacular process of opening up, although it would be some time before Moscow would be admitted to GATT or the IMF. By the end of 1988 the United States, which up till then had been very hostile, seemed willing to become more tolerant in order to bolster Mikhail Gorbachev's perestroika.

RENEWED BUT CONTAINED INFLATION

Would the terrible affliction of the 1970s, inflation, return? This was the question asked by economists, given that the recession they predicted would occur after the 1987 Crash had not happened. Despite strong pressures, particularly in the United States and Great Britain, the rise in retail prices remained limited. The exceptional dynamism of world economic activity was the prime cause of this slight increase in inflation. There were production factors (raw materials, labor, and capital) and the partial, often temporary, imbalance between strong demand and insufficient or badly directed supply also affecting prices. However there was no great upheaval. Booming industry needed raw materials. Having hit an all-time low in mid-1986, raw materials' prices took off, so that nickel doubled in a year. Strong demand, drought in the United States and Canada, as well as in the Sahel, contributed to a massive increases in food prices, such as maize and soya.

Economic growth — overheating in some countries like Great Britain — also contributed to new problems on the labor market. The shortage of qualified workers, the creation of new jobs, and high wage demands led to significant increases in wages. This occurred in the United States, where unemployment hit 5.4 percent, its lowest point since the end of the 1970s, and workers demanded much higher incomes.

This strong growth put pressure on capital. Several countries, notably the United States, used their productive capacity at its highest rate since 1979. In several sectors, industrialists found themselves caught in a vice. Commodities were rare — world savings remained low in many countries — money was very much in demand. Its price — the interest rates — went up, especially since the state, notably the United States, also needed to borrow. So there were inflationary pressures on raw materials, labor, and capital: but they did not lead to a massive rise in prices for the consumer. In fact, several factors diminished these pressures in 1988. The oil price dropped back again to the 1986 level, about $14 a barrel, and compensated for the raw materials' price increases.

Important rises in productivity, mainly in industry, allowed it to absorb easily nominal increases in wages. Also the monetarist policies became particularly restrictive from spring onward and prevented these pressures from being passed on as increased prices to consumers. In most countries the level of demand influenced the level of inflation.

A NEW DROP IN UNEMPLOYMENT

Not only did unemployment drop in most Western countries, but job creation was vigorous almost everywhere. The OECD, which was usually cautious, noted that the upturn, started in 1983, was "the longest since World War II." Extremely pessimistic and numbed by years of recession, commentators were used to being skeptical and pointing to the rare exceptions, the United States, Great Britain, and more recently West Germany and Japan. The trend was long-term and affected several foreign economies, even France, which was lagging behind.

Globally, the OECD countries enjoyed a 1.6 percent growth in employment in 1987 and 1.8 percent in 1988. The worst cases, only four a year earlier (Ireland, Greece, Finland, and New Zealand), had fallen to two (Ireland and New Zealand). Within the EC, Italy, Portugal, and Spain also created new jobs. There were still about 28.5 million seeking work within the OECD in 1987, but this was a significant drop on the 32 million of four years before. It did not prevent the return of problems that had long disappeared. Here and there, there were many jobs which remained unfilled. "Disconcerting," wrote the OECD experts, which meant that the unemployed "did not have the necessary skills to fill the vacancies."

Old problems reemerged, at a time when it seemed just as difficult to reabsorb unemployment. This meant that in spite of the recovery a large section of the population did not benefit. The mass of long-term unemployed could become unemployable and excluded from society. Nonetheless, despite the common trend, there were many differences between countries and it was often difficult to make out the advantages or disadvantages of the different policies adopted. The United States seemed to be benefiting from deregulation. In some ways, Great Britain was drawing on the dividends of its extreme flexibility, as was witnessed by the fact unemployment had dropped for 27 consecutive months, thanks to fabulous aid programs.

With the benefit of a declining working population since 1986, West Germany could restructure and improve its competitiveness. But countries which were rigid and had good social security, like Sweden, were also doing well. Only France had a different experience, because job creation could not absorb all the new arrivals on the labor market, which would continue until 2005 or 2010, as a result of the rise in the working population.

RECASTING EMPLOYMENT

It was in services that there were new jobs, particularly restaurants, garages, or odd jobs. Skills and wages suffered as a result, particularly since the jobs were part-time, for women, and relatively precarious. There were not such strict laws as previously, and there was more self-employment, sometimes a cover for proper jobs. These tendencies were very strong in English-speaking countries and showed how employment was changing. Traditional, male jobs stagnated or regressed while there were more women employed part-time. Women's employment in Great Britain went up by 2.9 percent between 1979 and 1986, while full-time employment dropped by 4.4 percent and part-time work increased by 7.3 percent. The same phenomenon occurred in France, West Germany, Japan, and the Netherlands. But not in countries where there was less unemployment like Sweden, Norway, and the United States. There was a tendency to adapt, which would involve a recasting of employment and unemployment.

15. 1989 — An Eastern Wind

CAPITALISM WAS TRIUMPHANT

BREAKING DOWN THE WALLS

The wind of freedom swept over Eastern Europe as the people rose up from Poland to Romania. The breaking down of the Berlin Wall on November 9, was a symbol of the triumph of democracy after 40 years of totalitarianism. State bureaucracy and authoritarian planning had not created a brave new world but empty shops. The upheavals in the East were a rejection of oppressive communism and showed the lure of Western materialism. The free market and consumer society was what was on offer in the West, and everyone wanted it. The 24 OECD countries enjoyed their seventh consecutive year of growth, after the 1982 recession which had hit the United States particularly hard.

Since 1987 to the end of the first half of 1989 the annual rate of growth had reached an impressive 4 percent. This was largely the result of being pulled along by productive investments, guarantees of the future, and of exports, which for the first time exceeded $3,000 billion. West Germany, at the center of Europe, was the most impressive performer of the EC and at the end of the year the Deutschmark surged ahead. This happened with relatively weak inflation, although prices had been moving upward for three years. At the same time some of the external imbalances were adjusted, mainly the US deficit and Japanese surplus. Monetary pragmatism and banking fastidiousness produced good results in the sphere of international cooperation. The US-Soviet summit at Malta in early December was another example of this.

For the sixth consecutive year unemployment dropped, from 8.7 percent of the OECD working population to 6.6 percent in 1989. However there were still 25 million unemployed in the OECD countries — almost 16 million in Europe — and employment could sometimes be unsure, either precarious or badly paid. The marginalized city-dwellers contrasted sharply with the stock market whiz kids.

In the end capitalism seemed to have triumphed. There was the risk of the environment suffering and culture disappearing, with money dictating all. The success of ecology and the resurgence of religion — as witnessed by the visit of Gorbachev to Pope John Paul II at the Vatican — demonstrated a reaction against the dictatorship of economics and materialism. Faced with a spiritual void, would the Eastern wind, full of hope, lead to a new, more caring Europe from the Atlantic to the Urals?

NO TO ULTRA-CONSERVATISM AND THE MARKET

In the West the market was king and with its laws dominated the end of the decade. Since the early 1980s conservative policies (pushing back the state, deregulation, privatization...) undoubtedly contributed to spectacular growth in almost all the Western countries. In 1989 economic activity held up. Yet conservatism — or rather ultra-conservatism — was being questioned in many countries. It was probably the last year to be inspired by Reaganism in the United States, but elsewhere as well. In many areas reregulation took over from deregulation. While the West questioned the limits of the market, in the East as in the South a new religion emerged: that of the market. Supply-siders, the priests of ultra-conservatism who had advised Reagan in the 1980s, went East. They were more likely to be seen in Moscow than in the corridors of the White House. It was the end of centralized planning, state ownership, and the Communist Party's leading role. The market triumphed over Marx.

In the Western countries, growth continued to be strong in 1989, though it was slightly down on the exceptional results of 1988. After 4.4 percent growth in 1988, economic activity grew by

3.6 percent in 1989 in all the OECD countries. World trade also had a good year, growing by about 7 percent, according to GATT experts. The recession was over, more and more economists began to say. All the indicators pointed to capitalist economies' excellent health. Industry — undergoing worldwide restructuring — was profitable again and investing in capacity. The services sector (tourism, air transport, computers) was booming. Household expenditure held up well and European car manufacturers thrived. As in 1988 this newfound growth created jobs and was not accompanied by the return of inflation. However public opinion and financial experts remained circumspect. The number of unemployed was still high and in some countries consumer prices were rising. Inflationary tendencies were sometimes strong, even if for the moment they were restrained.

GROWING INEQUALITIES

During this crucial year the capitalist countries did not perform identically. There were many financial imbalances. Asia, with Japan in the lead, increased its economic and financial power: economic activity grew by 5 percent in Japan, 9 percent in Singapore, more than 10 percent in Thailand. West Germany also increased its power in 1989 and had a growth rate of 4 percent. Tokyo and Bonn continued to accumulate gigantic trade and balance of payments surpluses. By contrast the United States was running out of steam and was heavily in deficit.

In each of these countries the mechanisms of the market proved themselves. But at the end of an exceptionally long period of growth, they also reached their limits. There was persistent unemployment in Europe, increasing inequalities in the United States, general deterioration of public services: the "less state" slogan of the 1980s was being substituted by that of another kind of state. The reduction of income tax deductions — one of the aims of the decade — was no longer regarded as the top priority, even by Margaret Thatcher. The new slogan was the laws of the market but not those of the jungle. Almost everywhere and in different sectors, from finance to air transport in the United States mainly, deregulation was replaced by reregulation.

The Eastern countries had become the devotees of the market. There the absence of market forces had provoked a crisis. In 1989 economic activity — already in difficulty — was disrupted by political revolutions which resulted in the dismantling of the economic bureaucracies that had held sway for more than 40 years. All the taboos were broken — even private property. With the interested aid of the Western countries, Eastern Europe and the Soviet Union got ready for a difficult, uncharted transition with no experience to draw on. This would be the theme of the first year of the next decade.

THE END OF THE RECESSION OR NEW PROBLEMS? A TURNING POINT ON INVESTMENTS

Would investment, which for the last three years had been the motor of world economic growth and had led the industrialized countries out of the recession, continue at a very high level? This question was even more pressing given that investment traditionally depended on demand, which must be strong, and to a lesser extent profits, which must be comfortable. These two indicators of investment were less certain than they had been a year before: world demand, while holding up, had been going down slightly; profits were dropping in the United States and Great Britain.

Japan had another problem: the exceptional growth rate in investment for the last two years (more than 35 percent in volume during 1988-89) threatened to produce overcapacity given the needs of the international market. It also called into question the choice of export strategy, which risked provoking protectionist measures from Europe and North America. A classic analysis of the situation led one to be skeptical that spending on new plant would continue to pull the economic growth of the industrialized countries. This skepticism was apparently confirmed by the collapse of investments in the United States. But was this true given that the communist regimes were collapsing and the heads of enterprises had to adjust their strategy to take into account new markets? Also increasingly fierce international competition often led to overinvestment to stay ahead, and also led to the replacement of perfectly profitable plant. In Europe at least there was no problem of a slowdown in investments. The communist bloc countries, which were trying to reform politically and economically, had huge and pressing needs.

INFLATION WAS IN THE CARDS

There was bad news as well as good in 1989: the return of inflation, the old number one enemy. Would there be further stagflation (slow growth and price increases) as in the late 1970s? Was the inflation cost pushed or demand pulled? Would existing policies be able to deal with the monster?

The 1989 results showed stagflation was unlikely. Although economic growth was slightly less strong than in 1988, it held up. There was much investment, proof that companies were looking to the future. There were definite signs of a slowdown in the United States, but they did not indicate a collapse or recession. It was not easy to find the underlying causes of inflation. Some production costs had gone up. The market in energy sources had turned around: demand for oil overtook the record levels of 1979, which firmed up prices, also of natural gas and coal. However other raw materials, the price of which held up in the first quarter, dropped afterward.

Wages remained stable everywhere, apart from in Great Britain. Demand has not led to overheating. Demand at home, according to the OECD, was less strong than in 1988 in the United States, Japan, West Germany, and France. Still the rates of utilization of productive capacity went back to the record levels of 1973, before the oil crises. The vigor of international trade explained a large part of this: exports were one of the most powerful motors of growth, as was seen in West Germany. There foreign demand led to an increase in GNP, which reached a new high during the first quarter of 1989.

The incipient inflation during the first quarter noticeably dropped during the second. Did this show that economic policies were working effectively? They were based mainly on interest rates, but there were other contributory factors, such as increased competition. The United States set the example during 18 months by following a strict monetary policy. After June 1989 this was greatly relaxed, given that inflation had dropped to cruising speed. By contrast Japan, West Germany, France, and mainly Great Britain raised their interest rates (the stability of money was regarded as proof against inflation).

On the whole, the industrialized countries made use of the boom to reduce their budget deficits or increase their surpluses. The OECD estimated that for the seven most important countries the public borrowing requirement went from an average of 2.4 percent of GNP to 0.9 percent between 1987 and 1991. The previous years' attempts at adjustment had been less fruitful. While in 1988 there had been a general rise in interest rates, everywhere the central banks were increasing the cost of borrowing to safeguard against overheating and inflation, with differing results in 1989. There were real about turns, the cost of borrowing dropped gradually in the United States in the second half after initially holding firm and the European central banks agreed to take a stand against inflation, under the guidance of the Bundesbank.

$3,000 BILLION OF TRADE

The year 1989 was a high point in international trade: it grew by 7 percent in volume, after the 8.5 percent growth in 1988, according to GATT. World trade reached a peak at $3,000 billion in value (current dollars), without including some 20 percent extra represented by goods and services which grew at a slightly lower level. This divergence between the growth of trade and that of production, which had accentuated over the years, showed the integration of national economies into the world economy. Almost everywhere foreign trade's share of national production was on the increase, imposing norms of international competition even on those so-called "protected sectors" as opposed to the "exposed sectors," the former of which were waning.

BETTER FOR EMPLOYMENT
APART FROM A "HARD CORE"

Usually confident, the OECD drew the following conclusion (in Perspectives on Employment): one can create jobs, and most countries saw them grow by 1.8 percent in 1988, at a superior rate than that which they had obtained for ten years, without it affecting the hard core of unemployment. Worse still, distortions had worsened over the years of recession so that outlying regions had twice the rate of unemployment as that of other regions. The number of unemployed went down from 26.8 million in 1987 to 24.5 million in 1989, that is 6.6 percent of the OECD working population, with no prospect of further improvement. According to forecasts, 1990 would see an increase in unemployment and numerous signs showed that it was the end of a cycle. It was no coincidence that the United States had hit an immovable barrier at 5.3 or 5.4 percent of unemployment, despite the creation of 200,000 jobs in November.

16. The Recession was Born of a New World

THE NATURE AND CAUSES OF THE RECESSION

PROFITABILITY WAS IN CRISIS: RECESSION WAS BREWING

Since the mid-1960s postwar growth suffered from structural problems, which were invisible at first. It was less and less possible for capital to produce large enough profits to guarantee indefinite expansion. In fact, one of the characteristics of the contemporary period was the drop in capital's profitability, due to poor use but also because of modifications in social factors affecting production. The more regular rises in wages, often stronger than before, and improvements in social protection modified the distribution of added value in favor of wages rather than profits. Since at the same time working hours were diminished and absenteeism increasing, the utilization time of capital dropped, accentuating the slim returns on invested capital. This provoked a natural response from employers almost everywhere to invest less; then later to try replacing men and women with machines (thanks to investments in productivity) and increase the profitability of invested capital.

This was a logical step in the quest for profits but it produced a double effect on the economic crisis: further deterioration in employment and an increase (in the first phase of the process) in inflation because costs, investments, and the cost of maintaining the new plant were passed on to the consumer within the framework of price freedom, when the market could accommodate it. Of course, countries responded with austerity programs (aimed at controlling prices) slowing down economic activity and downgrading employment (the period between 1974 to 1981), but this risked aggravating the crisis.

THE MONETARY CRISIS: THE FERMENT OF DISORDER

The US dollar policy definitely sowed the seeds of world inflation and then contributed to its increase.

The United States undermined the bases of the Gold Exchange Standard to its profit, provoking a dangerous flood of Eurodollars, then it devalued — in fact the year that preceded the crisis — the currency which was the basis of the international monetary system, finally scuttled the system, and installed floating exchange rates and their worrying facilities (at Jamaica in June 1976). It was responsible for seriously disrupting the economic mechanisms within which contemporary capitalism had developed. The United States' Western partners allowed Washington to do this, and their banks became swamped in Eurodollars, thus encouraging excessive secured, and unsecured, international credits which fueled inflation.

After 1974 the avalanche of petrodollars — $180 billion in five years, the surplus of the OPEC countries, after paying for equipment, consumption, and armaments — aggravated the problem, while increasing inequalities between countries. In 1980 the new rise in oil prices provoked an even bigger flood of petrodollars, of which the floating part exceeded that of 1974 by 25 percent. Thus the inflationary spiral, which had contributed so much to the monetary crisis seven years earlier, went out of control.

THE FATAL TRIANGLE

In 1973-74, the crisis was not sparked off by the stock market — as it had been in 1929. It occurred because of an insidious combination of world phenomena: expansionary phases in all the leading industrialized countries, which put a lot of pressure on raw materials prices; this imported inflation, contributing to the internal upward pressure, led most governments to take anti-inflationary measures, to rein in demand without slowing down production; the gap between demand and production led to a massive buildup of stock. These were then dumped on the market by companies, which also cut back on their activity. The drop in production had a knock-on effect on purchasing power, as well as demand and investment: the crisis was in full swing.

THE PETROLEUM TRIGGER

This stagflation (stagnation and inflation) was a symptom of the West's depression, along with the exceptional length of the crisis. The increase in oil prices, almost ten times more expensive than before 1973, also featured. It was thought that in two stages (1974-75, 1979-80) there was a 3 percent drop in average national production because of the extra oil price burden. Retail prices also increased by about 3 percent as a result of the 1974 quadrupling of oil prices, the doubling of price in 1975 had a similar effect.

THE TWO "OIL SHOCKS"

The first shock, after the Yom Kippur War, in October 1973, showed a vulnerable and punch-drunk West as well as OPEC's newfound power. The quadrupling of oil prices in four months aggravated inflation in the developed countries and massively increased the poorest countries' debt. At the same time the nationalization of the oil industry, begun in 1970, accelerated in 1975-76 in all the OPEC countries. It broke the hundred-year monopolies' of the large companies — "from well to pump."

The second oil shock in 1979, in the wake of the Iranian revolution, was accidental. Even more brutal, it had a profound recessive effect, coinciding with a change in US monetary policy and a jump in interest rates. In three years, prices almost trebled, disturbing the consumer countries' trade balance and leading them to launch or speed up a vigorous program of energy self-sufficiency.

STAGFLATION'S INSTIGATED DEDUCTIONS

The fact that the industrialized countries had to pay twice as much (on average) as in 1973 for the raw materials they imported led them to deduct from their resources the part which would have gone on consumption or investment. The resulting deflationary effect increased unemployment without reducing inflation; on the contrary the price increases effected this transfer.

OIL WAS NOT THE ONLY FACTOR

The rise in oil prices had unequal effects on many countries. Beneficial to some, more or less tolerable to others, and catastrophic for the last group. Nonetheless the gravity of the crisis was not only related to how much each country depended on foreign supplies of oil, but also to the way authorities reacted to OPEC's decisions. That was true for the consequences on the balance of payments and disruption at home, particularly the stability of prices. From the point of view of the balance of payments, it was noted that Japan, which in 1974 imported $26 billion of oil, and West Germany, which imported $10 billion, were able to reestablish their balance of payments within a few months. Other countries, which did not import so much oil, accumulated large deficits over a period of time. So the notion of oil deficits lost much of its meaning.

On the home front there were many differences. During the three previous years price rises had been very uneven from one country to another, while the oil price rises had been universal. On the one hand, they had less impact in some countries, such as West Germany, Switzerland, or the Netherlands, than in France, Great Britain, and Italy. The long term outcome was even more varied: after one or two years of increases, some countries regained stability (at 1 percent) or relative stability (4 to 5 percent), while others continued to have inflation rates which bore no relation to the price of oil.

There were two reasons behind all these variations:

* The first was that certain governments (West Germany, Switzerland, the United States, and Japan) immediately responded

to the increase in oil bills: they used rigorous monetary, fiscal, and budget policies to reduce the increase in the national standard of living, at the cost of slowing down economic activity and employment. These governments accepted the idea of an OPEC tax, and managed to secure a transfer of real wealth, about 1 or 2 percent of national income, by reducing consumption at home and increasing exports to oil-exporting countries. This was certainly the case for West Germany, whose exports to OPEC countries exceeded 5.9 billion Deutschmark in 1973 but climbed to 20.7 billion in 1976, while imports of oil from these countries went from 7.9 billion Deutschmark in 1973 to 22.7 billion in 1976, without increasing the deficit.

* The second reason — which lay behind the first — was that in those countries public opinion supported the transfer, while in others the loss of purchasing power resulting from inflation was not accepted as a necessary evil but was regarded as robbery. Thus workers, and more generally, the people resisted making sacrifices and demanded wages which would maintain their purchasing power. Therefore the basis of these political divergences was very marked sociological differences.

OIL AT THE FOREFRONT OF THE DEFLATIONARY SPIRAL

The global incidence of price increases happened in three ways:

* *The transfer of real wealth* from the consumer countries to the exporting countries meant that effective solutions within a nation led to stalemate on a global level. As we have already seen, the countries which first adopted rigorous stabilization policies had a commercial advantage over others by finding new markets for their exports, not just in OPEC countries, but in all markets. Thus they largely escaped the widespread difficulties in currency exchange and balance of payments. It did not follow that the strategy was generally applicable and that the policies which had worked in three or four countries could have been applied with the same results in all the Western countries. In fact the OPEC

countries' capacity to absorb wealth and services was limited, and it only grew slowly — 4 to 5 percent a year —, and for an indeterminate period, consumer countries would only be able to pay a fraction of their oil bills in kind.

* *Financial transfers* had to be looked at by distinguishing between local and global problems. Each country had a legitimate right once they had exhausted export possibilities to follow a policy of adjusting demand at home to get their balance of payments on a even keel. This was desirable because the countries with deficits were also ones with high levels of inflation. However if these national programs were applied on a global scale then the combination of these policies led to a deflationary spiral. The depressive phase of Western economics — which hit its nadir in 1975 — was attributable to the combination of policies of adjustment necessary at the national level.

* Finally, *costs* meant the additional energy charges lay behind the stagnation of the world economy. On the one hand, the additional energy charges accelerated price rises in the countries with surpluses as well as those with deficits. But also the stabilization policies resulted in the flattening of company profits. This was true for European countries and Japan. The end result was feeble industrial investment, aggravated by lack of confidence in the future, greatly affected by the knowledge that there was always the possibility of further price increases. In these circumstances companies hesitated before investing in any sector which depended on the cost of energy. The result — except in the energy sector — was a slowdown in investment which threatened the length of any upturn.

NEW COMPETITORS AND CONTESTED OUTLETS

The Third World's growing share of international trade sometimes had the same effect, but along different lines. The share was still small: in France, for example, it was no more than 4 percent of the total imports of manufactured goods; in the OPEC countries it was nearer 10 percent. But, besides the fact that it was on the increase — competing more and more with the developed countries' national production —, it limited the latters' outlets abroad. The upturn in Third World production and in South-South trade (to the benefit of producers in Brazil, India, and the workshop countries of Southeast Asia) reduced exports from North to South; in particular in textiles, steel, food products, leather goods, household goods, simple machinery, small-scale shipbuilding, etc.

Many of these competing products come from Third World factories, built by Western multinationals to maximize their profits by using cheaper labor and profiting from less stringent social and fiscal laws. But to change the famous dictum what was good overseas for General Motors was not necessarily good for US wage earners and consumers. As the economist Gerard de Bernis pointed out as long as the world was not ready for the internationalization of political power, the internationalization of the means of production could not explain the depth and length of the actual crisis.

Everything happened as if the "delocalization" of the big Western industries reproduced the contradiction at a national level between rapid growth in production (low wages overseas produced high levels of profits, which led to more investment and greater company activity) and insufficient consumption (Third World wage earners' purchasing power was low, while unemployment was growing in industrialized countries because of the closing down of uncompetitive industries).

This dissymetry between production and consumption at a national level used to be reduced by state intervention, by distributing direct and indirect revenue and jobs. But the absence of the equivalent world political unit allowed this major contradiction to grow, which the multinationals, even if they could agree on a common line, had neither the desire nor the means of surmounting.

THE "SOFT CRISIS"

The current crisis did not have the same profile as the "classic" crises. Between 1974-80 production tended to decelerate, the year 1976 (with strong growth) was a good exception, just as the years 1974-75 were bad exceptions. But this time round there was neither the strong depression usual in the Juglar cycles, nor the habitual consecutive recovery. The comparison in prices is even more striking: it followed a complete reversal of the classical model, prices rose almost as fast as activity dropped.

THE CLASSICAL JUGLAR CRISES

We can compare the current situation with the cyclical, Juglar crises, which featured in the development of the West before World War I. From 1815 to 1914, the capitalist world had 11 crises each lasting eight years: five before the 1870 Franco-Prussian War and six after. Each cycle could be divided into two roughly equal parts: four years of expansion, four of depression. There were usually four phases: after an initial period of increased production, prices, wages, profits, interest rates, and stock market prices, there followed the spectacular bankruptcy of a bank or company. It was unable to raise the credit needed to pursue its operations or collect its debts from overextended clients. The domino effect meant a whole series of banks and companies were affected; caution became the watchword and others slowed down their activity. The reduction in the number of jobs affected wages; demand dropped and hit prices, which caused the bankruptcy of the least competitive firms which were no longer able to sell their output at prices that covered their costs. So there was further unemployment, disposal of stocks at low prices, the buying up of closed-down factories by the surviving companies.... When stocks had run out and the fall in prices had given rise to new demand — in spite of low wages — production took off, and with it, employment, prices, and profits. This cycle was regularly repeated throughout the century.

STAGFLATION: A SIGNIFICANT SYMPTOM

Another singular feature of the period was that during the two years of serious depression at the beginning of the crisis (1974 and 1975), prices had increased by record levels in the larger Western countries (an average of 12 percent), even though unemployment had doubled. After this, the rhythm of inflation dropped slightly during the 1970s, but remained high and in 1980 neared 1974's exceptional rate. Stagflation had not occurred during previous cycles. Statistics showed that during the last few years inflation had increased in line with unemployment. Phillips' secular "law" (unemployment and prices progressed in opposite directions) was disproved during the 1970s.

The general speculation in raw materials like gold, currency, land, etc, was the result of supply and demand going out of control thanks to inflation. Little by little inflation neutralized the free market's primary regulatory force, the discipline of covering one's costs. In fact the adjustment factors, which had previously automatically come into force (prices and employment), stopped regulating the Western economies. They became invariables, which sabotaged national policies aimed at recovery. These policies were often contradictory. The cleaning up of finances and "trimming the fat" in employment aggravated unemployment, while job creation schemes tried to counter the trend. The increasing number of social protection laws (well justified) put a burden on cost prices, at the same time that governments talked about fighting inflation. The takeover by the state of company expenditure (fiscal and social) to improve their profitability and the vaccine of public contracts, which did not lay down performance criteria, did not lead companies to improve management structures or performance, contrary to official objectives. The acceptance of international monetary slackness, which benefited the strongest, led to the failure of national credit policies, all in the name of the free market.

REACTIONS TO THE CRISIS AND POLICIES

There were thirteen years of oil maelstrom (from the first shock in 1973 to the counter-shock in 1986). After a spectacular rise, the price of "black gold" fell back to its real level in 1974. Consumers won out and the previously all-powerful cartel, OPEC, was left staggering. Did this mean a return to the starting point? In fact the oil crises had permanently transformed energy policies. The Iranian revolution (1979) had further deprived the oil companies of their traditional resources. The largest ones regrouped by accelerating the exploitation of new oilfields outside OPEC, in the North Sea and elsewhere.

Finally the disruption of supplies and the disintegration of industry stoked up the "free" market in oil. Prices were negotiated day by day, cargo by cargo, and soon escaped the producer countries' control. The results were that after 1979, for the first time in ages, world consumption of energy fell. Oil demand fell even more quickly. OPEC was caught between the fall in consumption and rise of "new" producers. It was forced to cut its official prices and constantly cut back on oil production to prop up the market, which was threatened by overproduction. Its share of the oil trade, both crude and refined, had reached 77 percent in 1979, but by 1985 it was 44 percent. In December 1985 the cartel's resistance was exhausted. OPEC stopped propping up oil prices and unleashed a drop in oil prices as sudden as the rise had been.

1983: A HISTORIC TURNING POINT

The year 1973 was a key date for most people in the history of energy, since it was the year of the first oil shock. However, *1983 was the year of the countershock*, marked by the first official drop in oil prices by OPEC. This difficult decision, taken on March 14, after several weeks of bitter negotiations, was a turning point on the oil market, begun in 1981.

The continual drop in world demand since that date, largely due to the economic recession in all the developed countries, but also to the economic measures and diversification of the consumer countries after the two shocks on 1973 and 1979-80 had put OPEC in a critical situation.

The prospect of penury had haunted consumers for more than ten years. It disappeared, along with Sheikh Yamani, the famous Saudi oil minister, symbol of OPEC's glory days. Was the "oil crisis" a mirage? Oil in 1985 was less important than in 1973, not would it ever play the same role again. Prices fell again but investments had already been committed.

In the consumer countries, industrial processes and the oil products themselves used much less oil, also there were environmental factors. Alternative sources of energy had been pushed to the fore. American automobiles, Japanese refrigerators consumed two-thirds less than in 1973. In Sweden the amount of energy needed to produce a ton of steel was down by a quarter. In France nuclear power produced two-thirds of electricity consumption....

UNEQUAL EFFORTS
WHICH SLACKENED WITH EXPANSION

The rise in energy prices pushed the Western countries to stabilize individual energy consumption during 1973-78, despite economic growth averaging 30 percent, thanks to rationalization and cutbacks. But these efforts were often unequal and gave way with the pivotal takeoff of growth in the 1990s. Western Europe made a considerable effort to cut back consumption, under the impulse of the EC's European Commission which launched research and development programs. But the recovery slowed these efforts and threatened the objective of the European Council of Ministers of a 20 percent reduction in "energy intensity" by 1995.

In the Soviet Union, however, individual energy consumption shot up by 37 percent after 1973: it did not slow down until 1982. In the 1990s there was a long term plan to reduce energy intensity by 40 percent, technically possible but difficult to effect. The United States faced urgent decisions because individual energy consumption remained high and increased dependence on Gulf sources of oil. Japan had, by contrast, stabilized consumption despite a 66 percent growth in Gross Domestic Product, thanks to industrial and technical progress (30 percent less energy was required to make a ton of steel). There was a system of soft loans to companies. The current oil détente is illusory and carries the germs of further trouble. For certain, there will be much talk about oil.

Among the producers the consequences of the two shocks were just as visible. The new oilfields opened up since 1973 in the North Sea, Alaska, Angola, Egypt, Mexico, Brazil..., were at full production. Since 1976, according to OPEC, some 8 million barrels a day from these new sources have come onto the market. Prices would have to remain well under $5 to 7 a barrel for these oilfields to close down.

The oil industry was profoundly changed by these turbulent years. The "big" companies lost their control of reserves, but also access to the cheapest sources of crude, that is OPEC. This led to a complete shake up in the use of reserves: the most plentiful and cheap crude remained underground, while those of the new producers, expensive but more profitable and reliable for the companies were extracted first. This aggravated the market's instability. Adjustments between supply, in the hands of the producers, and demand, in the hands of the companies, were just as jumpy as the price of crude, fixed on the open market, and subject to speculation.

ECONOMIC DIRECTION AIMED AT CONTAINING THE CRISIS

Possessing many detectors and more or less subtle intervention strategies, governments reacted to the crisis in many different ways, in terms of timing, intensity, scale. But generally they used an austerity program (against inflation), recovery programs aimed at investment and consumption, specific plans for jobs, or foreign trade.... Thanks to these counterattacks — and to the increased capacity of the unions and social legislation to protect incomes — the drop in private investment remained limited and consumption was stemmed in many countries.

Most of the industrialized countries were able momentarily to recover their trade balance, despite the increase in oil prices. As a result the loss of jobs never reached the terrible levels of the 1930s. There were many differences with the Great Depression.

WINNERS, LOSERS, AND OTHERS

Many governments claimed "the crisis is worldwide and affects everyone" thus avoiding blame. However West Germany had a less than 6 percent increase in prices while Great Britain and Italy had an increase of more than 20 percent. Japan enjoyed a 6 percent growth rate in 1979, while Great Britain stagnated during that year — the second oil shock. In 1980 unemployment affected only 2 percent of the Japanese working population, 8 percent of Italians, and yet again 7 percent of US. These results give an idea of who won and lost out in the crisis.

How can one account for all these differences? European experts examined the problem and came up with three principal causes.

* Firstly, there was an unequal effort to adapt. Japan, West Germany, the Netherlands, and, in some ways, the United States began earlier than others and with greater effort the industrial restructuring necessary to adapt to the new conditions and the economic emergence of the Third World. They closed down weak sectors, transformed others, stimulated new areas which paid off and maintained growth, and wiped out inflation.

* Social resistance to change varied from country to country and was the second important element in responses to the crisis. In West Germany, for example, wage earners realized that price rises were weak and thanks to joint management structures were able to contribute to industrial changes, at a company level as well as the shopfloor level. West Germany had a strong increase in productivity as a result — despite the crisis, it remained 50 percent higher than in most other European Community countries. Until 1979 it stimulated German export performance, which also saved jobs in spite of the deflationary effect of oil deductions.

* The third trump against the crisis held by some countries was the discipline of the European Monetary System (EMS), the snake. It was noticeable that the two countries facing the worst of it — Great Britain and Italy — were not part of the EMS. The measures they took, both social and financial, did not pay off. France left the snake then returned and this went some way to explain its average performance.

It was clear, given these facts, that the crisis, though general, did not affect every country in the same way, because of the different ways in which they reacted. Earlier we noted the same pattern when looking at the underlying causes of the current crisis. While no Western country could escape the depression, the different ways of coping and its consequences depended on the political will of a country and the therapeutic measures adopted.

We will have to translate the typical language of the OECD experts. The authors expressed their concern that wage increases would go back to levels that were in force before the crises: the indexation of wages to prices and productivity led to a shareout of value which was relatively favorable to wage earners (the famous equation wage increases = price rises + productivity increases). Thus the OECD was asking governments to disregard the rule of indexing wages on prices, in order to break inflationary tendencies, but mainly to restore profit margins to the level where they could stimulate an expansion in the market economy.

AGGRESSIVE MONETARISM (1980-82)

In 1981, as in 1980, the movements in world interest rates were determined by the United States. The monetary authorities' policies led to a new rise, during the summer, which profoundly disturbed the European financial markets. The only difference between 1980 and 1981 was that their profiles were completely opposite. In 1980 the first rise in American rates in the spring led to a 20 percent rate but was followed by a rapid decrease to 10 percent: the worsening recession, provoked in a large part by the draconian policies of the monetary authorities trying to fight inflation, forced the Federal Reserve Board to back pedal and hastily remove the restrictive measures it had imposed. After fall renewed inflation and increasing demand for bank credits led the Fed to harden its policies, which made the rates shoot up in the United States and on the Eurodollar market to a record level of 20.5 by the end of the year.

In 1981 it was the exact opposite. After a small drop to 17 percent in the spring, American interest rates were rising at the initiative of the monetary authorities, alarmed at the increase in money supply, which in May had exploded and increased at an annual rate of 14 percent instead of 6 to 7 percent fixed by the Fed. Through its president, Paul Volcker, the Fed reaffirmed its purpose to fight the roots of inflation by using high interest rates: the minimum lending rate went from 13 to 14 percent and a further 4 percent penalty was levied on banks which too often asked for help from the central bank. Thus the quasi record 20.5 percent level was reached in the summer, to the Europeans' great annoyance as they were forced to raise their rates to protect their currencies. This was the case for West Germany, where the central bank raised its Lombard rate from 9 to 12 percent at the end of February.

By the end of the September, in view of the first symptoms of a new recession and the announcement of a drop in demand for credit, the monetary authorities relaxed their policy. The extra penalty was gradually reduced and eventually removed, while the federal minimum lending rate went from 14 to 12 percent. At the same time the costs of borrowing money dropped in two months from 20 to 12 percent, which allowed banks to reduce in stages the prime rate which by the end of December had gone from 20.5 to 15.75 percent. By the end of the year the drop in rates had tailed off and more or less stopped.

THE SECRETS OF PAUL VOLCKER'S SUCCESS

Extract from *The American Trial* by Jean Pisany-Ferry, Syros, 1988:

"We can spend a long time trying to discover Mr Volcker's thinking. However there were no doubts about the results: in the space of two years, from the end of 1980 to the end of 1982, the inflation rate had dropped from 10 to 4 percent. Even more remarkable was the fact it stayed below this level in spite of the strong recovery, the decrease in unemployment, and the drop in the dollar.... The price of this victory was high: the 1981-82 recession was the most violent for 50 years.... *What was the magic ingredient of this victory?...* It mainly lay with wages. It was said that Paul Volcker, during the months he kept the American economy in recession, kept a scorecard where he regularly noted the results of collective bargaining from all over the country. He thought, in fact, that victory would follow a change in wage levels."

DISCIPLINING WAGES WITH UNEMPLOYMENT

In four years, price increases slowed down considerably in the principal industrialized countries. From 10.2 percent in 1980, the inflation rate went to 5.9 percent in 1983. At the same time these countries saw their unemployment rates go from 7.4 to 11.8 percent. Was there a cause and effect between these two results and did prices drop as unemployment rose? It goes back to the "Phillips law", in vogue during the 1960s. The British economist Phillips observed what had occurred in Great Britain during 1861 and 1957 and had drawn up a wages-employment graph. He formulated the law whereby wage increases dropped in inverse proportion to the increase in unemployment. He also found a relation between prices and wages, taking into account wages as a cost in production. Thus one could draw up the Phillips curve, using the rate of inflation and the rate of unemployment.

Economists lost no time in pointing out that underemployment helped reduce increases in wages. According to them, one way to fight inflation was to rein in economic activity to trigger off a cycle of unemployment-stabilization of wages-slowdown in consumption-stop in price rises.

But in the 1970s the Phillips law could no longer be used to explain the unusual results. The decline in the labor market did not stop prices from increasing as in the past. If one looks at 1974 they increased even faster: up 24.5 percent in Japan, up 19 percent in

Italy, up 16 percent in Great Britain. The Phillips law was no longer applicable. To take into account the new situation, economists invented the word "stagflation."

Would the Phillips law still apply? At the beginning of the 1980s after the second oil shock it did. In the larger industrialized countries prices stopped increasing in inverse proportion to the increase in unemployment. Was this a coincidence? Or was the Phillips law still applicable? Did not its dysfunction prove the completely unusual state of affairs of the economic system? To reestablish things, it should have been enough to modify the most disturbed element in the unemployment-wages-consumption-prices chain. This was what most countries tried to do in different ways, which resulted in a spectacular drop in inflation. The crisis had broken down resistance and given back to the market one of its functions which the power games between various forces (employers, unions, state) had destroyed. Maybe Phillips was right.

THE UNIONS WERE NEUTRALIZED BY AUSTERITY PROGRAMS

Unions did not enjoy a favorable environment. The improved economic climate did not lead to wage demands being met and they clashed with hostile governments, intent on restrictive policies. Even if some fared better than others, union membership was in decline.

THE EXPANSION SPIRAL

The return to expansion came from a combination of monetary medicine (mid-1981-1982), which led to the containment of wages, a cooling off of the economy. The slower growth reined in oil consumption and provoked the 1986 oil countershock. The drop in oil deductions stimulated demand without affecting inflation excessively. The slowdown in the costs of production (wages, energy, raw materials, etc) brought back profitability. The large American deficits (federal budget and foreign trade) stimulated world demand. North America was the locomotive of growth in the last years of the 1980s. Profits gained during a period of little money and high real rates of interest led companies to clean up their balance sheets. Companies paid off their debts. Saving had increased returns, real estate prices shot up, which led to a speculative bubble which burst in 1987 — the stock market crash which killed the speculation without adding to the recession. Order books filled up and the rate of utilization of productive capacities became very high (1988-90). After the second oil shock investment took off again because industrial investments looked attractive once more compared to the stock market, which regained its health but not its 1986-87 form. Industry was working flat out, employment rose, the opening up of the Eastern European economies provided new perspectives of a rehabilitated market economy. Europe with the prospect of a single market in 1993 pulled itself back from its position in the early 1980s. The 1990s could look forward to a prolonged expansionary phase. However there were several dark shadows: high real interest rates, the fragility of financial movements, growing inflation associated with shortage of labor, and especially gigantic levels of debt (household, Western states, and of course, Eastern Bloc and Third World countries).

17. Industrial Changes

NEW INDUSTRIAL PLANT

REVOLUTIONARY INDUSTRIES

Computers, nuclear power and production, space industries today are replacing the industrial changes begun in the early part of the century (cars and aviation) as well as the postwar boom in reconstruction. Biotechnology is very promising — and potentially dangerous since it touches on life — and is another field rich in changes, along those which have occurred in electronics, computers, telecommunications, production engineering, mechanical engineering, robotics, etc. Neologisms abound for these new technologies, and new words have to be designated for new concepts and objects.

TECHNOLOGICAL AND ECONOMIC COMPETITION

The industrial developments following the development of the steam engine and the harnessing of energy took more than a century, the electronic revolution occurred within a generation. On the one hand the rhythm of progress and discoveries accelerated and electronics could be applied to ever-increasing areas. On the other hand the economic crisis and international competition forced the industrialized countries' companies to improve their productivity in all spheres: industrial production but also administration. Technology offered better and better products, which revolutionized traditional working methods: robotics and new office automation.

This was the crisis' paradox. The more one invested, the more jobs were eliminated. The period of investments in productivity stretched from 1973 to 1986. Even if the new technologies created new jobs, there was a critical phase, when the industrialized countries had to pay more for energy, remodel their traditional industries, invest in the new technologies, and train personnel. All this within a short period of time, with money in short supply and expensive, and with almost zero growth rates.

It was not surprising that tension was mounting, commercial battles were intense, and countries like the United States were trying to protect their technology, and control transfers. Japan decided to concentrate on electronics very early on and it became the spearhead of its economy. It had to sell its calculators, TVs, Hi Fis, and other integrated circuits to the world and automate its industries because exports had to pay for its fuel and food deficits.

In Europe the situation was very tight. Traditional industries were in a state of collapse, there was competition from Third World factories using cheap labor, from factories in the countries with raw materials, and from robotized factories in Japan. The cradle of the electronics revolution was elsewhere. The future communications revolution occurred in the United States and Japan. The old world had not yet faced up to the inevitable, nor the tremendous upheavals.

In order to compete with Japanese and American firms, which had large markets at home where they could mass-produce goods on a large scale, large investments needed to be made, especially in research. European countries also had to increase industrial and technological cooperation if they wanted to preserve their autonomy, their rank in the world economy, and prevent a drastic reduction in their people's standard of living.

TELEMATICS, SYMBOL OF CHANGE

Popularized in 1978 with the publication of a report on the "computerization of society," the word telematics soon became a key concept. This was probably because the authors of the report, Simon Nora and Alain Minc, merely conceptualized what already existed. Telematics sprang from the osmosis between computers, telecommunications, and television. Each sector had undergone dramatic development during the last 20 years in the industrialized countries; the Third World countries, with a few exceptions, had been left far behind. All kinds of computers proliferated; telephone networks spread to link up with the most remote areas; most households (in the industrialized world) had a television set.

These diverse markets had up till now remained distinct. Technological progress and the fantastic drop in the relation between performance and price with the advent of microprocessors, made the connecting up of these diverse elements both possible and profitable. They were all based on information. There was also a complementary definition: telematics was the science that combined the treatment and distribution of information in all its forms, even the broadest sense of the word. In our society, information was already, and will be for a long time, as necessary as energy. There is no doubt that the increase in energy prices accelerated the process of electronization and the irruption of telematics. Thus long-distance communications, weak consumers of energy, replaced physical travel. In reality telematics was not an industry like any other because of its economic, social, cultural, and political implications.

STRENGTH SHOWED THE OBSESSIVE JAPANESE SUPERIORITY

For decades, Japanese technology had spread far and wide. After developing electronics, the Japanese concentrated on hi-tech, robotics, materials, biotechnology, energy, and space. Sometimes this was to maintain their advance, sometimes to make up for their backwardness but mainly to be well-placed in the economic wars.

Japan Tried to Conquer the Electronics Markets

Electronics became an important part of the international economy. Europe continued to decline. In 1980 European companies had a 26 percent share in world production, in 1985 it had 21 percent. Japanese competition took 6 points away (15 percent of world production in 1980 and 21 percent in 1985), the United States maintained its supremacy (46 percent of world production in 1980 and 47 percent in 1985). Computers were the most important market in electronics, representing about 34 percent.

Abel Farnoux, in a report published in April 1982, concluded that "It is difficult to understand why highly industrialized countries, which with tenacity and success have established strategies in the space and defense industries, have neglected to apply the same energy and concert to electronics." The year 1987 was particularly rich for the electrical and electronics industries, but the dominant feature was the commercial war between the United States and Japan. Concerned about the erosion of its position in hi-tech, the United States imposed customs duties of 100 percent on some electronics imports from Japan, on the pretext that Japan was dumping semiconductors. At the same time it rejected Fujitsu's acquisition of Fairchild.

The New Japanese Strategy in Cars

Is Japan invincible? Starting from zero, the Japanese have become, after three decades, the world's leading car maker in 1980, overtaking the United States. The home market had been protected by a 40 percent import tax, which has now disappeared. Inversely and despite serious setbacks at first, exports have fueled growth. In 1975 manufacturers exported 1.8 million cars, 40 percent of their production. Ten years later, the record figure of 4.5 million was achieved: 60 percent of their assembly line production.

Cars were the best example of the Japanese model of accumulating surpluses at the expense of their American and European partners: hardly any imports and massive exports. In 1984 the United States decided to put a limit on Japanese car imports at 2.3 million a year. This policy of quotas had been adopted by several European countries in the 1970s — France, Italy, Spain, and Great Britain. Following these protectionist measures, Japanese corporations decided not to go as fast as they had in electronics (TVs and stereos), where they enjoy worldwide supremacy after 15 years, having wiped out American competition.

But obstacles were overcome very quickly. The corporations responded with three plans: paring down production costs, opening up the home market, and investing abroad. With the rise of the yen, it became profitable to invest abroad, even if the dollar's rise in 1989 to 140 yens trimmed the profit margins. Nobuhiko Kawamoto of Honda confirmed that his factory in Marysville, Ohio was doing well, producing 360,000 cars a year, and the Canadian factory produced 80,000 a year. Symbolically Honda exported 5,000 cars from the United States to Japan.

Toyota had already set up a 50/50 company with General Motors in 1984 and produced 300,000 automobiles in California. It almost doubled production in Kentucky (200,000 cars) and Canada (50,000 in 1990). Nissan produced 440,000 cars a year at its factory in Tennessee. To cross the Pacific other smaller Japanese corporations preferred joint ventures. Mitsubishi went 50/50 with Chrysler, Suzuki 50/50 with General Motors, Mazda with Ford, and Fuji had a 51/49 agreement with another Japanese company, Isuzu. In 1991 total Japanese manufacturing capacity in the United States reached 1.7 million vehicles.

This trend was repeated in Europe, mainly through Great Britain. Honda joined with Rover (taking up a 20 percent share). Nissan opened a factory in the north of England, followed in the summer by Toyota. When Europe opened up as a single market in 1993, the Japanese had the capacity to produce 700,000 vehicles.

THE SOUTH TOOK ON THE WORLD

A More Diversified Production

The Third World can no longer be written off as a producer of raw materials and purchaser of finished goods. From 1970 to 1981, manufactured goods went from 22 to 51 percent of deliveries — excluding oil — from South to North. Even if we leave out the Far Eastern exporters, the share doubled from 15 to 30 percent, and these structural changes were happening very fast.

For the most important countries (India, Pakistan, and Brazil), industrial products for several years represented more than half of exports. In all, after much stagnation (in India) and reverses (in Thailand), despite difficulties arising from recession and indebtedness, the competitiveness of Third World industries was surprisingly resilient. The growth of sales in the United States reflected an undoubted diversification in the South's industrial activity. The Third World made definite advances in all sectors: equipment (19.7 percent of imports to the United States), but also semi-manufactured goods (28 percent), chemical products (14.1 percent), and the addition of new goods. The deliveries of equipment ($17.5 billion) had almost exceeded sales of consumer goods. Despite increasing in value by $2.2 billion, consumer goods dropped their position. This was the sector long considered the reserve of countries with low wages — and the Third World supplied more than 54 percent of the United States' requirements. This drop was probably due to a dip in deliveries from the South of 80 percent in US imports of clothing.

In fact, specialization did not disappear but became more extensive, and at the same time Third World producers became more competitive. The developing countries confirmed their dominant position in telecommunications and electrical goods (49 percent of imports to the United States). They also performed strongly in non-electrical equipment (8.4 percent of imports to the United States): the Latin American countries doing as well (up 39 percent) as Asian countries. In fact motors and spare parts represented two-thirds of exports from Latin America. But accessories and spare parts for computers, semiconductors, and microcircuits were the booming sectors. Countries in the South provided 30 percent of American imports in this sector and shared the market with Japan (48 percent to Japan's 52 percent). The Korean company Samsung worked its way within a period of months from 18th to 13th place in world production of semiconductors, while none of the American producers was in the first five world producers in 1989.

Powerful Performances in Steel and Shipbuilding

There were adjustments in steelmaking: at the end of 1986 the 24 members of the OECD produced less steel than the rest of the world. The new producers pursued their expansion but Latin American producers did not grow as fast as their Asian rivals: the former had increased their production by 34 percent since 1980, as opposed to 61.6 percent for the latter (Asia excluding China, North Korea, and Japan).

In shipbuilding, Japan was the world's leading builder but its huge yards were rivaled by those of South Korea. The two countries were engaged in a commercial war, from which South Korea emerged less than glorious with the results of all-out expansion and dumping. The losses of the four principal South Korean shipyards amounted to $100 billion in 1986 and $235 billion in 1987.

MERGERS, JOINT VENTURES, AND RESEARCH

With the abundance of acquisitions and mergers, economic power was redistributed throughout the planet. Spurred on by the 1987 Crash, this development predated it: the delocalization of multinationals, worldwide movements to privatize, corporate raids, the deregulation of the financial markets were all aspects of the globalization of the economy and the subsequent need for industrial and financial organizations to reposition.

Schneider's takeover of Telemecanique, the attempted purchase of Firestone by the Japanese Bridgestone, the French company Hachette's takeover of the American publisher, Grolier, the takeover of Martell by Grand Met and Seagram — and the counteroffensives launched against these maneuvers — came from clear strategic objectives. Small companies needed to merge if they were to survive on the world markets. In the already highly concentrated area of tires, both Pirelli and Michelin responded defensively to the Japanese Bridgestone's attempt to buy Firestone. They had to grow or perish, as well as preventing others from growing, especially if they were Japanese and in car-related sectors, to safeguard against future pain.

Thus the trend to form conglomerates was an inevitable response to the globalization, and for the Europeans certain areas had to be restructured (energy, for example), faced with the prospect of 1992. Company capital was spread too thinly, as was seen with Belgium's Generale and the prevalence of family companies. These industrial problems predated the October 19

Crash, which reduced the price of companies, creating bargains. In any case the crash was not accompanied by the expected purge, and as companies became more profitable, large sums of money were involved: almost 9 billion francs each for the purchasers of Belgium's Generale, 6 billion for Firestone, almost 5 billion for 51 percent of Telemecanique.

This trend demonstrated the growing overlap between industry and finance, since in order to attack or defend industrial activities huge sums of money were needed at a moment's notice. Capitalism was becoming stateless. An Italian used a French firm to get control of a holding company which controlled a vital part of the Belgian economy. A Canadian took over a French company (Martell) to make the most of its Far Eastern sales network. For a long time capitalism had been closely connected with the state — in the 18th century financiers managed the public purse, in the 19th and first half of 20th century through colonialism — but it now seemed to be distancing itself. Global strategies were needed for the global markets.

In Europe companies merged to make the most of the 1993 single market: the German insurance company Colonia was bought out by the Victoire group; and in industry the German MMB (the aeronautics and military electronics group) was bought by Daimler-Benz, which consolidated its place as Europe's leading conglomerate. In Spain small companies were written off as inviable and sold to foreign groups — the truck manufacturer Pegazo was bought by the Germans, Man and Daimler-Benz.

MERGERS ALL OVER THE PLACE

Seven computer manufacturers — four US IBM, Apollo, DEC, and Hewlett Packard, and three Europeans Siemens, Bull, and Nixdorf — decided to join up and develop a new standard, based on the UNIX system, to challenge the number one telephone company, AT&T and its recent ally, Sun. The latter were accused of trying to seal up the market and control the future development of the telephone software.

For a long time there had been general chaos in computers. In the first years' euphoria, each manufacturer carved out its own niche, without worrying about the competition. However in the age of communication, incompatible computers could not talk to other machines. Users suffered as manufacturers seemed unable to achieve compatibility between their own machines of different sizes.

The large US companies radically changed strategy. They stopped denouncing the disloyal practices of their Japanese rivals. They no longer wanted to take them on, knowing that apart from in computers, they could challenge the Japanese. They decided to join them. The US companies thought their technical backwardness was too great and the best thing would be alliances to gain that technology. General Motors decided to join forces with Toyota to build a new model. There were further agreements in car manufacturing. General Motors held 34 percent of Isuzu Motors, Chrysler had 15 percent of Mitsubishi, and Ford 25 percent of Mazda Motors. The new Chevrolet was built in Japan by Isuzu.

SAVED BY RESEARCH AND INNOVATION DIFFERENTIATED DEVELOPMENTS

The most inventive French company was Thomson, which took out an average of 600 patents a year. Its Japanese competitor Hitachi took out 12,000 a year. That was twenty times more patents on double the turnover. To compare world rates: France had 11,000 patents a year, Great Britain 20,000, West Germany 50,000, and Japan 165,000.

TECHNOLOGY IN THE THIRD MILLENNIUM

These would be, according to the experts, the communications and command technologies: computers, robotics, telecommunications, and biotechnology. The specificity of the enormous technical change depended on the staggering rhythm of innovations in each of these areas. Also they had to crossover since developments in one area had immediate repercussions on the others. Biotechnology could assure the mass production of proteins from unicellular organisms using substrates of natural gas or agricultural debris. This would lead to a solution of the world's food problem and revolutionize agriculture, calling into question how it was organized and how we see the rural world. But biotechnology could also revolutionize computer science by creating microprocessors where biochemical molecules could be used instead of silicon or gallium. The molecules would have the same capacity to store information as living cells.

EUROPE GETS ORGANIZED

François Mitterand said the White House's Strategic Defense Initiative (SDI or Star Wars) demonstrated Europe's backwardness. He launched the Eureka project in April 1985, as a response to SDI and to stop Europe from being a US subcontractor. It was also to relaunch the European idea. Eureka's backers were convinced that the EC could not move forward because of its bureaucratic and institutional form and they wanted to accelerate industrial cooperation to produce concrete results. Eureka was not just a program of research, it was a place where companies could come together with their own ideas. It was up to them.

The 1988 Launch of the European JESSI Program

Today Europe only produces 10 percent of the world's microchips. To challenge the United States and Japan, Philips, Siemens, and SGS-Thomson cooperated in research and development of submicrotechnology — because the thickness of the drawing line on an integrated circuit is less than a micron (between .5 and .3 of a micromillimeter). This would be necessary for the production of memory and microprocessors at the end of the 1990s. This was known as the Joint European Semiconductor Silicon (JESSI) and was part of Eureka. The three companies would perfect the manufacturing processes of the next generation of integrated circuits. Each would concentrate on areas they were strong in: Philips on Read-Only memory, Siemens on RAM memory, and SGS-Thomson on programable memory.

Considerable sums of money were at stake: to finalize the manufacturing processes — at least $400 to 500 million needed to be spent annually for seven years. This was the first large-scale project in Europe. Given the strategic stakes of the project, the industries received subsidies: if the European electronics industry was to survive producing consumer products like televisions or hi fis or in other areas like computers, armaments, telecommunications, etc, governments would have to help microchip research, which was the basis of electronics. The Japanese led the world in semiconductor production with 48 percent, the United States managed 39 percent, while the Europeans lagged far behind with 10 percent. Furthermore the Europeans were rarely at the cutting edge of technology.

Was European Culture against Technological Change?

Europe's backwardness in relation to Japan stemmed from its inability to adapt to change and its slowness in adopting new ideas and technologies. This was a cultural problem. Europe was also slow to adopt modern working methods: quality control, analysis of value, design, non-Taylor organization. Without adopting these methods, the introduction of new machinery or technology was doomed to failure, as had been shown by the poor performance of some of the larger, flexible workshops.

The Eureka program could not limit itself to technical developments, it had to address the methodological, organizational, and human environment, in order to succeed in the techno-social transformation. This transformation did not just mean the advent of a society of communication but a society of creation. People's intelligence and dynamism were just as essential as capital or machines to face the brave, new world.

NEW, PROFITABLE CHANNELS
ELECTRONICS: A HITECH REVOLUTION

In 1983, of all the industrial sectors, it was the electronics industries that saw the most spectacular growth. This was particularly noticeable in the United States, where the market grew by 15 percent following great progress in computer microtechnology. The electronics industries occupied an important place in the world economy. In 1986 with a total production worth $485 billion, it represented 4.7 percent of world Gross Domestic Product, excluding the Eastern Bloc. By 2000 it would total 8 percent.

BUT NOT IMMUNE TO MINICRISES

In 1985 there was the first "crisis" within the world computer industry. It was more of a hiccup, given it was just the slowdown in the growth of the US market. None of the big names, such as Control Data, Apple, Burroughs, Wang, were spared. During the first three-quarters of the year, IBM saw its profits drop. There were extremely complex reasons for this: there were over-optimistic forecasts of microcomputer sales and the premature announcements of new IBM models, which put orders on hold. In 1989 the market for semiconductors was slowing down, achieving only 10 percent growth, a feeble result in this sector.

SPACE-TELECOMMUNICATIONS: RAPID GROWTH

Telecommunications were pushed by computer science developments and saw stunning progress: networks which allowed the simultaneous transmission of text, image, sound, and data, were being put in place in Europe; mobile telephones were available, etc. There was almost euphoria in air transport because everyone began to use aircraft to send passengers and goods. The air carriers anticipated 5 percent growth until the end of the century. This rise almost reached 10 percent. In Europe the first months of 1989 saw 12 percent monthly growth rates, in Asia it was even more.

MORE TRADITIONAL CHANNELS
CHEMICALS: CRISIS AND RECOVERY

Following the toughest crisis since World War II, lasting four years, there was a recovery in 1983 but whose benefits were not immediately felt. At the beginning of spring, Rolf Sammet, president of the German group Hoest, the world's leading chemical manufacturer, said it was like a "fragile plant." The plant would rapidly regain its vigor during the second quarter and especially during the second half. The year's results were the best since 1979.

The upturn in the chemicals industry was nothing less than superb. The intermediate results published by most companies were spectacular: an increase in profits of 23 percent for Bayer and the West German BASF, 34 percent for Hoest, and 25 percent for the US Du Pont. Rhone-Poulenc, the number one French company, did even better with a 40 percent growth in profits in September. Chemicals had done well out of the consumer boom.

FULL PRODUCTION IN CARS

During the bleakest years, many predicted that the car manufacturing industries would have to merge and some would disappear altogether. In 1988 reality contradicted the experts, there were some irreversible mergers and much scaling down. With a total of 33.3 million cars, production was back to the 1978 level.

OLDER CHANNELS
STEEL: HALTING THE DECLINE

The year 1982 had been disastrous and 1983 was no better, except in the United States. World production had stabilized at a very low level the previous year (400 million tons approximately). Steel makers worldwide took on board the problems and there were few optimists. Steel needed a strong upturn in GNP. As long as GNP did not pass the 2.5 or 3 percent growth threshold, the steel market was in trouble. Since the macroeconomic perspectives for the 1980s did not leave much room to hope this level could be achieved, the market would remain flat during the 1980s. The threshold could be explained by the decline in massive infrastructure works, which were blocked in all countries for lack of credit, as well as the end of the housing boom. As well as these two structural developments, there was a drop in investments, mainly in mechanical goods, thus steel, and the slimming down of numerous consumer goods, including cars.

The problem was knowing whether the technological developments would accelerate, leading to the inevitable reduction in the requirements for steel in plant as well as consumer goods. In either case steel would be hard hit. However, after 15 years of crisis, marked by large-scale closures and redundancies, Western steel manufacture knew a period of respite, because of the world upturn. Even "older" industrialized countries had good years: with few exceptions, their companies went into the black, thanks to price adjustments caused by growing demand.

SHIPBUILDING

The year 1985 had been one of crisis in world shipbuilding, but 1986 was the year of collapse. According to the Lloyds Register of Shipping in London, Great Britain, the tonnage of ships on order at the end of the third quarter was the lowest it had been for ten years. Throughout the world, there were widespread redundancies and restructuring. Thus, in 1988, Margaret Thatcher's government decided in early December to close down the nationalized yards in Sunderland, northeastern England, with the loss of 2,000 jobs. At the end of the year there was some movement in shipbuilding. Japan, Spain, Brazil, and Taiwan benefited from this recovery, while there were considerable drops in the number of orders in Yugoslavia and Denmark.

TEXTILES: CONTINUAL SLOWDOWNS

The 1989 trends in the world textiles were market stagnation, mergers and company modernization, with the developing countries holding their own. World consumption grew very little or even collapsed, as in knitting yarns, so textiles industries continued their investments in modernization and improved productivity, to the detriment of employment which continued to fall.

THE SOUTH:
BACKWARDNESS OR A TECHNOLOGICAL GAP

There were about 3.5 million patents in the world, of these 6 percent or 200,000 had been taken out by underdeveloped countries. Using the classic distinction between "national" and "foreign," (a legal distinction which does not take into account the different ways control can be exercised abroad), only a sixth of that 6 percent belonged to nationals of Third World countries. Since Third World companies had hardly any patents abroad, it followed that these countries only owned 1 percent of all the world's patents.

In the Third World, human resources were not the only resources to be exploited insufficiently. Much industrial equipment was under-utilized. The setting up of factories, which benefited Western exporters and local bureaucracies, usually ended in disaster. In the absence of a real industrial culture and of a rigorous training program for workers and technicians, the plants broke down, and some even stopped working. Much of the developing countries' surplus from manufacturing production and agriculture was plowed back into rehabilitating existing factories.

The transfusion of knowledge contained risks which Thomas Dakati-Kamga, Cameroon's Minister of Equipment described thus, "A technology developed within a particular physical or socio-economic environment cannot be transplanted into another, without encountering more or less serious rejection or negative secondary effects." In fact there was an opposite transfer of technology, since the elite from many Third World countries became desperate about change at home (material, cultural, and political) and emigrated to the industrialized countries.

THE ASIAN DRAGONS

In 1979 the major event for the island-state of Singapore and its neighbors was the redeployment of economic activities, the second industrial revolution. Faced with growing protectionism in the Western countries and competition from Hong Kong, Taiwan, and South Korea, the Singaporean economy had to respond. It abandoned down market electronics and cheap textiles to concentrate on industries which required a lot of capital and few workers. These included advanced technologies like precision engineering, aeronautics and car components, medicines, oil equipment, computers, insurance, banks, and tourism. The city-state took an increasingly large part of the value added to the state's exports. The first stage in the state's attack on industries producing down market goods and using a lot of labor was to increase wages by 20 percent. Similar wage increases were to follow in successive years, to force out industries which could not adapt to this second industrial revolution. The government spent a lot of money on professional training: its slogan was "high wages for better qualified work."

In South Korea, after 1979, it was thought that 15 percent of an electronics component, 25 percent of a car for export, 5 percent of a car for the home market, and 20 percent of a nuclear power station was produced abroad. South Korea tried hard to reduce this. To achieve this objective, it devoted 3 percent of its GNP to research and development. It was to be seen whether this Korean haste was compatible with research which generally takes a long time to come to fruition given their lack of suitably qualified personnel.

Thailand's extraordinary growth over the last decade had not been problem-free. There was a serious shortage of engineers and technicians. Almost 2,700 new engineers graduated every year, when 7,000 were needed. There was also a dearth of technicians in electronics, car manufacturing industry, and even in textiles, jewelry, and shoe manufacture.

INDIA BETWEEN TRADITION AND MODERNITY

India was a country of great contrasts: on the one hand there were thousands of pilgrims visiting holy places and women carrying rocks on their heads; on the other there was television, satellite launching, the green revolution with India exporting rice, space travel, and one day the management of the monsoons. There was the huge, illiterate peasantry, with poverty, the problems of caste system and the untouchables, the stifling traditions of religion, which preached accepting fate.

There was also a middle class, still very much a minority, but dynamic and in search of success, which traveled by scooter or car, listened to local pop music, drank local Cola, ate pizzas made in India, did aerobics, went to seminars in Goa, had videos, watched and copied the West to the point that women wanted to become air hostesses.... There was little synthesis, even if the first Indian astronaut did weightless yoga and if trucks were blessed before being put on the road.

TECHNOLOGICAL TRADE
BETWEEN SOUTHERN COUNTRIES

There was much competition in the Third World between the leading technological sectors — ready-built factories, major works, engineering. From 1978 to 1980 the newly industrialized countries had become the second largest provider of industrial goods in Asia, then in Latin America and the Middle East. The year 1981 was one of stagnation marked by a slight drop in the export of manufactured goods from the industrialized countries, it confirmed the importance of South-South trade and the competitiveness of the newly industrialized countries in all sectors.

In order to win contracts for ready-built factories, engineering, and all sorts of major works, the most advanced newly industrialized countries only competed on the international market after years of experience at home. Backed up by teams of technicians and the reputation of its plants, India installed in a few years more than 150 industrial plants (in textiles, chemicals, steel, machine tools, as well as electric power stations, telecommunications networks) from South Asia to Libya and from the Middle East to East Africa. About 50 Indian engineering companies with 15,000 technicians worked in the Third World, as did some Brazilian firms.

This competent engineering services' activity showed the Third World's emancipation and cleaned up the market by contributing to the break-up of the monopoly of know how. National companies took the initiative in these areas. The still low value of these contracts was less significant than the confirmation that the newly industrialized countries could do the work.

THE EASTERN BLOC: OBSOLETE TECHNOLOGY

The non-capitalist Eastern and Central European countries' economic situation was parlous because of their infrastructures, investments, and institutions. The infrastructures, that is the roads, railroads, water and sewage works, telephone systems, hospitals, schools, etc were in a deplorable state. The inventory of state assets had hardly been developed and on top of that had been badly maintained, so it was in a poor state and inadequate. These inadequacies were a barrier to developing the economy.

Productive investments were not in any better state but the main problem was that there were not the right factories and machines. The productive plant in most of these countries was technically obsolete and sectorally poorly adapted. The inefficient blast furnace was an example of this. The technology behind the goods and the productive processes were 15 years behind that of the industrialized countries and 10 years behind that of the newly industrialized countries.

THE SOVIET UNION: A COLOSSUS WITH FEET OF CLAY

The Soviet Union would like to have had the means to resist a new "blockade" by diminishing its economic dependence, that is developing as much as possible its own technology. Thus it decided to increase its efforts in scientific research as well as its application to the economy. Few speeches or reports failed to mention the better use of scientific results in agriculture and industry, the more efficient development of technical improvements designed to increase work productivity, and the more rigorous integration of research to the production processes so that it moved from the extensive to the intensive. It was only when the Soviet economy met these conditions that it would pull out of the crisis, which had made it fragile and weak relative to the United States. Much was at stake..

The planners talked about a "new exploration of scientific and technical progress." Special programs were launched, and the 1982 budget at 24 billion roubles, up by 5.2 percent, represented 5 percent of the world's budget. In February 1982 the president of the State Committee summoned the foreign ambassadors and scientific attaches to announce "We have reached a stage where we no longer need Western aid to develop our technology. It is only a matter of time." Was this hot air? Possibly, but it showed the Soviet Union did not intend to be moved by US threats and that if it wanted to recognize that a break with the West would involve a substantial delay in the fulfillment of its programs, it was not about to admit that they would be compromised definitively.

It all depended how long the delay would be, but those who thought that it would only take the Soviet Union a few years to overcome its main handicaps, pointed out that it had been able to obtain remarkable results in the military and scientific fields. These may have been helped by industrial espionage, but they would continue and all the Soviet Union had to do was concentrate its efforts on civil production.

But there lay the problem. While the Soviet Union could develop prototypes (scientific or military), it was unable to put them into production. So the Soviets built military and scientific computer hardware which were well adapted to their purpose, but they had quantitative and quality problems producing computers for economic use (planning, management, control), particularly for very small and very large systems.

Mikhail Gorbachev was the first Soviet leader to have traveled abroad before his arrival in power. He could see that the Soviet Union was very backward. He did not hesitate to point out that many Soviet goods were inferior to world norms. The Soviet Union produced large quantities of oil, coal, steel, synthetic textiles, cotton, wool, leather, etc. But it was still unable to provide its citizens with the household goods, shoes, and clothes they wanted to buy. The production and distribution networks seemed to lead to waste, as goods spent much time on dusty shelves. In the other communist countries the technological backwardness and the desire to modernize were persistent themes.

DIVERSE BUT SIGNIFICANT BACKWARDNESS

Hungary

The delays in modernization of several key sectors (for example, steel) and poor productivity were severe problems for an economy particularly vulnerable to the repercussions of the world crisis, because it relied on foreign trade for more than 40 percent of its revenue.

Czechoslovakia

The development of the Czechoslovak economy was held up by technological backwardness. Despite great efforts particularly using robotics, the results were inadequate. The country's leaders were concerned about the ageing of the production machinery, especially those used for foreign trade.

Poland

The results of the 1986 plan were not encouraging, despite a 5 percent increase in industrial production. The per capita income remained about 20 percent lower than it had been in 1980. The modernization backwardness only got worse.

Romania

Nicolae Ceauşescu's Romanian economy was at least 40 years out of step with Europe. It had shortages of basic necessities, hot water was supplied in pathetically low amounts, electricity came under a quota system (22 kilowatt per month for one room, with the threat of being cut off if it was exceeded). These general shortages, which were getting worse, were due to the leadership's incompetence but also to an unproductive agriculture directed to producing exports — destined for the Soviet Union — and industrial plants which were as gigantic as they were obsolete.

East Germany

The objectives of the annual plan were realized and often improved upon with an increase of 5 percent in national revenue. The growth in industrial production (8 percent in 1984) was almost all due to productivity. The introduction of new technologies allowed the saving of almost 572 million hours of work in industry and construction, using 11,700 new industrial robots to go with the existing 27,000. In 1986 some 62,200 industrial robots were already in use and the production of microprocessors had accelerated. East Germany wanted to catch up with the West by 1990: production in electronics and microelectronics increased by half in less than four years. However quality did not go hand in hand with quantity.

NECESSARY RECOURSE TO THE WEST

It was thought, for example, that the Soviets had gained five to ten years thanks to the sophisticated machinery supplied by the United States for the Kama truck factory. This gain contributed to the war efforts in at least three ways: directly because these trucks were used in Afghanistan by troops; indirectly given that this ultramodern equipment could be used by them in diverse military operations; even more indirectly in that the savings on economic resources were assigned to the army.

However the difficulty the economy faced in digesting the Western technology, acquired over the last few years, went some way to explaining the drop in industrial contracts with all the capitalist countries, which had supplied the Soviet Union (since the end of the 1970s).

COCOM: DEFENSE BEFORE TRADE

Since the beginning of the Cold War, the transfer of technology, conceived of as a transmission of know how, was reduced. In November 1949 the Cocom (Coordinating Committee for Multilateral Export Controls) was set up to harmonize the technological restrictions between NATO (except Iceland) and Japan.

Any help from the West could be used for military purposes. Of course, hitech industries were more closely scrutinized, even if they represented only a feeble percentage of foreign trade, and even if, as it is rumored, they are out of date immediately they have been installed. With detente, trading relations were opened up again and accelerated after the end of the 1960s, particularly between 1972 and 1975. After 1975 this changed : trade in machinery slowed down while that in food increased. Paradoxically, it was when transfers were declining that the invasion of Afghanistan (1979) and the Solidarity crisis in Poland led to the West tightening up.

At the Malta summit, Gorbachev obtained from the United States the promise that the Soviet Union would eventually be integrated into international economic and financial institutions. The first stage should have been GATT, but the general *rapprochement* accelerated and made nonsense of the restrictions on technological exports to the former "evil empire." This was good news for the Soviet economy, as well as for the Western ones.

18. Feeding the World

According to the FAO (the United Nations' Food and Agriculture Organization), in 1989 out of 4.8 billion human beings, there were 1 billion undernourished, 500 million were hungry, and 12-18 million died of hunger. In the early 1990s 35,000 children died each day of starvation. At the same time the FAO estimated there were 900 million overfed people....

THE UPSIDE DOWN WORLD

In 1989 cereal production grew by 120 million tons to reach 1.88 billion tons. But as the director general of the FAO, Edward Saouma, noted this improved harvest did not prevent demand from outstripping supply for the third consecutive year. Food stocks diminished and were back at the level they were in 1970. Production went up in the developed world, but in Third World countries it improved marginally (1 percent). The situation in Ethiopia deteriorated. A preliminary survey of the 1980s revealed that malnutrition had worsened and affected 500 million people.

THE WEST MANAGED ITS SURPLUSES

The second half of the 1980s was dominated by a quasi-general overproduction of food, which was more visible because of the relative stagnation in demand. This imbalance affected world prices, which had been accentuated by food subsidy battles in the developed world and the contraction in the trade in agricultural produce. The religion of market forces meant the big wheat exporters — the United States, Canada, the European Community,

Australia, and Argentina —,were engaged in a savage competition to sell their huge surpluses. This was done at any price and using any means, regardless of the real needs of their client-countries and the future of their farmers.

During 1975-1990, world wheat production went from 350 million tons to 520 million, under the double effect of increased yield and guaranteed prices. In developed countries this was accompanied by greater intensification: more wheat, fewer farmers. There was the prospect of limitless expansion of world demand, which effectively doubled between 1970 and 1980 from 50 to 100 million tons. After this it had stabilized at 85 million tons in 1985. The result was overflowing silos and a surplus among the exporting countries of 80 million tons. This led to the trade war, fighting for shares in the market.

At the same time world demand had considerably changed: some of the larger, traditional buyers, such as India and Pakistan, were not so needy; new, socialist clients appeared. The Soviet Union and China were at the same time the world's largest producers and importers. The rest of the surplus was sold throughout the Third World. In most cases this wheat was sold on the open market, food aid, which continued to decline, represented only 10 percent of this.

However, the insolvency of many of the importing countries, the drop in oil revenues, regional conflicts, and geopolitical factors led many of the big exporters to use food as a bargaining tool in bilateral agreements. This was particularly the case in the Mediterranean area, a battleground between the United States and the EC. Solvent clients got the best deal out of this economic cycle which favored them, making prices drop and influencing market shares. This was the case with the Soviet Union, always looking for self-sufficiency in cereals.

Wheat was at the heart of the problems provoked by the world crisis. There was famine and deficit on one side, and surpluses and waste on the other. There was an obvious solution. But world trade was as incapable of resolving the South's food problem as it was of finding outlets for the North's farmers. The distribution and level of trade reflected the inequalities in development, the degree of integration of each country in the world economy, and the struggle for hegemony between the most powerful countries.

THE SUBSIDY PROBLEM

The leading agricultural producers were in the grip of a paradox. While world cereal production hit a new record of 1,679 million tons (including rice), there was constant talk on both sides of the Atlantic of the need to reduce surpluses and limit, or even eliminate, the subsidies which caused them. The United States took the initiative, July 4, 1987, by proposing "zero option" for developed countries: the complete dismantling of the subsidy program within 10 years — the elimination of export grants, customs barriers, farming subsidies. The Reagan administration specified that, during 1976-86, the EC and the United States had spent $296 billion to maintain agriculture, that was more than the Chinese GDP....

Even if no one could quite contemplate the complete suppression of subsidies, in 1987 it was obvious that there had to be an end to agricultural losses. Further subsidies were needed to find outlets for overabundant produce, while elsewhere with the drought conditions in the Third World, subsidies to subsistence farmers were as rare as rainfall. The effect of the costly food aid programs and sales at knock-down prices (thanks to grants of as much as $40 on a $120 ton of wheat) was that the United States devastated certain developing countries' agriculture, by disorganizing their foodstuffs market with massive injections of its cereal surpluses. The American proposal of "zero option," to eliminate all subsidies within ten years, did not achieve any consensus, as was demonstrated in the growing stalemate of negotiations on GATT between the United States and the EC.

The drought which hit the United States' great plains that summer, precipitating a 20 percent drop in US cereal production, could have led to the cleaning up of world agricultural relations. The United States could have made the most of the ensuing higher prices to revise downward their subsidy program and follow a more reasonable policy. This was a missed opportunity which did not recur. Despite the growing imports by India and especially China, the cereal market contracted. For many developed countries the time had come to diversify away from wheat, maize, soya, meat, or sugar, where there was growing competition. It was time to concentrate on the products, often quite elaborate, of the agrifood industry, where the value added brought in money. In Europe as in the United States, there was such a big food surplus, it was impossible for the subsidy race to stop abruptly.

FREEZING THE LAND

There were three ways of helping the milk market: direct intervention; stimulating animal consumption at home (particularly the premium for converting into powdered skimmed milk to feed calves); helping exports and protecting against imports.

SMALL CALCULATION FOR COMMUNITY USE

The intervention mechanism, in broad outlines, was as follows: every year the EC fixes an "indicated price" and an intervention price for milk. Using the indicated price as a base line, the dairy farmers negotiate the real price, paid by the milk processors to the farmer. The real price is generally about 90 to 97 percent of the intervention price, depending on profitability. The milk processors buy up all the milk production.

Let's imagine a milk processor buys up in a year one million liters (US convert) of milk, of which 500,000 liters are transformed into yoghurt and 300,000 liters into cheese. The remaining 200,000 are converted into butter or milk powder, according to the EC list of charges and "taken for intervention" by the ONILAIT. The milk processor receives from the farmers the "co-responsibility tax," created in 1977, which is paid to the FEOGA, via the offices of ONILAIT, according to the quantity delivered.

In 1983 the EC's inventory grew enormously: the butter mountain was 853,000 tons, almost three times larger than in 1982. Some 870,000 tons of powdered skimmed milk was bought up, an 87 percent increase on 1982; 34 percent of European production ended up in the EC's stores. Denmark put 62.7 percent of its production of powdered skimmed milk in store, compared to 11 percent of France's production. The reason for this massive increase in stocks was the collapse of third party purchases, mainly the developing countries.

To read the US press, the planet was threatened by a serious food crisis... harvests and stores were too abundant. To prevent the total collapse of prices, the Carter government restored the system of "freezing land," which had been in use until 1973, to reduce the possibility of using it for cereals. It was in 1987 that the EC agricultural ministers launched an ambitious program: to reduce by about 20 percent the volume of cereals, beef, and wine by freezing land or introducing more extensive farming. Why not leave land to lie fallow? Agriculture had been too successful and production had to be limited to the available outlets, because genetic engineering meant less land produced more. Also aging farmers had fewer heirs than in years gone by.

THE FAILURE OF THE SOCIALIST SYSTEM

* *In the Soviet Union* — On March 15, 1989, during the Central Committee of the Communist Party of the Soviet Union's plenary session, Gorbachev admitted that the Soviet Union had lost 22 million hectares in 25 years. Of this, 3 million were the best irrigated land and 10 million were flooded fields, the result of badly run irrigation schemes or misconceived hydraulic projects.

* *In Poland* — Farmers and farm laborers represented more than 30 percent of the population, and 48 percent of the population was employed within agri-food sector (compared with 12 percent in France). The agri-food sector was the most difficult area in social terms: every time there was a price increase, there were strikes, as happened in December 1970 and July 1980. This occurred despite the fact that in 43 years of rule by the Polish Communist Party, heavy industry had been prioritized.

Of the 600,000 farms in Poland, only 36,000 had running water. This was the case of the Slotys family — father, mother, three children aged five to 13 years — who had a seven hectare farm in Barchow (some 60 miles from Warsaw), of which five hectares produced cereals — wheat, maize.... Mr. Slotys did not own a single farming machine: "I rent them," he said. "I do it with my family. I repay them in gasoline." Normally the rent of a combine harvester was 28,000 zlotys an hour — the private sector rate was 30,000 — which was the equivalent of a quarter of the average monthly salary in Poland. In fact the Slotys lived, like most Polish peasants, hand to mouth. "We sell our produce to pay taxes, buy clothes and anything we cannot produce, if we can find it on the market."

In Poland 80 percent of agriculture was private. The land belonged to the peasant and any attempt at nationalization (between 1956 and 1958) had failed. Also Polish agriculture's structure barely advanced during 30 years and reforms were undertaken only in the large state units (on average more than 3,000 hectares/convert to US).

There were grave deficiencies in equipment: there were just about one million tractors (of less than 30 horsepower), there was little mechanization, and there was a shortage of spare parts, if machines broke down. Poland used 190 kg of fertilizer a hectare a year, which was the lowest rate in Europe. Almost all pesticides were imported, an annual bill of $200 million. There was much waste resulting from poor stock and storage management, and the length of time taken to preserve produce. Witold Trzeciakowski, the president of the Economic Council, explained "some 30 percent of milk and meat products were wasted because there was not enough refrigeration space or because of badly organized transportation."

Shops were not empty because the Polish farmers did not produce enough but because they did not sell. According to Leon Podkaminer, a professor at the Academy of Sciences and economic adviser to the OPZZ union (close to the CP), the depreciation of money and the lack of consumer durables led to the hoarding of agricultural produce.

DIFFICULT REFORMS TO EFFECT

"Rent a few hectares. Why bother?" In a comfortable cottage with red flooring, an elderly Ukrainian grandmother played deaf. Gorbachev could repeat ad nauseam that the peasants must manage their land, she did not think about it. Her mind went back to the 1930s, when she first arrived on the collective farm. "We worked night and day. You had to come back home on foot. Now I'm at home at 6 in the evening. We were serfs, now we're the masters." Nikolai Sopchuk, president of the "40th Anniversary" collective farm's council, nodded "the people do not want to be slaves again. If they take back the land, they will not be able to use the industrial techniques, which the collective farm uses."

The inhabitants of the rich Ukrainian countryside deserved the title of Resistants to *perestroika*, which Muscovite intellectuals gave it. According to an agricultural specialist at the Novosti Agency, a hundred farm workers had taken on individual leases, mainly in the Baltic republics. The estimate was low, probably too low, but it reflected the lack of response of the population. Even if the breakup of the collective farms was not on the cards, their management had already changed. On the "40th Anniversary" farm, autonomous teams had been set up to look after some of the farmland. They have a contract with the collective farm's council, which meant they have to achieve certain targets. Any surplus produce provided extra income for the farm workers.

The program was ambitious: to give the peasants a sense of ownership, use the carrot of wages to make them work, allow the enterprise spirit to flourish — this among a class that was liquidated during collectivization. For every well-managed, high-performance collective farm, there were many run-down, almost medieval, farms, run by local managers worried about their jobs. "One in ten farms was good," said Viktor Kirichenko. "Out of 50,000 collective and state farms, more than 1,700 were run at a loss, 20 percent barely broke even, 10 percent were profitable and could have become private companies. Others had indifferent results." The agri-food businesses, set up as joint ventures with Western firms (including Interagra), and the lease of 500,000 hectares in the Ukraine to the Italian company, Ferruzi, were examples of the reforms. But the peasants were not behind it.

THE PERSISTENCE OF FAMINE
IN THE THIRD WORLD

The richer countries kept more than 350 million tons of cereals in reserve, while food aid never exceeded 10 million tons a year, 500 million people suffered from malnutrition, and 280,000 people died each week. Hunger was more than ever part of the economic and political, in truth ideological, struggles in the world. Dr Paul Lunven, director of the FAO, estimated an individual needed to eat 1.4 times her or his metabolic rate, an absolute minimum of 2,500 calories per adult. By this measure the number of undernourished rose to 494 million in 1980.

In 1985 were there more or less undernourished individuals than 15 years before. In fact it was both more and less. More because the number of undernourished had risen due to demography (the affected countries were very populous); less because the proportion of undernourished in the Third World population fell slightly, for example, from 28 percent in 1970 to a bit more than 20 percent 15 years later.

THE FOOD DEFICIT:
SLIGHT WORSENING IN THE YEAR 2000

The FAO scenario, Horizon 2000, gave a Third World food deficit bracket of 52 to 100 million tons of the equivalent-wheat.

Globally since the 1970s there was a definite improvement. According to the FAO, from 1984, 34 countries, whose population totaled 1.7 billion, that is half of the Third World population, had exceeded the daily 2,500 calories per human level. These figures hid massive discrepancies between regions of the Third World emerging from chronic malnutrition (mainly India and China) and those where it is still prevalent (Africa); discrepancies within countries (India had 200 million malnourished people), or sometimes whole countries (Vietnam, Cambodia or Kampuchea as it was then known, Laos, Afghanistan), to pockets of poverty within continents where the situation was improving; finally between town and country, because extreme poverty was concentrated in the Third World urban sprawls of Lagos, Kinshasa, Calcutta, Karachi, Mexico City, etc.

AFRICA ON THE EDGE OF DISASTER

More than ever Sub-Saharan Africa was in a crisis: agricultural, demographic, ecological, financial. According to the FAO statistics, the 45 Sub-Saharan African countries would need 4.5 million tons of food aid by 1988, an increase of 47 percent on 1987. The contributing countries had only promised 3 million tons. The rest would have to be found by commercial imports, thus increasing the debt burden. To put it simply what was not paid for or given would not arrive. In Africa, where less than 80 percent of food needs were met, malnutrition could only get worse.

CUSTOMS VERSUS THE GREEN REVOLUTION

"It's too bad." Within 15 years, despite considerable foreign aid, two severe famines had hit several countries south of the Sahara. Could they not make a green revolution like the Asian countries? There, with a few exceptions, the stores were full and past disasters could be averted, even though there was still malnutrition.

We must compare the plateaux of India with those of the African countries with similar geographic conditions, Zimbabwe, Zambia. In India they could sustain 200 people to the square km, while in Africa it was only 10 or less. Therefore, apart from high risk areas like the Sahel where there was insufficient rainfall, large areas of Africa could feed a larger population, with new techniques. In Africa women cooked food on a fire using three stones. Given the demographic pressure, firewood had become rare. So the experts said "let's teach women to use clay ovens as they do in Asia. They would use half the wood." However it was not that easy. You needed good soil, adequate cooking time, and skill to make a prototype clay oven.

Another example was trying to improve wells by using a pulley with the rope. In countries which had only recently begun to use wheels, this did not prove easy. In agriculture the gap between the hoe and plow was enormous. In Asia one man could push the plow and manage the cattle. In Africa the cattle needed to be trained. At first several men held the plough while others guided the cattle. This innovation disrupted the traditional division of labor between herders and farmers, between women and men. As for the use of irrigation to extend land use, without historic precedents, there were too many distributaries.

The political instability of many states and the lack of administrative cover did not facilitate technical innovations. This was also true of the scattering of villages and the dreadful state of the roads. All these problems were underestimated when these countries gained independence, around 1960, but they were not catastrophic. They could have been overcome with time, strong leadership, and decisive administrators.

In spite of the population increase which every day widened the gap between traditional ways and needs, there were several hopeful factors. African farmers had been able to innovate in the past and they could today. They had managed to grow American plants like cassava, maize, peanuts, and peppers, before the colonial period.

The green revolution achieved remarkable results in production but it necessitated the purchase of agri-business products like seeds, fertilizers, pesticides, machinery, heavy equipment, dams, and canals. Poor farmers became indebted, redistributed land was sold, official programs helped well-off farmers because they gave a better return on investments. Countries lost the necessary autonomy to decide on local food priorities, because they had to agree to strategies imposed by developed countries. For smallholders, land and work became hard to get. They fled to the cities, swelling the already huge urban masses, increasing the food needs and justifying further development programs.

THE SPECTER OF PENURY ROSE UP

In 1988 there was a drought in the United States, Canada, and China, agricultural waste in the Soviet Union, land lying fallow in Europe, swarms of locusts in Africa, and late monsoons in India. Security in food, built on stocks which were thought to be inexhaustible, continued to crumble. In eight years Africa had had three years of drought, the 1988 one seemed the worst of the century... while waiting for the next one, because in the United States the cereal growing area shrank year by year as the semiarid zone spread.

The 1988 results showed how world agriculture had suffered: cereal stocks had dropped by 111 million tons and production by 57 million tons. The green revolution of the 1970s, with its hybrid wheat and maize, and its incredible battery of fertilizer, seeds, and machines, let people believe in eternal abundance. It seemed science had allowed agriculture to triumph over nature but 1988 had exposed its Achilles' heel. This proved the wisdom of having surpluses as the cereal prices rose. The grain mountain disappeared surprisingly fast.

A report written by the US economist Lester Brown for the Worldwatch Institute, which specialized in research on development, contained a note of alarm. He could see two major dangers, the increased degradation of the environment — degrading the soils, growing shortage of water, global warming — and overpopulation. Economists recommended conservation of the soil and demographic controls. Malthus would have done the same. Brown also pointed to the downward trend in *per capita* world cereal production since 1984 (down 14 percent), while from 1950 to 1984 it had grown by 40 percent. For five years the best Third World agricultural producers — China, India, Mexico, and Indonesia — were stagnating or declining. Elsewhere the overuse of the soil led to the loss of the equivalent of Australia's cereal area each year. Finally, the Earth's population increased by 86 million each year, agronomists thought potential productivity increases would be limited. The most pessimistic thought agriculture would follow the law of diminishing returns.

It would be foolish to underestimate the speed of progress, but the climatic disasters of the year meant food had again become a diplomatic weapon, one which had been long buried by years of overabundance. In 1988 it hit the Third World first, which had to pay twice as much for its cereal imports. The Soviet Union would suffer a similar fate if it could not escape the collective miasma.

19. State Intervention

FROM ONE CRISIS TO ANOTHER

The economic crisis revived a public debate which had opened in the 1930s. The capitalist world had been in a crisis then, that only ended with World War II. The most renowned participant in this debate, John Maynard Keynes, won it and his theories had been followed ever since, even if not always faithfully. In France forty years ago Jacques Rueff started to question Keynes' wisdom but the fiercest critic in the English-speaking world was the Austrian Friedrich von Hayek, who had held a chair at the London School of Economics since 1931. In 1974 he had received the Nobel prize in economics. He was now back in Austria, living in Salzburg, but spending a lot of time in the United States, where the "Austrian School" was very lively if rather small.

At a symposium organized by Monex International on "The Economy in Crisis," the US economist Patrick Boarman, a very interesting exponent of monetary theory, read an address from Professor von Hayek. He was in New York putting the finishing touches to his second volume of a trilogy of memoirs (he was born in Vienna in 1899). What gave his address particular weight was the fact that he was one of the few economists to have predicted in early 1929 that there would inevitably be an economic crisis.

The U turn in economic orthodoxy will be difficult to achieve since it implies on the part of all official experts admitting a fundamental error.

EXORCISING THE KEYNESIAN DEMON

According to von Hayek, if Keynes had lived a bit longer he would have been one of the principal adversaries of inflation, and this was why his untimely death (in 1946) was such a calamity. How was it that this error could have turned the minds of so many economists, and through them influenced a whole generation?

Meanwhile was not the drop in demand the reason for the current slump. The reason industrialists were all cutting back on machinery programs was because they could not see any tangible prospect of an improvement in consumption.

According to von Hayek, the recovery would only come with a resurgence of investments, however, these had to be carefully made. It was not the offer of subsidies or reduced interest loans that would spark off a healthy growth spurt. What von Hayek recommended was the opposite of what most governments were doing against common sense. The governments and employers thought that by stimulating demand new investments would become profitable but this was only true if the investments merely increased production using yesterday's techniques. In fact, productivity had to be stimulated, that meant providing a given work force with greater capital. In this way by reducing costs, the economy would be back on its feet....

Von Hayek raised an old controversy, a source of many heated arguments, in apportioning the blame for the 1929 crisis being prolonged by 15 years (instead of two to three years) on erroneous policies which sought to cure the depression by increasing wages. This policy was launched in the United States by President Herbert Hoover and adopted by President Franklin Roosevelt. Another factor in the unnecessary length of the depression was the absence of a healthy international monetary system, according to the Austrian economist.

WHY WAS THE STATE SO OVERWHELMING?

It was a sign of the times that the US economist James Buchanan won the Nobel prize for economics in 1986. For 15 years there had been a renaissance in economic conservatism in the

West. James Buchanan, along with Gordon Tullock and the Public Choice Society, had long questioned the need for the state to intervene in society. Buchanan had two objects in mind. On the one hand he asked "who and what benefits from public spending?" On the other he was following the Italian and Austrian tradition of the early 20th century in carefully dissecting the procedures by which individuals allow the state to receive taxes and then the state spends those resources to finance public policy in their name.

The new Nobel prize winner decided that individuals simply wanted to follow up their private choices by public ones. There was a unity of action. It was not possible to separate the economic and the political. The two areas were interlinked, or at least should be. If they were not, it was because the democratic processes were too weak. The elected representatives created financial illusions (making it appear that public services cost little or were free, minimizing the importance of taxes) or introduced bureaucracy: in league with technocrats, they let public services grow to increase the directors' prestige.

Thus Buchanan, who was not afraid of delving into political science, insisted on individual participation on the political market. The only objective of private and public choices should be the well-being of all and the consumer or user-taxpayer-voter should be considered as acting in a coherent manner. According to the professor, opinion polls should be extended, in the same way that purchases were daily decisions, it was no longer enough to choose "those who are going to choose." Everyone could be an expert on public life.

Buchanan's original contribution was that new constitutions not only contained general agreements on the existence of this or that public service (school, hospital, local services, etc), but also covered public deficits by withdrawing from the elected representatives part of their budget powers. Buchanan explained the reasons for the constitutional Gramm-Rudman-Hollings amendment, which obliged the American president to reduce the budget deficit, in the following way: Keynesian economic ideas had impregnated political institutions too much and skewed the functioning of democracy. Fiscal and financial responsibility had disappeared with Keynes's dicta, by showing that what was folly in private life could be prudence or good management in public affairs. Public deficits were really abuses of power, even if they were authorized by the elected representatives. Taxpayers did not know what the costs were, since every asset or public service had a hidden cost, either from inflation, or from future taxes, which were needed to pay off the public debt incurred now.

ULTRA-CONSERVATIVE MYTHS AND PARADOXES

There was a curious paradox in the 1980s. There was a public outcry almost everywhere and in almost all sections of society. There was too much state, too much bureaucracy, and too many taxes. However any analysis of that decade's economic successes showed they were the product of state intervention, born of the conviction that human will could influence the course of history. Reaganism was the opposite of conservatism. It was traditional Keynesianism. Massive increases in defense spending and budget deficits, coupled with a reduction in direct taxation, were the motors of US recovery. As for Japanese and Korean economic policy, there were not many historical examples so systematically interventionist in monetary, financial, technological, and industrial terms. Of course, there were too many rules. Of course it was a vain and inauspicious task to try to stem the flow of blood from the millions of arteries in the body-politic, but the new conservatives were even more dangerous because they failed to monitor the heart and brain.

THE DISORIENTED STATE
AND STOP AND GO POLICIES (1974-80)

The states themselves were riddled with gangrene. How many restrained themselves from lurching between stop and go, hoping recovery would reduce unemployment and fearing a worsening trade deficit; or else showing themselves ready to stimulate the economy by running up a budget deficit but giving up prematurely for fear of stoking up inflation and weakening the currency. Valery Giscard d'Estaing's expensive-looking policies found followers abroad. By reducing the size of economic movements, it avoided the worst depressions, but it did not lead to a complete recovery.

All recovery policies, which were not based on a draconian control of inflation, failed. The recent US and Japanese growth was attributable to the control of inflation. The US budget deficit was so large that it did not allow the growth to last. The Japanese example was more convincing, because a constant but controlled budget deficit allowed steady growth thanks to a negligible rate of inflation. If inflation exceeded 4 percent, growth was not possible.

BACK TO THE ORIGINAL KEYNES

The 1980s did not quite know which way to go. Successive policies were like the same sequence over and over again until finally it was realized that.... The exit from the 1982 low point could be explained by the application of neo-Keynesian therapies: voluntary and automatic deficits abounded. Budget control seemed to work again, at least in countries like the United States where the dollar's attractiveness (1983-86) rendered the accumulation of external deficits "harmless" (as it was put). More astonishing, the relaxation of monetary policies in operation since 1984-85 in different countries was curiously accompanied after 1987 by the pursuit of disinflation.

Last but not least, the drop in taxes and deregulation, when it exceeded the limits of the first percent of variation, had perverse effects. Thus the most obvious experience of privatization, that of Great Britain, showed that what was done was not as simple as it was supposed to be: the multiplying of hybrid enterprises allowed one to believe in the glory days of the mixed economy. In the United States, learned economists, like Rudiger Dornbusch of the Massachusetts Institute of Technology (MIT) or Alan Blinder of Princeton University, favored Keynes as the least risky recipe for economic success, along with new accents on the microeconomic, which must be respected when following macroeconomic policies. Laurence Summers of Harvard University (a specialist in measuring world product) did not believe in the "capacity of the market to raise the maximum investments and to allocate them in the best way."

All these factors pointed to a return to the primary source, to the real Keynes whose work had not been fully exploited, in the eyes of leading economists. Keynes recommended the "socialization" of investments but at the same time much latitude so that there could still room for initiative and private responsibility. Keynes thought the traditional advantages of individualism should be maintained and that the microeconomic should above all be preserved; Keynes had been against austerity measures to deal with recession but was also the instigator of the compulsory loan, and said he was in favor of compressing consumer spending to avoid overheating the economy. Keynes believed the money supply should be managed very subtly for many reasons: because it represented a social convention, a state of mutual confidence, arbitration between different interests at a given moment (access to credit led to strong competition between brokers); because it allowed society to define the degree of confidence it had in the future (to sit on a stockpile of cash and to refuse to invest in real goods were both signs of lack of faith in the future); because financial institutions do not like to be brutalized by drastic monetary policies. In Great Britain Keynes was neither a conservative nor a labor supporter.

DEVELOPMENT MODELS

At the end of the 1950s, some of the best of the world's economists forwarded a report to the UN on the future of those countries which had just gained their independence. They predicted a brilliant future for Belgian Congo, which had few people and plenty of raw materials, but they were not impressed by South Korea's prospects, under US tutelage and badly damaged by the war. Since 1960 Zaire's (the former Belgian Congo) per capita income decreased by 2 percent a year, while that of South Korea increased by almost 7 percent.

The economists got it wrong because they saw economic growth in terms of the accumulation of "production factors," that is, raw materials, qualified work, technological know-how, and especially capital. As well as the accumulation of production factors, growth depended on the allocation of resources and the choice of development strategies.

STATISM VERSUS CONSERVATISM

Two successive doctrines were adopted to conduct the poor countries' development strategy. Historically, the first was industrialization regulated by the state and geared to the substitution of imports. After the 1970s this doctrine was followed by the conservative credo and the opening up of the world markets. Nowadays both paradigms have been questioned not just because of their mistakes, but also because development led to problems they had not mentioned: social demands, cultural preferences, and the hierarchy of power.

For those countries which gained their independence after World War II, the basic model of development was that of the construction of a national industry, which had to be as heavy as possible. The Soviet Union's example was the historical justification for this, nationalism the political justification; the fear that opening up frontiers and that *laissez-faire* would lead to the domination of foreign interests were less obvious economic arguments. All these reasons combined to explain the adoption of a state model heavily weighted to industrialization in countries as different as Nasser's Egypt, Boumediene's Algeria, Nehru's India, and even in the most unexpected cases, such as N'Krumah's Ghana.

It is difficult to draw up a balance sheet for these experiences. On the one hand, it is an undeniable fact that China and India succeeded in establishing industries from steel manufacture to consumer durables, shielded from foreign competition, and affording them real economic independence. But in other cases the enormous price of industrialization, paid for by poor people, often resulted in disappointment.

THE FAILURE OF INDUSTRIALIZING INDUSTRIES

The example of Boumediene's Algeria (1965-78) was significant in this regard. This country decided on an enormous effort to develop heavy industry, devoting more than 30 percent of its GNP and sacrificing the development of its agriculture and certain social infrastructures like habitat. By the end of the 1970s what was left was a truncated productive machine, largely under-utilized, employing a very small number of wage-earners and unable to supply the basic necessities of its population. Such a failure could not be explained purely in terms of bad management. It sprang from the choice of the very nature of model of development. In fact, the self-maintained growth assumed that all production would engender an income surplus capable of absorbing this production.

But if productive capacity exceeded potential demand, capital was under-utilized, leading to the waste of scarce resources. Precisely, during the first phases of industrialization, a large part of demand was directed at improving wages or importing industrial machinery, which proportionately reduced demand for national goods. On top of this, the techniques used were transferred from already industrialized countries and were most often capital intensive and did not allow the training of wage-earners capable of consuming the goods produced.

In addition the national industries enjoyed the position of monopolies, shielded from external competition, and were able to impose high prices curtailing consumers' purchasing power. Only large countries, like India and China, which already had captive demand, or countries which enjoyed a source of foreign currency, were able to improve simultaneously production and global demand.

Since the 1970s the internal market's deficiency led some countries like Brazil to look for outlets abroad for goods which the national markets could not absorb. At the end of the decade, China and India both opened up so they could acquire the techniques and necessary capital to sustain growth. During the 1980s most Third World countries looked abroad, to be ruled with a rod of iron by international organizations like the World Bank, in the hope, often disappointed, of achieving an external balance by increasing exports.

THE CONSERVATIVE STRATEGIES IN EXPORTS

The adoption of an export strategy was often accompanied by deregulation and debureaucratization policies, the return to market mechanisms was supposed to lead to increased competition and eliminate monopolies and more generally allow for a more efficient allocation of national resources. The sometimes brutal instruments of this new paradigm were the lifting of protectionist barriers, large devaluations, the sale of public enterprises, and the respect of a tightly balanced budget. For example, all these policies were put into action in Chile between 1975 and 1982 under the guiding hand of the "Chicago Boys," but they also inspired the economic policies of Turkey, Egypt, and Indonesia, though in a less brutal way.

Did this conservative strategy get any better results than the more interventionist policies? It was true that competition was a powerful motor of development and those countries which were best able to conquer expanding markets were the ones that had the highest growth rates. However, the conservative recipe did not allow a return to growth and attempts to open up and deregulate were sometimes accompanied by major crises, as in Argentina and Chile. Following the 1982 devaluation, this country saw an 18 percent drop in its per capita GNP.

The reasons behind these failures came from the nature of the insertion in world trade and the perverse effects of the market. Firstly, the poorest countries can only offer the world market unskilled work or raw materials. Thanks to the generalized automation of the industrialized countries, cheap labor was less in demand. As for raw materials, their real price dropped after 1980 by almost 20 percent, because of the overproduction of some tropical produce and the use of new materials instead of traditional minerals. As well as the impossibility of insertion in world trade, there were the perverse effects of internal liberalization. The economic opening up and deregulation often led to the destruction of small national producers and the buyout of state enterprises by outside parties.

SPECIFIC SUCCESSES CANNOT BE GENERALIZED

As for the lifting of controls on the movement of capital, often it led to capital being moved from productive structures into speculations, as is evidenced today in Mexico. We are a long way from the paradigm which stated all that was needed was to put the market in place to achieve the most efficient allocation of resources. Faced with these opposed strategies of development, more pragmatic solutions were called for. South Korea was able to conquer foreign markets by protecting its internal market. This country's example also showed that the administration can guide and control industrialization by relying on private firms, from large groups to small subcontractors. The problem was that the experience of countries like South Korea and Taiwan could only serve as examples, if their phase of takeoff occurred in very particular historic circumstances, when cheap labor was a decisive asset in international competition. The countries which tried to emulate this example 20 years later, like Tunisia and Mauritius, had to come down a peg or two.

There were two lessons to be drawn from the failure of these models of development. The first was that one must not confuse growth in production with raising the people's living standards. Secondly, economic development cannot be imposed in an authoritarian way, but rests on the widespread decentralization of initiatives.

NEITHER A STATE STRAITJACKET
NOR UNBRIDLED CONSERVATISM

The Algerian and Brazilian experiences showed that a strong accumulation guaranteed neither work for all nor even the meeting of the people's barest essentials. By the end of the 1970s Algeria under Boumediene had only created 370,000 industrial jobs. In spite (or because) of strong growth, income disparities in Brazil became more acute. Some estimated that 10 percent of the richest households received half the national income while 20 percent of the poorest only had 2 percent. The bitterest lessons to be drawn were in the spontaneous explosions in Iran, Egypt, Mexico, and

Algeria. These popular uprisings contained many unpleasant surprises for many economists. They had long considered that high growth necessitated forced savings, and only strong government could ensure this.

Too much emphasis on economic logic exacerbated social resentments, paralyzed individual initiatives, and made the people's fundamental problems more and more difficult to express. The most widespread phenomenon of Third World economies in the contemporary world was the extraordinary capacity for people's invention and organization to meet their needs, from Chinese farmers to *pobladores* in Santiago. These initiatives had to be free from the administrative straitjacket, market mechanisms had to allow the poorest people access to land and the means of production, and decisions had to be really decentralized.

20. World Trade and the World Economy

TRADE'S GOOD LUCK

Since 1963 the world economy enjoyed a quarter century of almost uninterrupted growth, apart from 1975 and 1982. Like production, trade expanded in volume (that is, without taking into account the effects of prices and exchange rates), but with a different dynamic. During this time, which covered the end of the 30 glorious years, the 1974-83 crisis years, then the boom of the late 1980s, total production multiplied by 2.7, while trade multiplied by 4.

The autonomy of trade had accentuated for five or six years, which allowed Arthur Dunkel, the director general of the General Agreement on Tariffs and Trade (GATT), to write in his December 1989 report. The American postwar doctrine, according to which free trade was the instrument of general prosperity, had not been contradicted. In 1962-63, in response to the setting up of a new commercial bloc in Western Europe, the European Economic Community, the democratic US government relaunched multilateral trade negotiations. The Kennedy Round (1964-67) led to the reduction of average customs duties to less than 10 percent on industrial goods, while recognizing the specific interests of developing countries for the first time. The next two GATT cycles, the Tokyo Round (1973-76) and Uruguay Round (1987-92), enlarged the multilateral negotiations: about a hundred countries were involved and the ground covered was not just customs but all non-tariff restrictions (reserved public markets, norms, subsidies). Finally, agriculture and services were also discussed.

Nonetheless, the brilliant world trade results and the quasi-permanent negotiations on free trade should not lead to any illusions. There were winners and losers in commercial competition. The developing countries as a whole belonged to the latter category. Specialized in trading raw materials, both agricultural and mineral, they suffered an almost permanent deterioration in terms of trade — with the exception of the oil-producing countries for a brief period in the 1970s. Japan was a winner during the 1960s, then the new dragons of the Far East, because they based their economic takeoff on mass market consumer goods (cameras, watches, toys, and electronics). Others also, like Brazil, developed consumer goods or intermediary industries, which allowed them to take over a considerable share of the world market.

The rich countries' domination of world trade did not diminish. It even strengthened. Also, without ever really threatening free trade, there were great tensions in world trade. Politics intervened more than once in commerce. For example, there were the Cold War COCOM restrictions on technological exports to Eastern Bloc countries, or the US cereal embargo to the Soviet Union after the invasion of Afghanistan. The oil weapon was twice used by the Arab oil producers against Israel and its Western allies. South Africa was boycotted by trading nations because of its apartheid policies.

Apart from these relatively rare cases, daily tensions between trading nations were present, particularly in steel and agriculture. The United States, by far the most important world importer, progressively lost its export supremacy from the beginning of the 1970s. The advent of a massive trade deficit in the mid-1980s revived protectionist tendencies. Even though Reagan and his successor George Bush used their vetoes on openly protectionist laws proposed by Congress, they reinforced their legislative arsenal against "unfair practices," reserving the right of judgment in a unilateral way.

Two countries accumulated considerable trade surpluses, Japan — especially in trade with the United States — and West Germany — especially in trade with the rest of Europe. The other large trading nations France, Great Britain, Italy, Switzerland all found themselves with trade deficits (marginally compensated for in services). A third category of country, those of the Eastern Bloc, saw trade between themselves and the rest of the world grow less quickly than the average for world trade. The conversion of these socialist countries to the market economy, will eventually enlarge the area of free trade. The multiplying of US and EC trade agreements shows how much hope the Eastern Bloc countries place in hard currency trade — while waiting for trade between them to normalize. After the conclusion of the Uruguay Round in 1993 world trade should prosper.

THE DOMINATION OF INDUSTRIALIZED COUNTRIES

Developed countries dominated international trade. What was true in 1963 is even more true today. Their exports represent more than 2.5 times that of the rest of the world in value. The rules of the commercial games set by multilateral negotiations and by the evolution of terms of exchange worked to the advantage of rich countries. In a quarter of a century, sales multiplied by 20, those of developing countries by 18, and those of the Eastern Bloc by 15.

The composition of goods traded was also altered. In 1963 agricultural produce represented 29 percent of the total, and mineral products 16.8 percent. Some 25 years later they only represent 13.5 percent each, while manufactured goods make up 73 percent. This trend was unfavorable for the large producers of raw materials such as the Third World and the Soviet Union. But the developed countries are also the main exporters of agricultural produce (more than half the total), which leaves the rest of the world only a slender part of world trade, which was otherwise very vibrant. The emerging countries of the Third World learned that they would face competition from industrialized as well as unindustrialized countries. Also rich countries must not arm themselves with more or less disguised forms of protection, which were denounced by GATT in its December 1989 report.

FROM EUROPE TO THE PACIFIC BASIN

Ten countries control 61 percent of world trade, both in exports and imports. They were the same ten years ago. West Germany took the poll place in exports between 1986 and 1988; but the United States ousted it in 1989, according to GATT's estimates. Behind the astonishingly stable group of leaders, there came many new entrants. Between 1978 and 1988 Hong Kong, Taiwan, the People's Republic of China, Singapore, and Brazil appeared in the top 20 world exporters; South Korea and Spain climbed up and Switzerland, Australia, and East Germany fell back. By the end of the nineties which of the new countries will have climbed into the top 10?

There was a considerable flux in trade between the rich countries. While the 1963 chart showed that the currents of world trade were essentially European and transatlantic, that of 1983 revealed a change in favor of the Pacific and Asia. In a quarter of a century North-South trade did not grow in relation to the world total, with the exception of the Far East. For a quarter of a century the United States had continued to dominate international trade. But it went from having a surplus until the 1970s to having a record deficit in 1987 of $170 billion. Was the strong performance in exports since 1986 the answer to the trade deficit?

Since the early 1960s, West Germany had sold more than it bought, even during the oil crises in 1973-74 and 1979-80. In 1986 West Germany achieved a record $200 billion exports, overtaking the United States. However the United States took out its irritation over its massive deficit on Japan; West Germany bought more than Japan and had a smaller surplus with the United States, since most of its surplus came from trade within the EC. West Germany's foreign trade displayed the same upward trend as the Deutschmark.

In 1963 Japan was only a small trading nation. Some 25 years later in 1988 it had multiplied its exports' value by 50, while the United States had only managed 14. In the 1960s Japan had had deficits, every oil crisis led it into deficit. But Japan compensated for its vulnerability in terms of raw materials, particularly energy, by its industrial productivity. This was also the case for the other major shock experienced by Japan with the revaluation of the yen vis-à-vis the dollar in 1986-87 (the dollar fell from 250 to 150 yens). The Japanese surplus over the rest of the world dipped and in 1989 it dropped markedly for two reasons: imports clearly increased, and the delocalization of production led to a decrease in exports.

THE PRINCIPAL EXPORTERS OF SERVICES

In developed countries services represented more than 60 percent of GDP, while in developing countries the proportion lay between 30 and 70 percent. Unlike goods, services did not need customs documents. Definitions and nomenclatures differed from country to country. Nonetheless GATT evaluated services at 20 percent of world trade. The leading exporters of services were also leading exporters of goods. But there were a few variations: France followed close behind the United States; West Germany was third, and Japan trailed behind being in 6th place. The over-representation of transport and tourism in the exported services explained the French share and the presence of several Nordic countries among the top 20 exporters of services.

CONSTRAINED AND UNCONSTRAINED COUNTRIES

In their April 1979 report, the Cambridge University economists centered their analysis of the world crisis on international trade. One of the major innovations of the report was a world model drawn up by Francis Cripps, one of the economists' leading lights. This group, strongly influenced by Keynes, was out of line with the current teaching of general theory; the principal economic variables affecting activity and employment were no longer those which governed home demand, but those which were linked to foreign trade. The group's analysis also strongly opposed the traditional theory according to which employment and the pressure of demand in each country were independent of the level of world trade, the latter being "balanced" by price adjustments which laid out the market share of each country. According to the authors, the analysis of the world economy rested on observation of the great stability in the medium term of the market shares of exported manufactured goods, as well as different countries' propensity to import (the part of imports in national production). Observation of these key variables in different groups of countries led the Cambridge group to formulate a fundamental distinction between constrained and unconstrained countries, applicable in the medium term. The group called the constrained countries were those which had to adjust home demand to prevent their current deficit from becoming excessive. This was the case for almost all countries. However, unconstrained countries could adjust their demand to achieve national objectives (full employment, growth in GNP, reduction in inflation), without worrying about their current balance. In 1975 only Japan, West Germany, and the OPEC countries fell into this category. Thus Great Britain, a constrained country, had a strong propensity to import (14.2 percent in 1975) and its share of exported manufactured goods in world trade was fairly weak (7 percent in 1975). For Japan, an unconstrained country, its shares were 2.4 percent and 11.5 percent respectively.

According to the Cambridge group, the level of world trade in manufactured goods played an important role in sequencing the variables. How was this? A fairly simple analysis led to a formula showing this variable in relation to the unconstrained countries' volume of imports, their commercial deficit in manufactured goods, and their share of world exports.

Thus the determining variables of the level of world trade were:

1) the dividing up of countries into constrained and unconstrained;

2) the level of home demand fixed by unconstrained countries which with their propensity to import determines the volume of that country's imports;

3) the unconstrained countries' share of the world's exported manufactured goods;

4) the volume of trade deficit in manufactured goods that constrained countries can finance.

According to the Cambridge group the current world recession was not inescapable. An examination of the different variations in the model showed that better performances could be attained if other policies were adopted. In this respect the two countries which appeared to play the crucial role in determining the actual level of world activity were Japan and the United States (more than OPEC). Because of its trade surplus (at least until 1978, the last year for which statistics were then available), Japan could set its rate of growth to match its internal priorities; by increasing its volume of imports of manufactured goods and reducing its share of world exports, it could contribute to sustaining world growth. US economic policy was also crucial to the rest of the world. The current risk was that the United States would undertake deflationary policies to reduce its trade deficit; in fact the strong elasticity of imports in relation to home demand was a major obstacle to attempts at recovery in constrained countries. The pursuit of a similar deflationary policy was likely to provoke a marked slowdown in world activity.

The Cambridge group proposed an alternative way out of this situation; it constituted a way out of the current dilemma recession-trade deficit. The United States would expand home demand and restrict imports of manufactured goods to keep them at their previous level. The object of the restrictions was the rapid growth in GNP while avoiding a reduction in the total volume of imports. Thus paradoxically recovery and a freeze on the volume of imports at the previous level would harm world activity less than deflationary policies, which would inevitable reduce the level of imports. This was the reports' principal idea, which distinguished the Cambridge group from the free traders whose doctrines had until then influenced high-level international economic meetings. Beyond the role of motor played by the two countries, the results given in the world model showed how concerted international action could allow world trade to reach an optimal volume. This concerted action would include, in outline, expansionist policies by unconstrained countries, a reduction in Japan's exports, limiting the growth of constrained countries' imports to allow their economies to recover, and active discrimination in favor of developing countries' exports. This international solution presupposed a high degree of coordination between blocs, but would allow optimal growth compatible with keeping balance of payments in equilibrium. According to the authors, this growth could be as high as that enjoyed by the world as a whole before the current crisis.

THE QUESTIONING OF FREE TRADE

Trade had often led to the reinforcing of wealth and minority rights in developing countries. It was probably easier to establish relations abroad than to worry about the disinherited and landless. Thus the directors of multinationals, which now controlled almost half of the world's trade, and the socialist and developing countries' leaders were working hand in hand, this being facilitated by improvements in communications. In many cases those in charge lost sight of the real needs of farm workers and bought instead goods whose true utility was lost on the country's citizens. One should not forget the scandalous arms trade, in which all countries share responsibility.

Currently the world is in the grip of a serious crisis and habits, whether intellectual or other, need to be changed. Already plans have initiated new maneuvers based on the fashionable concept of redeployment. They are aimed at a fairer distribution of the cards. According to this plan, which was outlined in the 1979 OECD study, the newly industrialized countries (NIC) have to be accommodated — Mexico, Brazil, South Korea, Taiwan, etc. The industrialized countries should abandon traditional sectors of industry to these new Japans, to concentrate on more sophisticated manufacture. The NICs would leave simple manufacture to other Third World countries, just as Japan gave up textiles long ago. Thus a relay system would ensure a new world distribution of work to the greater good of international business.

Such an adjustment would leave the leaders in their place, preserving their knowledge and defining the way forward. In the developing countries the elites, who already have access to the consumer society, would be tempted to follow this route, which would increase the distance between the new bourgeoisie and the rest of the population. Trade would then have facilitated an extroverted and limited growth. Free trade was not the guarantor of universal prosperity. On the one hand an integral application of its laws led in the Western countries to excessive specialization, while it was better for socio-economic reasons to maintain a greater diversity of activity. On the other hand in the Third World trade, which gave rise to export industries, led to the growth of shanty-towns, the abandonment of traditional cultures, and rootlessness. Thus foreign trade needs to be controlled, perhaps within the context of regional organizations.

21. The Monetary System, World Debt, and Finances

THE INTERNATIONAL MONETARY SYSTEM'S
GOOD AND BAD TIMES

The monetary conference, which was held from July 1 to 22, 1944, in Bretton Woods, in New Hampshire, was particularly significant in the last, critical 70 years of monetary history, marked by many fruitless attempts to reestablish an international monetary order. While the war was still raging in Europe and the Far East, the foundations were laid of what was to prove one of the most durable and grandiose attempts to restore a stable monetary system. In fact it was the installation of a system of fixed rates of exchange conceived at Bretton Woods, which in its application resembled the old gold standard of the 19th and early 20th century. On many essential points it was innovative by providing a backup system for countries going through difficult trade balance problems.

Some 44 delegations were invited to attend the conference which took place in the Mount Washington Hotel. However two delegations dominated the proceedings. Firstly the US delegation, led by the remarkable Harry Dexter White (later accused by the McCarthy commission of being a member of the Communist Party). In the end the US team won out over the other influential delegation, Great Britain, whose prestige was enhanced by being led by the most celebrated 20th century economist, John Maynard Keynes. With hindsight, we should be thankful that the US's proposals were adopted as they were simpler (which in this matter was a quality) and more constructive than the British ideas.

Keynes represented a country which possessed all the exterior attributes of power, but was in reality poverty-struck and badly in debt. The British proposal envisaged the maximum protection for debtors, which could only be accomplished by artificially extending all the means of credit facilities, whose extensive use would have led to general financial insecurity. The Latin American countries were over-represented in relation to the role they played in the world economy (but the war had temporarily enriched several of them), while Europe was represented by delegates from governments in exile. This was the case with France, whose delegation was led by Pierre Mendes France. He opposed some of the United States' more excessive claims. Finally the Soviet Union participated in the discussions but never ratified the Bretton Woods agreements.

The aim was to respond to the Axis powers' declared intentions and to prevent a return to the terrible disorders of the Great Depression of the 1930s, with its millions of unemployed and closed down factories. Nazi Germany wanted to create a unified Europe and Japan wanted a Greater Asia Co-prosperity Sphere, out of the debris of the world economy, which had foundered under protectionism and the breakdown of the international monetary system after the 1929 Wall Street Crash.

To meet this double challenge, there was only one way: ensure the return to free trade by laying down mechanisms to help the weaker countries adapt. It was understood that if international trade was free, there also had to be some discipline to avoid anarchy. It was the monetary system which would fulfil this function and assure economic freedom. Some 730 delegates took part in the July 1944 conference, but a lot of work had already been accomplished before the conference. The British and US experts had been holding discussions since the signature of the Atlantic Charter in August 1941 between the US president and the British prime minister.

Keynes presented five different versions of his plan, which involved the issuing of an international currency, the *bancor*, to be used by the central banks of the members of a common fund. Harry White and his team also redrafted their proposal several times before coming up with the version which was very close to the final agreement. It established a system of fixed exchange rates based on gold and the dollar and set up the International Monetary Fund (IMF) to give credits to help with balance of payments problems, and the World Bank to give long-term loans to finance development projects.

The principle behind the proposed monetary system was to ensure the free convertibility of currencies, which was a precondition for free trade. Each country had to guarantee this free convertibility, at least for nonresidents. But the Bretton Woods agreements, signed in July 1944, ten months before the end of World War II, went even further. The members of the IMF had to ensure the convertibility of their currency at a fixed rate.

THE MAIN POINTS OF BRETTON WOODS

* Each country agreed to ensure their currency's convertibility with all others and particularly with the dollar standard of exchange.

* The dollar was fixed to gold according to the equation $35 were worth one ounce of gold. It was theoretically possible to obtain gold, which remained the ultimate theoretical standard (hence the gold exchange standard).

* Countries had to define the fixed rates of exchange and be prepared to defend the value of their currency within a one-percent margin of fluctuation.

* Competitive devaluations were not allowed and remained unusual.

* A supranational organization was founded, the IMF. It had to monitor the enforcement of the Bretton Woods rules.

It was only after the end of 1959 that the European countries and Japan were able to make their currencies convertible. It was only after this date that the Bretton Woods agreements were really in force. The system collapsed when the currencies began to float in 1971. However this did not undermine the principal mainstay of Bretton Woods, which was to ensure the convertibility of currencies; from then on the convertibility was at variable rates.

THE BRETTON WOODS ANOMALIES

As it was put into practice, the Bretton Woods system contained a serious anomaly. The United States was almost exempt from the obligation to defend its currency on the foreign exchange markets, because the dollar was used as a reserve currency, and thus the Americans could cover their external deficit by issuing dollars. In line with the Bretton Woods agreements, the creditor nations could demand the conversion of their dollars into gold; but as soon as the United States began to worry about its currency's solidity, these countries refrained from effectively exercising this right as a rule.

The result was that it was incumbent on the central banks of countries other than the United States to defend the value of the dollar. The central banks in question bought back the dollars on the market by issuing their own currency, which provoked serious inflationary tensions. It was to reduce these that they decided in 1971, and more definitely in 1973, to stop buying dollars automatically every time the dollar looked like falling below its level.

JACQUES RUEFF'S WARNING

Jacques Rueff saw the Bretton Woods monetary system, qualified by the specialists as the gold exchange standard — as a means for the United States to accumulate "a deficit without tears." The US creditors reinvested their dollars in New York (instead of asking to be reimbursed in gold) as and when they were accumulating, which gave the US the possibility of disposing of the same quantity of income as if their balance of payments had not lurched into the red.

The Bretton Woods system did not collapse at once. It came down in stages, each of which, not just the last one, involved the abandonment of an essential part of the system. It is perhaps arbitrary to say the first serious crisis came with the pound sterling's catastrophic devaluation on November 17, 1967. It may be fashionable today to affirm that a system of fixed exchange rates can accommodate periodic parity "adjustments," but these can aggravate existing imbalances if they affect a leading currency and if they are not accompanied, as was the case, with the necessary measures to make the new parity credible. This was what happened in the months that followed the sterling devaluation. It led to intense speculation in gold, which led on March 17, 1968 to the breaking up of the gold "pool," then step by step to the destruction of the subtle mechanism of Bretton Woods.

THE GOLD POOL

The gold pool was drawn from the leading central banks and was supposed to maintain, with adequate interventions in the area of $35 an ounce, the price of gold on the free market. It was responsible for ensuring, for the benefit of private individuals, the free convertibility of currencies into gold at a fixed rate. From the moment the central bank members of the pool decided to get out, there stopped being a fixed gold price.

The double market in gold was in reality fatal for a system of fixed exchange rates: such a system can only be perpetuated indefinitely if official transactions in gold do not play an important role. The central banks have to be able, in this way, to reabsorb at least a fraction of the currency purchases which they had to accumulate by intervening on the market. If the reabsorption became impossible, as a result of the free convertibility in gold being eliminated *de jure* or *de facto*, the gold exchange standard developed all the pernicious effects so accurately denounced by Jacques Rueff.

The markets did not recover after the decision taken in March 1968, despite the agreement made at the same time over the creation of a new instrument of reserve, of which everyone expected the earth (the Special Drawing Rights or SDR). In August 1969 the French government, without warning, devalued the franc, and in October that same year the German government revalued the Deutschmark. Within less than two years, the three leading European currencies, sterling, the Deutschmark, and the franc had changed value, thus letting the price of gold "float" freely on the open market. More was yet to come.

NIXON'S BLOW

On August 15, 1971 President Nixon openly drew the logical and implicit consequence of the dissolution of the gold pool: he embargoed gold. At the same time, he destroyed the reality of an official market in the precious metal. This decision led all foreign governments, which had not already done so, to stop maintaining the dollar (West Germany and the Netherlands had already done this in early May that year). This was followed by a period of more or less free fluctuation. It would end on December 18, 1971, with an agreement signed in Washington DC, signaling the dollar's first official devaluation.

Hailed rather hastily as a historic event, the Smithsonian Institute agreement was destined to fail, because it was attempting the impossible: reconstituting a system of fixed exchange rates in the absence of the regulatory element of the monetary authorities' obligation to defend a fixed price for gold. During 1972 the central banks had to continue absorbing huge amounts of dollars to try to maintain the new parity. Then the US government devalued the dollar again, February 12, 1973, which instead of curbing speculation fueled it. After this, the pseudo-system of fixed exchange rates so laboriously assembled at the end of December 1971 crumbled.

From 1968 to 1973 all the mechanisms meant to assist the functioning and the perpetuation of a fixed exchange rate had been abandoned one after another. Such a regime could only continue if the deficits and surpluses on the balances of payments were only temporary. The countries with deficits would have to have a policy of relative monetary contraction and those with surpluses would have to follow a policy of monetary expansion to restore the balance. These processes of adjustment, which experts advocated in vain for many years, could never function because of the dollar's privileged position.

The floating exchange rates were an enormous obstacle to a lasting recovery of the world economy. A growing number of business and industrial leaders in both Europe and even the United States shared this opinion, even if the IMF experts disagreed and went so far as to write: until now there was nothing to indicate that this (the fluctuating rates) would seriously hinder world trade growth. However world trade contracted substantially. The question was not which of the two systems was best. The floating exchange rates was not a system, but the result of the abandonment of all the rules laid down to establish an international monetary order.

Nonetheless nothing could be worse than to repeat the disastrous experience of December 1971. What was the use of fixing new parities if one did not ensure there were means to maintain them? It is obvious that none of the necessary conditions to achieve this were in place. In all likelihood, apart from a last-minute change of heart, monetary nationalism would slowly lead to an economic downturn for countries and groups of countries.

THE DOLLAR CRISES

The years 1971-73 signaled a rupture. The world lurched from the stability of the dollar, a universal reference currency, to chronic instability. The May 1973 decision to let the dollar float marked the end of the Bretton Woods agreements. These agreements were to have led to the reconstruction, once peace was established, of the international monetary system, after it had been dislocated since the early 1930s. It was supposed to avoid a return to the disastrous experience of competitive devaluations and floating currencies of the interwar period.

Since the beginning of the crisis, some 15 years ago, this climate reigned once again on the foreign exchange markets. The year of the 1987 Crash was particularly eventful: rarely had the US government's intention to allow the dollar's value to drop for purely commercial motives been pursued so openly since the September 1985 Plaza agreements and with so little success. It was especially worrying that the dollar continued to be perceived as overvalued during the 20 years in question, whatever its rate. Also the US external deficit was the constant subject of international monetary negotiations.

What did change was the political exploitation of this double phenomenon. At first, it was Europe that decried the effects. In February 1965 General Charles de Gaulle launched a diatribe on the dollar's hegemony, which allowed the Americans to put off sorting out their own affairs and enabled them, with their strong dollar, to buy up the old world's companies, despite their balance of payments' deficit. However at the end of the 1960s, when it was clear that the official gold stock of the United States, valued on the basis of the intangible price $35 an ounce, was no longer enough to meet the value of the dollar purchases accumulated as reserves by foreign central banks, the Americans embarked on a new doctrine, which continued to inspire them, apart from the period 1981-1985. This doctrine, called benign neglect, was summarized thus: the United States did not need a strong dollar to ensure good profits for its companies competing, both abroad and within the national boundaries, with foreign producers. Therefore the best course was to treat the external deficit with amiable indifference.

WORLDWIDE WORRIES, IMBALANCES AND PLANS

Washington went from ignoring the external deficit to being obsessed about it. During Reagan's first term, the policy of systematically downgrading the dollar was abandoned; on the contrary the new chief executive proclaimed the virtues of a strong dollar, symbolic of a strong United States. It recovered more than previously experienced, and experienced harmful side effects. But it seemed this path had been given up reluctantly.

The persistence of the deficit and the inability of the dollar to find a stable level, under the new floating rates system as well as under the previous fixed exchange rates, gave rise to the following question: Given the nature of the international monetary system, would the dollar not remain largely immune to US and other "intentions"? Sometimes the governments took stabilizing measures (the Louvre agreement of February 22, 1987, for example), sometimes they resigned themselves to having to fix new, more realistic rates. The most famous example of this was the December 18, 1971 realignments of parities, marking the first devaluation of the dollar since 1934, which Nixon called "the most important monetary agreement in history."

All these attempts soon proved to be inoperative. The probable reason was that there was an underlying cause for the dollar's decline, which was slow or fast depending on circumstance, even with low or almost zero inflation. The central banks could not accumulate massive reserves of dollars without buying on the foreign exchange markets, and if they were doing this, it was to halt a fall or slow it down at least. However the mechanism maintained itself: the dollar reserves were placed in US Treasury bonds. It was as if all the non-American central banks were giving the United States permanent credits; in this way they were condemning the United States to a permanent deficit, by supplying the means to pay which had not been created by its own economic activity.

As long as the dollar was fixed to the price of the weight of gold according to the Bretton Woods agreements (conserving the gold parity fixed by Roosevelt in 1934), the accumulation of dollar reserves was slowed down, because the Bundesbank, Banque de France, Banque de Suisse, Banque de Belgique, etc, asked for the conversion of part of their dollars into gold. It worked even better when the leading central banks ensured the free convertibility of currencies into gold at a fixed price between December 1961 and March 1968.

The world, unaware of its benefits, had a gold standard. The point needs emphasizing because it is almost impossible to ensure long-term fixed exchange rates between currencies, which have ceased to be exchangeable against the weight of gold or any other goods chosen as the defining standard of value. Historically floating exchange rates were applied to inconvertible currencies or at forced prices. It had nothing to do with the market economy, as some people claimed. The unfortunate monetary experience did not go against the lessons of history.

THE LIQUIDITIES EXPLOSION

The most important fact in the last 20 years of monetary history — whose consequences on inflation and indirectly on economic activity were considerable — was the massive accumulation of dollars by the central banks. Since 1970 their total had risen ten times; this was a multiplying coefficient of the same size that we see for the rise in the Eurodollar market. The dollar always appeared overvalued because its price dropped further, if it was not artificially maintained by these purchases.

The two major periods of world inflation were both preceded by an orgy of interventions on the foreign exchange markets: 1970-73 and 1977-78. The oil crises were made possible by the prior dollar crises. There were further massive interventions after the end of 1986. By buying back dollars from the commercial banks on the foreign exchange markets, the central banks allowed the former to increase their ability to provide credit. This abundance of credit fueled the stock market inflation which led to the 1987 Crash.

WHO PAYS FOR THE US DEFICIT?

Until 1976, the US external deficit was traditionally calculated on the basis of official transactions. This meant that the current balance of payments' share of the deficit, covered by the flow of foreign private capital, was not seen as a deficit. The only part that counted was that financed by loans from official foreign institutions, by the skewing of subscriptions to US Treasury bonds resulting from interventions on the foreign exchange markets. In fact the 1976 change in presenting the deficit did not make much difference, as we can see today: the net assets of private capital had almost ceased since the loss of confidence in the dollar during the last quarter of 1976, since then at least three-quarters of, if not all, the current balance of payments' deficit during the first quarter of 1987 were covered by the central banks' intervention on the foreign exchange markets.

The interventions on the foreign exchange markets were a powerful destabilizing factor. The foreign central banks held their currency reserves in US Treasury bonds. Thus they indirectly allowed the issuing of new bonds in the US public debt and maintained its budget deficit. Why? Because a deficit that was easy to finance tended to persist.

The non-American banks of issue held about 10 percent of the federal state's accumulated debt; 10 percent was held by the Fed which was, on New York's money market, a buyer of US Treasury bonds. A fifth of the US public debt was in official hands, which also took on half the support on the market for US Treasury bonds.

In the absence of this support, how much would these bonds have been worth, supposedly perfectly "liquid"? And what would the interest rates' level have been (they went up when the value of the bonds dropped)?

REFLECTIONS
MILTON FRIEDMAN, EURODOLLARS AND INFLATION

In a famous and still useful article, published in 1969, the US economist Milton Friedman analyzed the international monetary system. He showed that deposits in dollars in foreign banks multiplied in the same way as bank deposits did inside the United States because of the multiplicator of credit. A bank has to keep some of its assets in liquid form to allow it to deal with any unusual events. In a national system, these reserves are often compulsory and take the form of deposits with the bank of issue (and on which commercial banks can draw on sight). In practice, these precautionary reserves need represent only a fraction of the customers' credits. This is so because banks are constantly in receipt of funds from other banking bodies, and they are also paying out on innumerable transactions. In these conditions banks try to limit their liquid reserves (part of its assets which do not bring in any profit) to what is necessary to meet the difference between sums paid in and out or against depositors' unexpected withdrawals. The multiplicator is the number by which the amount of liquid reserves has to be multiplied to get the amount held on deposit.

It has been argued that the reason the Eurocurrency market is a source of inflation is because its multiplicator coefficient is very high because it develops freely without the guidance of a central bank, thus Eurobanks hold their liquid reserves in accounts at sight opened in their names in private US banks (a French bank holds an account with New York's Citibank on which it can draw dollars at sight). As the bank is the only one which can judge the risks involved, it determines the extent of these reserves. From this comes the idea of having an agreement between leading countries to regulate this — but there is the problem of getting Singaporean and Bahamian banks to respect this.

It is not just that this would be difficult to enforce. There is no serious study showing that banks are more imprudent in their operations on the Eurocurrency market than in their domestic operations. In the absence of cast-iron statistical data, the argument above becomes meaningless. The absence of a central bank, which functions as a lender of last resort, probably leads to most banks being in solid arrears (but there was also the possibility that the US banks which hold their reserves started to be in difficulty).

LAXITY IN RESPECT OF DEBTORS

It was as if the national banking system provided the Eurobanks with reserves. On a larger scale, it resulted in a system in which the European, Japanese, and now OPEC central banks held their reserves in dollars, which were placed in the United States in different forms (US Treasury bonds, short-term investments, etc). This was precisely the duplication of credit which Jacques Rueff denounced in the gold exchange standard.

Nonetheless this last mechanism was more lively than ever and added to the problems. It no longer merited the name gold exchange standard, since US money was no longer convertible into gold with the US Treasury. The elimination of gold removed a big obstacle from its rise. Since spring 1977, the central banks' purchases of dollars had reached even higher levels than during the time of the last convulsions of the Bretton Woods system.

SDR OR SPECIAL DRAWING RIGHTS

Since 1970, the IMF had to manage the SDR which were made up of a basket of five leading currencies — dollar, Deutschmark, French franc, yen, pound sterling — and which were part of a country's foreign exchange reserves according to which a mechanism of attribution of quotas in theory proportionate to the country's economic weight or needs. The more a country drew on its rights, the more it became expensive and necessary to put rigorous policies in place which would tackle the problem of private and public accounts.

The IMF continued to publish the breakdown of "international foreign exchange reserves," by adding up the reserves of each member country, the drawing facilities on the IMF, and the IMF's reserves. In September 1978 the IMF general assembly decided to raise each member's quota by 50 percent. The figures produced reached incredible levels which no longer had anything in common with those before the big upheavals which occurred between 1971 (when the link between the dollar and gold was stopped) and 1973 (the abandonment of the fixed rates of exchange and the dislocation of the Bretton Woods system).

At the beginning of the 1970s, the total reserves of the system were estimated at some $77 billion. By the end of June 1979 they had reached $260 billion, and that was only what was held in currency mainly in dollars. To this had to be added the metal reserves which potentially came to the same amount. These statistics were impressive but they no longer meant the same as in the past. Implicitly the notion of reserves refers to the idea that each country, and the system in general, possesses the means to pay. What did this mean, when it was known that in 1978 countries, even those with large deficits, saw massive increases in their foreign exchange assets because the total of their borrowing exceeded their immediate financial requirements, apart from a few exceptions? Previously the total had acted as a constraint on the reserves but it had been eroded by the complete opposite: instead of the deficits being limited by the ability to finance them, it was the volume of credits that adapted almost automatically to the total deficits to be met.

TWO TURNING POINTS IN MONETARY HISTORY

Many people cite March 1973 as a major turning point in monetary history. It was the beginning of the floating exchange rates. Another important date was January 31, 1974 when the US government lifted all restrictions on US bank loans abroad. This decision was prepared several months earlier and came a few weeks after OPEC's quadrupling of the oil price. It gave an extra boost to the development of international credits. From then on one could get dollar loans in New York, London, Zurich, Paris, etc and it also boosted off shore centers like the Caribbean and the Bermuda. The existence of the Eurobanks allowed the US banking system to gain interest, since dollars on deposit in the United States could be lent by banks in London (or Paris or the Bahamas), without affecting the US banks' resources. This devilish trick of inflation meant countries with deficits came out ahead.

In March 1973 many countries, such as West Germany, Switzerland, and Japan thought they would gain but they were thwarted. The advantage of no longer having to support a floating dollar was to cut off one of the principal sources of inflation (when the Bundesbank bought dollars to stop it dropping, it issued an equivalent amount of Deutschmarks). This had happened before but the inevitable result had been a rise in the Deutschmark, the Swiss franc, the yen, which had repercussions on the German, Swiss, Japanese, and other economies. Thus in the recent past countries with a strong currency got into difficulty which they only escaped provisionally after beginning (in the last quarter of 1977) to support the dollar — or stop its decline. This also stoked up inflation in West Germany, Japan, and Switzerland.

The new interventions on the foreign exchange markets were massive: during the period from September 1977 to November 1, 1978 some $70 billion dollars were bought by the central banks. This was the same amount of the total reserves of the international system in 1979. Since then there was an important reflux, but after the summer of 1979 the Bundesbank had to intervene again to stop the dollar's decline, which had dislocated the EMS, six months after its launch. That was why Germany asked for and got a revaluation of the Deutschmark.

To loosen the dollar's ascendancy, the diversification of foreign exchange reserves was necessary. All the world's central banks had to increase their holdings in yens, Deutschmarks, and later on it was hoped in ECU (European Currency Units). Was this wise? it might aggravate the whole system's instability. What would happen if the banks decided to sell their dollars and buy European and Japanese currency at the same time?

THE FINANCIAL BUBBLE
AND THE CASINO ECONOMY

There was a general crash in 1987, and a minicrash on Wall Street in 1989: the financial system was shuddering. The multiplication of new financial instruments and the new methods used by raiders frequently produced destabilizing effects on the world economy. By the end of the 1980s it was like a casino economy. When a saver wins without any risk or even know-how, there were substantial financial costs to the real economy.

A description of what happened in Wall Street in 1989 shows clearly the markets' volatility as they responded to the least rumor. Computers programmed to buy and sell automatically and the development of speculative operations were part of the financial scenario. In 1989, as in 1987, the bursting of the financial bubble did not mean the real economy suffered a brutal shock because the monetary authorities knew how to compensate for deflationary losses on the market with injections of liquidity. But the real economy was penalized by real rates of interest that were too high but necessary to attract the speculators' hot money.

EUPHORIA AND MINICRASH

There were two important dates on Wall Street in 1989: Thursday August 24 and Friday October 13. They showed the vigor and fragility of the US stock market: the first date was a record high and the second a minicrash. After two years of slow growth (4 percent in 1987 and 11.8 percent 1988) the New York stock market recovered its mid-1980s form. The Dow Jones index rose by 25 percent within 12 months, as in 1985 and 1986. Tuesday January 24 saw Wall Street lose the last traces of the October 1987 crash, when the Dow Jones hit the same level it was at before Black Monday. The market continued to rise in the following months, as it was still confused by the risks of resurging inflation and recession. As months went by and particularly in the summer, investors became euphoric with the good economic cycle, and convinced that the situation was under control.

People were beginning to take seriously the hypothesis of the soft landing (slowdown in growth without any inflationary pressure). There was also a drop in interest rates and the foreign exchange tensions were lessening. The US stock market made the most of this. Thursday August 24, Wall Street finally passed its highest recorded level, reached almost exactly two years before. This upward trend continued until October 9, when the Dow Jones stood at 2,791.41 points. This trend was also helped by talk of takeover bids. It was precisely the raids and their finance system that led to the stock market crisis. Friday October 13, almost two years after the crash, the Dow dropped by 190 points (7 percent), registering its biggest drop after the 508-point drop of October 19, 1987. That day, less than an hour before closing down, US stocks collapsed suddenly, causing panic on the Big Board.

The origin of the 1989 minicrash was the announcement of a consortium's failure to buy United Airlines, the second largest US air company. The consortium had been made up of United's personnel and British Airways. It was a deal worth $6.75 billion and it followed the failure of the Canadian Robert Campeau attempt to buy Federated Stores. Investors thought that if these bids could not raise the finance then several other takeover bids might fail. Junk Bonds were often used to finance these operations and they lost all credibility. The shakeup was short-lived, since after a week, the losses of Black Friday were restored. Shares continued to rise sporadically until the end of the year.

This minicrash prompted a new debate on program trading, which led automatically to tens of millions of large companies' computers selling when prices hit a certain level, also programmed in. Most of the large brokers were against this mechanism, but no one had decided to stop it. For two years Wall Street had been laying off staff and this continued. Experts estimated there still needed to be a further 20 to 25 percent reduction in staff, 35,000 out of 145,000.

THE DISCONNECTION BETWEEN
THE REAL AND FINANCIAL ECONOMY

During times of floating exchange rates, the rates tend to be influenced by the movement of capital, which were not connected to productive activities as such (buying and selling, investments, etc). Variations in exchange rates no longer reflected the more or less divergent inflation rate. Thus in the United States and Japan, consumer prices had increased in line, yet in 20 years the dollar's value in Tokyo had dropped from 360 to 123 yens, three times less. Prices had risen 3.5 times in the United States and by less than 2.2 in West Germany, but the dollar's value at Frankfurt had dropped from 4 to 1.60 Deutschmarks: there was no relation between the two.

INTEREST RATES: ANTI-CRASH EXPEDIENTS

The United States failed to criticize vehemently West Germany or Japan over their interest rates policies. In 1971 the United States adopted a policy of low rates but West Germany did not follow suit much to US annoyance. The truth of the matter was that the US interest rates were held at a much lower rate than the real market would warrant. This was still true now. In October 1979, this policy threatened to lead to a mass exodus from the dollar and the collapse of the markets. Paul Volcker, the new head of the Fed, courageously allowed rates to climb. The markets misinterpreted their steep rise: they saw the beginning of soaring inflation — hence the brief rise in gold prices — while they should have realized it signaled a return to normalcy. The rise in interest rates made the existing situation, which had profited those taking out loans, untenable and presaged a deflation of credit. Now the governments desperately tried to avert the prospect of further stock market crashes by an artificially low interest rate — a perilous maneuver.

DEBT FOR THE POOR CREDIT FOR THE RICH

After being ignored for a long time the Third World's debt became enormous and in 1982 exploded, so that the world economy was threatened with serious imbalance. On August 23, 1982, when the Mexican government admitted being unable to meet its commitments, the international authorities were at a loss. Ten years of easy money created by the rise in oil prices and petrodollars investments since 1973 had engendered a false feeling of euphoria. Throughout this time banks competed fiercely to invest in developing countries the surpluses accumulated by oil exporters. The leaders of industrial countries always encouraged the Third World to take advantage of the bonanza to speed up industrialization and purchases. Promises of imminent prosperity made the governments of debtor countries feel light headed and they did not always examine the soundness of their operations.

THE FINANCIAL BOMB

Amid general indifference debt had more than doubled between 1970 and 1975. During the next seven years it went up 4.5 times. In 1982, after the Mexican shock, countries began to do their accounts. It would take several weeks to find out the exact total of Mexico's debts, a stunning indictment of the lack of reliable data from the creditors and well as the debtors. A Mexican bankruptcy would have entailed that of several large American banks, heavily involved in Latin America. The risk of a chain reaction and of the collapse of the international financial system were soon confirmed by the growing difficulties of other indebted countries, from Brazil to the Philippines, passing through Africa.

Governments, central banks, international bodies, and commercial banks avoided the worst by taking temporary measures and rescheduling payments. The first cracks were dismissed as straightforward and temporary liquidity problems. But with the rise in the dollar and interest rates, the international community discovered that a simple budget purge was not enough for the debtor countries to go back to the path of growth, especially with increasing social discontent at home. Countries decided to join together and follow the Baker plan, named after the secretary of the US Treasury.

Launched in fall 1985, the Baker plan did not work. Within two years, Third World debt had increased by 1.2, while in 1987 *per capita* income was lower than it had been in 1980 in the most indebted countries, on the whole Latin American, as well as in the poorest African nations. The fall in raw materials' prices and the drop in the oil price at the end of 1986 reduced receipts as well as the capacity to pay. The governments continued to tighten up their budgets. Investments, signs of future growth, dropped. The vicious circle of debt was inescapable.

During this second phase, however, many taboos were broken. Banks, for the first time, admitted that they did not expect all their loans to be repaid completely. Learning from their previous carelessness and their sudden vulnerability, they increased the provision for bad debts and cleaned up their balance sheets. The parallel market, where written down debts were exchanged, grew. In 1987 some $15 billion was treated in this way, a total which was likely to reach $27 in 1988. Those countries which were the most in debt but whose economic potential was still attractive, generally the Latin American countries, became *a la carte*. Creditor nations' governments were anxious about African countries, as their debt was mainly public or guaranteed by the state.

CREDITORS BECAME PRAGMATIC

The year 1988 was the third phase in pragmatism's assault. Persuaded that the Third World would only regain its growth rate if its debt was reduced, not just spread out, the seven leading industrialized countries adopted in June the Mitterand proposal. The most severely indebted countries, which accepted the need for rigor, would benefit from a new deal with the Paris Club: the cancellation of a third of their debts or a reduction in the interest rates they had to pay. Some, like the United States, only proposed to lengthen the terms of payment.

The six years of rampant crisis afforded several important lessons: the indebted countries were unable to form a cartel and countries would still be dealt with one by one. The IMF and the

World Bank had to relax their policies and take into account the social costs, often enormous, of austerity policies in the Third World. It was to be hoped that future dealings would be less haphazard.

Nonetheless the debtor countries' vulnerability was still glaring. The least shake, the smallest boom or rise in interest rates, would tear the precarious safety net. Since Asia had fewer debts, the threat hung over Latin America and Africa: the banks' weariness was equaled by that of the debtors, which could not escape debt's trap, even if they followed rigorous policies.

AUSTERITY RULES

To find the means to pay off their debts, all the indebted countries followed the path laid down by the multilateral organizations: restrictions on imports and a kickstart for exports using massive or slow devaluations. In 1987 sub-Saharan Africa's imports were down on the 1978 level, both in dollars and in current prices, those of Latin America had dropped to the 1979 level. This global tendency covered many diverse situations: in 1987 Nigeria imported less than half of what it had done in 1978; South Korea had increased its purchases of foreign goods by 1.5 times in ten years.

The general effort to adjust external trade could be seen in the figures. After 1982 for Latin America, two years later in Africa, trade balances went back into the black. These regions did not feel any benefits from their austerity policies: thanks to the deterioration in the terms of exchange and the weight of the servicing of their debt, their current balance of payments was still in deficit. Again Asia was the exception, its surpluses rose dramatically after 1987, thanks to the four dragons' (South Korea, Taiwan, Hong Kong, and Singapore) dynamism.

THE PRICE TRAP

At the same time as raw materials' prices collapsed, after being the principal source of receipts for indebted countries, their payments (both interest and capital) increased. In 1970 the servicing of the Third World debt stood at $5.44 billion, by 1980 it reached $55.5 billion, in 1983 $72.23 billion, and in 1987 $105 billion. Oil exporters had even more brutal ups and downs, the massive increases in 1973 and 1979 were replaced by a fall at the end of 1985, followed by the hope of a rise in 1988. Basic commodities' producers faced constantly depressed export prices. This price trap made the economy's medium-term planning even more difficult.

The year 1983 was a bad one for the most heavily indebted countries, mainly Latin American. Until then, as with all developing countries, they had continued to receive more than they were paying back. These positive net transfers suddenly became negative. The drying up of new credits and the progressive loss of new foreign investors made the financial inflow fall, while the debt servicing continued to rise and increase the outflow. These negative transfers stood at $9.9 billion in 1983, but they reached $26 billion to fall back to $22 billion a year later, thanks to the rescheduling of payments and increase in debtors' arrears. Between 1985 and 1987, this withdrawal of money represented about 3 percent of the debtors' GNP, at the same time as austerity measures hit national wealth.

THE TIDAL WAVE

With hindsight, these damaging transactions look like a tidal wave, especially if we remember the weight of the debt in 1970. Then Third World indebtedness stood at $67 billion and the banks' claim stood at $8.3 billion. Some 17 years later the developing countries' debt stood at $1,200 billion, and the banks were looking to regain most of their loans, some $430 billion. The geographical distribution of this burden was significant. Almost marginal in 1970, the North African debt has considerably grown, reflecting Morocco's, and especially Egypt's, sometimes ill-considered recourse to foreign loans. There was also the fallout from the Iran-Iraq War. By contrast, Asia's debt was less than it first appeared. The South Korean debt stood at $36 billion at the end of 1987. But its economic success meant it had the means to repay, and the accumulation of assets abroad allowed it the hope of being in credit by 1989, for the first time in history. However the $129 billion accumulated by sub-Saharan Africa were a setback, even if most of the loans were preferential. As for Latin America's $440 billion, they showed the credit race between those countries with the greatest potential, Brazil, Mexico, Argentine, and Venezuela, for long the Third World giants of debt.

A FUTURE MENACED BY DEBT

The chain of events was implacable. Apart from Asia whose average *per capita* income had continued to grow since 1970, thus disposing of the financial means necessary to invest and modernize, the indebted countries were paralyzed by an unfavorable downturn: less growth in industrialized countries, the main export market, and a drop in raw materials' prices reduced their external receipts. The weight of the debt servicing and the growing pressure from multilateral organizations and Third World creditors led the governments to reduce their spending at the same time. Brutally interrupted, growth was replaced by recession at the beginning of the 1980s and for many countries this was worse than the 1929 depression had been for the industrialized countries.

Population growth remained strong in Latin America and particularly in Africa, so the economic setback led to greater poverty, and, in the countries with an emerging middle class, a drop in living standards. This relative impoverishment was accompanied by an almost constant reduction since 1981-82 of that part of national revenue devoted to productive investment. Infrastructure, where it existed, grew older. This situation would hang over the debtors' economic future.

THE BRADY PLAN, A DEBT-CONSCIOUS POLICY?

In 1989 the creditor nations' governments and banks seemed to take on board the fact that they would never recover the money they had lent the developing countries. At $1,290 billion (in 1988 it had stood at $1,284 billion) the developing countries' total debt continued to grow slowly: commercial banks' loans in 1989 went down (mainly because of anticipated reimbursements from

Malaysia, South Korea, Romania, and Thailand), but state overseas aid increased dramatically. Nonetheless, while global transfers of resources to Latin America climbed annually to $35 billion in 1982-84, they only reached $7 billion in 1986-89. That year was also notable for the slowdown in the conversion of claims (into liquid assets, into securities, or into other forms of debts): the total of these operations after culminating at $22 billion in 1988, fell back to $7 billion in 1989.

In the developing world growth was dynamic in 1989 at 4.2 percent, but it was very unequal (6.3 percent in Asia, 2.5 percent in sub-Saharan Africa, and 1.2 percent in Latin America) and the *per capita* GNP continued to drop in the last two areas. The servicing of debt represented 27.5 percent of exports in 1989, a bit less than the previous year. But Latin America and the Caribbean continued to devote 40 percent of their exports to repay their debts. After the Toronto initiative of 1988, which prioritized the African countries with poor revenues, those with medium revenues also benefited from a lightening of their debt. On March 10, 1989 the US Treasury secretary, Nicholas Brady, asked the banks to accept the transformation of part of their claims into receivables of a lower value, or to allow reduced rates of interest. The Brady plan was not such a surprise, since France and Japan had already acted in this way and had asked that real reductions in claims should be made.

Rapidly several developing countries and committees representing creditor banks opened negotiations. Mexico, which had launched the debt crisis in 1982 by announcing its inability to pay its loans, was the test country for the Brady plan and in July announced that it had reached an agreement in principle with the banks' committee. The 500 or so of Mexico's creditors had the choice of converting their claims into securities of the same nominal value but with a reduced rate of interest, or exchange them for written down bonds, or of giving further loans. In September it was the Philippines' turn to negotiate a Brady agreement with the banks, whose principal tool this time was the exchange of claims on the secondary market. The Costa Rica reached a similar agreement, while many countries with moderate revenues, which followed economic adjustment plans, were also engaged in a similar process.

It is too soon to draw any conclusions about this country by country approach, because no one knows what the total amount of canceled debt will be under the terms of these complicated arrangements. For the moment, the World Bank estimates that a 2 percent increase in real interest rates will wipe out the gains of the reduction in the debt and its servicing. The process is in motion. After the poor countries and those with moderate revenues, it may be the turn of those who have been able to pay their debts to benefit from annulments of claims. Until now it was natural that the initiatives were taken to help those countries having difficulty meeting payments or whose claims were, as a result, written down on the secondary market. Nonetheless those countries which had chosen to repay their loans on the nail, regardless of the cost, should not be ignored. Hungary, for example, increasingly has the classic problems of a developing country, the high cost of servicing debt and an unpopular economic policy.

22. The Organization of Work Changes

TAYLOR WAS QUESTIONED

THE NEW CREED OF THE ENTERPRISE CULTURE

According to Mr Ravelau, formerly of the AFCERQ, a French organization dedicated to improving quality, "With the rethinking of management, we face the end of an industrial era based on the exchange of labor for a wage, within which better social conditions could only be granted from above. With the questioning of this exchange, the person who yesterday gave his/her labor will tomorrow put in his/her intelligence, creativity, and capacity to adhere to those values. In exchange, s/he expects a share of the company's economic results but also an acknowledgment and identification with the aims of the firm. In this future enterprise system, there will be values of dignity, respect for the individual, authenticity, esthetics, and equality at all levels.... We can only mobilize personnel on quality if there is transparency. With our Taylorian culture, we have only sought to measure groups' returns on investments. But we forgot that by improving communications on all levels, we were attacking the very brakes, which slowed down enterprise such as demarcation and lack of respect for individuals. That cannot be measured."

TOTAL QUALITY

"Think of the client. We do not want to sell a bad tire. We do not want to send an incorrect bill. So we search out the flaws and we attack it in its infancy." This statement, addressed to the quality control heads at Michelin, dates from... 1926. The spirit of quality is there! But the road seems long and winding that leads to the perfection of a product, or service, in truth, for the most ambitious, the improvement of relations between all in a company.

"In five years, we will no longer talk about quality but management." Herve Serieyx, the president of Eurequip, third largest management consultancy group, was in a hurry. When many companies were only just entering the era of "total quality," he was already since 1984 into "enterprises of a third type" and since 1989 into "no contempt." Who cares about those he has lost on the way. The Lesieur group, for example, under his guidance in the early 1980s experimented in participatory management before exploding, in 1986, and reverting to more classical management methods. "For Lesieur's directors," Serieyx affirms today "the search for quality meant putting icing on the Taylorian cake and getting rid of it when things were getting rough. It could not work." The French edible oil group did not give up the search for quality, but adopted a low profile regretting that it had moved too fast in that direction, and allowed consultants to impose a parallel hierarchy, harmful in times of crises. The group was bought by Ferruzi and concentrates on achieving quality control in its different divisions.

Was quality just a fashionable catchphrase? The specialists said it was a necessity. It should not be confused with the passing craze created by the quality clubs of the 1980s. "At the time every company had quality clubs because they had to have them," reminisced Joseph Conrad, director of quality at the glassmakers Saint-Gobain. "But short of a good definition of the problems to be solved, of competent leadership, of an objective, many of them went round in circles," he added. "Or else," specified the consultant Christian Potie, "they helped the bosses put their message across." As for Herve Serieyx, who in 1984 wrote that quality clubs were "one of the most effective levers in the complete transformation of companies," he considered today that they were "small gadgets to make managers appreciate the need for total quality."

In times of economic crisis or keen competition, the quest for excellence seemed unattainable, insofar as it is the clients who dictate and not *vice versa*, as in the times when only quantity had to supply demand. The Credit Lyonnais, which in 1989 decided to go for total quality, for example intends to be prepared for competition from cooperative or European banks in a marketplace where banking services "are banal and where quality will make the difference" according to Michel Krug, director of the group's quality. The possible outcome of an increase in the cost of banking services is not foreign to this concept.

There was the same objective in industry, where Sollac, a subsidiary of Usinor-Sacilor, the world's second largest producer of flat products (sheet metal), threw itself into "total quality" accruing 4.6 billion francs of profit in 1988, compared with 230 million in 1986. Valeo and Saint-Gobain also went for total quality and the factories that were threatened with bankruptcy showed the best productivity gains. The problems which emerged from a quality operation were, as Christian Potie specified, "almost exclusively" to do with the managers' behavior and attitudes or its management. Stirring up inertia and obstacles so that everyone could find his/her worth by taking responsibility, at his/her level, for improvements in the quality of his/her work and that management is transformed into leaders of responsible teams, that is what is at stake in total quality. It takes time.

THE SEARCH FOR EXCELLENCE AND TALKS

"The hardest task is to plug the holes, which every day hamper our search for excellence." For eight years director of a Valeo alternator factory at Etaples, Michel Poquet knows about this. He cites as an example the supplier of diodes, which changed its mode of production without notice, provoking at the end of the chain the quadrupling of the number of parts returned to the manufacturer by the PSA group. Or the stupid mixup of different pulleys which led to a drop in the quality of alternators sold to Renault.

Previously personnel would have overlooked these mistakes but now they take time to think. A sign of the times was that a tray full of bits of defective alternators had appeared at the end of all seven production lines. Each operator can see, in real terms and graphic presentation, the damage done by these hazards which pollute the assembly process. He or she can then measure a part against a quality chart, signed by the directors of Valeo's alternator-starter division, and since April 11, 1988 pinned next to the non-quality graphics drawn up by the operators. Each fault is now dissected, explained to the operators, and gives rise, if there is a need, to a special team being commissioned to resolve these problems. Some 360 out of 1,300 workers at the alternator division are in these teams (there are a hundred of them), in the workshops or offices.

Since the laying down of the total quality plan in 1988, 46 problems have been solved. Some proposed solutions, however, were turned down because of expense. "The important thing was to explain why to the group members," stated François Chereau, director of quality at the factory. The organization of work has also changed. In the old days an operator who had finished a manufacturing batch would call the supervisor, who in turn would call the flying squad of machine controllers. Now the operator decides for him/herself which batch takes priority, depending on the state of stocks made by the previous stage; s/he assesses the faults in those batches, as well as maintaining his/her machine. Each operator has an instruction manual for his/her equipment, his/her measurement tables, and a red box for defective parts.

"All these refinements, perfected by the interested parties, may seem trivial," François Chereau admits "but they have been very worth while." In 1986 1,200 defective parts were returned to the factory, in 1989 only 50 were returned. "In three years" explains Michel Poquet, "car manufacturers have become extremely punctilious about the way we manage two apparently contradictory objectives: producing quality at a cheaper price." Each one of them visits the factory to assess it according to a set of criteria. Manufacturers make a point of measuring improvements in industrial relations, the strict description of jobs, but also minor details like the locking of the red boxes for defective parts. These audits provide, according to François Chereau, an impartial view on what else is needed to accomplish total quality. This has to be done as well as "sweeping the doorstep," Michel Poquet specifies. He adds there is nothing worse than setting high objectives when you cannot even ensure the quality of the daily routine. All the more so since the personnel, now on the look out for quality, has become more demanding in relation to their previous standard of work. This policy of little by little seems to be paying off. Absenteeism (4.7 percent in 1989) has diminished by 0.5 percent in a year, and wage agreements were signed, for the first time in the factory's history, by all the unions.

23. Social Issues

FULL EMPLOYMENT, AN OUTDATED NOTION?

As countries gradually recovered, one by one, without exception, they discovered the limits of a return to full employment. It was an increasingly outdated notion, related to postwar principles, and which had been achieved after the "thirty glorious years." Today, whatever happens, some of the population will be permanently excluded and will never find a productive place in society. To reabsorb the rest of the unemployed, the OECD said obstacles to the development of untypical employment — part-time work, weekend work, or the most precarious arrangements which will draw on those too unskilled to be reintegrated into work — had to be removed. But social security needed to be adapted, that is reduced, and salaries had to remain compatible with weak productivity. Otherwise, a black market in labor would open, as already existed in many countries.

At the same time, those countries which had already tried these methods were learning the limits of these policies. In the United States and Great Britain, the income of workers with secure jobs increased more rapidly than average purchasing power and the lack of qualified personnel became a problem and accelerated the process. In West Germany and Japan, where the drop in the working population was happening before other countries, it added to the worry that the economy might not remain competitive, except by turning to delocalization.

Nonetheless the move of employment to services or self-employment had some disadvantages, as can be seen in the United States and Great Britain — there were many part-time jobs, temporary, for women, which were unskilled and badly paid. For every ten jobs in production, there were 26 service jobs in 1984, in the United States, compared with 15 in 1959. Most of the jobs created in Great Britain where nonindustrial and for women.

Under the cover of freelance work, often false, working practices developed which were based on a commercial contract rather than a work contract. This solution corresponded to phases of technical regression, as in construction where 10 percent of workers were on a salary. Also the new jobs profited women, 38.9 percent of whom did not work the usual hours, either they were part-time or temporary in the services sector. This may provide paid work but was it a sign of good health or proof of lasting economic vitality. One thing was certain: what was happening in these countries was a precursor to what would happen in other countries, including France. The signs were already there.

EUROPE WAKES UP

Despite the recovery, the adjustment of the social security system to the aging population of the industrialized countries and a high rate of unemployment was painful. This change, which had not happened overnight, did not only affect those countries with a welfare net (mainly Europe), but also presented serious problems to those without. Thus, in the United States in the last year there was much unrest over the financing welfare. In the name of competition, many companies refused to make any social security payments. There were several strikes, like the one at the telephone company Nynex in New York in the fall, which lasted more than three months. While the French were more interested in modifying the financing of rather than the benefits of social security, the Germans, whose demography was less dynamic, adopted in November 1989 an important reform to their old age pensions. For men the retirement age was to increase from 63 to 65 by 2006. For women and the unemployed it would go from 60 to 65 by 2012.

The year 1989 seemed like the commencement of a realization of the European dimension of social security. Long considered as marginal, this aspect of community construction — almost left out of the European Social Charter — began to emerge. Making the most of the presidency of the European Community, France proposed directives on the social economy and insurance. The French government thought that insurance companies benefited from the absence of European texts on mutual insurance companies. The latter wanted to create a community-wide network and required precisely worded directives. Social security in Europe achieved some progress in 1989, in spite of everything. The EC ministers sorted out an old difference between France and other countries on the allocation of family allowances. Henceforth a migrant worker's benefits would be calculated on the basis of the country of employment to work out what benefits could be exported to his/her family members, not living in France.

SOCIAL SECURITY: THE FACTS

Social spending tend to rise spontaneously more quickly than GDP; after the 1973-74 crisis, the slowdown in production was more striking than the slowdown in spending. But the 1980s austerity policies put a stop to this trend by slowing down increases in benefits and everywhere there was a drop in social spending as a percentage of GDP (notably in West Germany). Taxation was kept under control by supply-side policies, but tax deductions went up in line with insurance contributions, which increased more quickly than national wealth, and this despite the conservative pronouncements of most governments in the 1980s. State spending on social security decreased as a percentage of GDP only in West Germany and the United States and they stabilized in Great Britain. State spending resisted downward pressure in proportion with medical advances stimulating supply and demand for healthcare increasing as the population aged and the standard of living improved.

TAX DEDUCTIONS

In the same way more people retired spontaneously as there was a notable increase in those over 60 in the population and the market tended to lay off its oldest workers. Only family spending went down as the number of children requiring allowances dropped. Spending on unemployment dropped with the recovery at the end of the 1980s and reductions in beneficiaries' rights after a long period of unemployment.

HEALTH

Health was an area where social progress was most marked. Healthcare improved in quality, there was costly technical progress, and greater demand for quality of life combined to increase medical spending. Everywhere states cut back on demand financed by the state; thus the state only paid for 6.4 percent out of 8.5 percent spent on health in France (a quarter of health spending was paid for by households compared with 46 percent in the United States).

OLD AGE

The increase in old age spending was inevitable given the rights to benefits granted in the past. Everywhere states tried to limit these rights and increase contributions from the working population. Everywhere people were encouraged to take out their own insurance and pension schemes (you have to pay when you are young to receive when you are old). The state pension was the principal source of payments (it was today's working population that paid for today's pensioners and payments were only partly determined by what had been paid in the past).

UNEMPLOYMENT

The unemployed's social security was very unequal: of course those countries with long-term unemployment had to make a greater effort than others (particularly France and Italy). The OECD calculated how generous unemployment benefits were by measuring the size of benefits compared with wages. France led the way with a 36 percent rate, in front of West Germany (27 percent), Great Britain (21 percent), Japan (17 percent), and the United States (only 8 percent).

THE FAMILY

Spending on families was high in France but remained a constant proportion of national income; West Germany which had a low birth rate did not have any policies on this.

WHO FINANCES SOCIAL SPENDING?

Without doubt France was one of the countries where companies paid out most for social security. By contrast Japan and Great Britain had to finance social spending from the public purse. This unequal financing of the share of social contributions affected companies' competitiveness. The more companies had to pay in social contributions, the more indirect wage costs increased, and the more the total cost of work increased. The coming of the 1993 single market made the harmonization of the financing of social security a more pressing matter.

PENSIONS, EMPLOYMENT, AND AGE

In France in 1989 with those registered as seeking employment, those on early retirement schemes (191,500), and the unemployed exempt from looking for work (229,500), at least 15 percent of those over 50 were without a job. They were almost automatically — apart from those with "guaranteed resources" before 1982 — put into retirement as soon as they reached 60: especially men, if the age they started their career is taken into account, they have usually achieved the 155 quarters necessary to receive a full pension. In fact, if one leaves out those without work (for this generation mostly women), one in three of those reaching retirement did not really choose the time to go. It was the company that decided, a few years before.

At the beginning of the 1970s this trend began — when the large companies in France (Chrysler, SNIAS, Thomson-CSF, IBM, and Citroen) sent personnel off into early retirement for the first time in company history. But after 1972, with the creation of a guarantee of resources in the case of redundancy, early retirement became a "selective process," in the words of Xavier Gaullier (*La Deuxieme Carriere*, editions du Seuil, 1989).

The raising of the age of retirement in companies happened in different ways in different countries. In the United States, companies took it on directly by putting in place individual or collective systems of early retirement. In several countries invalidity pensions were used. In Sweden all workers aged 60 without work and having run out of employment benefit were declared unfit for work and put on a pension. In the Netherlands the numbers on invalidity pensions doubled in a few years; in Great Britain recent studies showed that many of those retiring for health reasons did so under pressure to avoid redundancy. In France there was an explosion of early retirements after the extension of the guarantee of resources in 1977. Retirement at 60 shut off access to a guarantee of resources and stopped the rising trend of early retirement, so the figures fell from 700,000 in 1984 to 400,000 at the end of 1987 and brought the financial crisis to an end. But it did not affect the principle. It consolidated it by lowering the age of departure. The system not only allowed social security to pay for the cost of company restructuring (even if it involved further criticism of the cost of these reforms) but also created a dynamic that was difficult to stop.

Delaying the age of retirement allows, in principle, both to increase the numbers paying contributions and to reduce the number of retired, and the length of payments of pensions. It is also relatively painless. To balance the pension schemes from now until the year 2000, according to the commissariat au Plan, starting from the premise of unemployment continuing at the current level, it was enough to add three years to the retirement age. Better yet, a delay in starting retirement seems necessary because of the demographic imbalance, predicted from 2005 to 2010, when the baby boom generation reaches retirement age and there are less numerous generations on the labor market. But what will its impact be on unemployment? Would it not result in moving in the opposite direction the financial demands for unemployment benefits and early retirement?

Those countries which have taken some measures in this direction, notably Japan and the United States, have decided to apply them in due course. In the United States in particular, the retirement age is going to be progressively put back from the year 2003 until 2027, by two months every year. This will allow the system to adapt to the quantitative change in employment. But this will not be enough if there is no other planned management of labor. In 1986 the Tabah report, prepared under the auspices of the commissariat au Plan, suggested a policy of age scales by using training schemes: "In other countries, notably in the Netherlands, experience shows that this is possible and that the age (of workers) is not an immovable obstacle to the success of a training program." Nonetheless such a practice, already recommended in the Laroque report in... 1962, remains negligible, even a taboo for companies. On the contrary the management of age results in aging workers being laid off and the limit being brought constantly forward.

24. Eastern Europe:
The Massive Transformation

COMECON, MYTHS AND REALITY

Founded in January 1949 as a counterweight to the Marshall Plan in Europe, the Council for Mutual Economic Aid or COMECON included ten members: the Soviet Union, East Germany, Bulgaria, Hungary, Poland, Romania, Czechoslovakia, Mongolia, Vietnam, and Cuba. It was based on the same central planning system as the Soviet Union. Its first objective was the reconstruction, then the economic integration of very different countries: the Stalin's Soviet Union dominated in terms of size its "satellites," the industrialized countries of East Germany and Czechoslovakia, as well as the agricultural countries like Bulgaria and Romania.

During its first two decades, COMECON was relatively efficient in its work of homogenizing economic mechanisms (central planning and the state monopoly of external trade) and in developing heavy industry. The Soviet plan to create a true "international socialist division of work" never worked. COMECON was never able to satisfy consumer demands either in quality or quantity any more than it could stop each country from pursuing different aims, developing its own price and wages structures, and from having, in the final analysis, its own political economy.

A FALSE COMMON MARKET

COMECON was often referred to as the Eastern Common Market, but it was never more than a zone of administered trade. It never had the three necessary ingredients to become a market: demand, money supply, and prices.

Instead of demand, COMECON had the previously identified needs of the five year plans. The rigidity of the system was aggravated by bottlenecks in production, so there were constant shortages, which could only be filled by imports from Third World countries, paid for in hard currency. This was the first failing of a system supposed to function in a closed circuit.

COMECON's trade was conducted in "transferable rubles," a misleading name since the ruble could not be converted. Trade was usually conducted between two countries, given the large numbers of annual or five-year contracts, and aimed at equalizing in accounting terms. When there were surpluses, they could not be used to buy goods from a third country (with which trade was also bound by a series of bilateral contracts). There was no point in having a surplus in transferable rubles, which explained the Hungarians' fury at the two years' of accumulated surpluses in trade with the Soviet Union, which failed to supply the quantities of energy and raw materials agreed in the bilateral contracts. The value of the transferable ruble was calculated by converting the world prices of a product in rubles at an official rate, which was always totally arbitrary. The debate on convertibility — bilateral or multilateral — was central to any reform attempts. The other facet was the price problem. COMECON always artificially set its prices based on world prices. But medium term planning meant that prices were fixed for a five-year period, which led to aberrations, for example in oil prices. In the 1970s the Soviet Union followed the world price rise with some delay: this subsidized its satellites, to such a point that a revision of the sliding prices had to be adopted in the early 1980s. But when oil prices dropped, Soviet oil remained high, to the detriment of its COMECON allies.

There were other serious price distortions. Industrial products were as a rule overvalued within the bloc, while raw materials were undervalued in relation to world prices. This led to waste of energy and the tendency to sell raw materials as they were or with little value added on the Western markets (almost a third of industrialized East Germany's exports to the West were reexports of hydrocarbons).

COMECON largely failed in its mission to develop trade between East bloc countries. For a decade the stagnation in the East's trade contrasted badly with the dynamism of world trade. Besides trade between each country and the West grew more rapidly than trade with its partners. If the constraints of medium term contracts were lifted, and if as the Soviets wished trade was conducted in hard currency there was a big risk that COMECON would disintegrate as everyone bailed out. But this would not happen overnight. None of the Eastern economies could compete with the West by giving up raw materials and orders from the Soviet Union. The COMECON giant, even greatly weakened, still controlled the game.

LARGE COMMON PLANS

The mystique of economic integration was sustained by the publicity given to exemplary joint projects:

— the pulp-producing complex at Ustlimsk in eastern Siberia, in which most of the COMECON countries participated in return for a share of the production;

— the oil pipeline which went from the wells at Orenburg on the Soviet Union's western frontier to Eastern Europe and whose construction was paid for, section by section, by the future consumer countries;

— the metallurgical complex at Katowice in Poland, which was mainly equipped by the Soviet Union, and whose gigantic scale led to some criticism from Warsaw;

— the cement works at Erfurt in East Germany, whose productive capacity was supposed to be 2.5 million tons a year and which was built with Polish, Czech, Yugoslav, and other aid.

THE COORDINATION OF NATIONAL PLANS

This process of integration developed on two levels: on the one hand the coordination of five year plans of different countries for the period 1981-85; and on the other hand, the finalizing of sectoral long-term plans (up to 1990) in areas where cooperation was the most advanced. COMECON's 31st session at Warsaw in June, saw the nine members' heads of government adopt for the first time a program of coordination of national plans. But in practice this coordination remained limited as national susceptibilities and difficulties in planning in each country made the socialist division of work unrealistic.

THE LONG-TERM SECTORAL PROGRAMS

* In 1978 the COMECON countries discussed the development of long-term sectoral programs which would allow the harmonization of industrial policy until 1980. This affected the three large sectors: energy, fuel, and raw materials; agriculture and food industries; machine building.

* Between the 33rd and 34th COMECON sessions (1979-80), 20 cooperation agreements were signed between member countries to effect long-term programs. One of them was about computers, which were becoming an urgent priority for the socialist economies. Others concerned the different stages of the process of nuclear power production.

STANDARDIZATION AND SPECIALIZATION

In 1979 to develop integration and accelerate construction, the COMECON countries wanted to standardize plant and to specialize in the production of certain types. Thus Czechoslovakia produced reactors, steam turbines, and generators, while Hungary would supply specialized maintenance and control machinery. COMECON members signed an agreement on the production of plant for nuclear power stations.

WHAT HAPPENED WHEN THE ECONOMIC CRISIS AND INDEBTEDNESS LED TO RETHINKING

After the second oil shock (1979), the rise in energy prices, raw materials' prices, and the crisis in the West had profound consequences on the socialist economies, notably the slowdown in East-West trade. Dependent on a quarter of their trade with capitalist countries, the socialist countries were relatively vulnerable to economic and financial upheavals there. It was understandable that they tried to lessen these effects, especially since their indebtedness to the West had reached fantastic proportions: from $14 billion in mid-1975 to $116.82 billion in 1989.

The reduced possibilities of growth in relation to the West and the fact that most Eastern European countries — apart from Poland in coal and Romania in oil — were dependent on the Soviet Union for their energy resources led to renewed integration within COMECON. Cooperation in energy became an urgent priority.

EXTERNAL TRADE: AN ECONOMIC WAR

* 1979 US embargo on wheat exports to the Soviet Union.
* December 1981: US embargo on technological exports to the Soviet Union.

The COMECON countries had a common worry: their indebtedness. Apart from Hungary (a member of the IMF since 1982 and with a good image in financial circles), the COMECON members were on the "at risk" list of Western creditors. All tried to reduce their debts to capitalist countries in the early 1980s.

OBSTACLES TO INTEGRATION TRADE TERMS WITHIN COMECON

The year 1976 (like 1975) was notable for the deficit the Eastern European countries had run up in their trade with the Soviet Union. This was a fairly new trend. In the early 1970s the reverse was the case: Moscow supplied less to central Europe than it received. Again the energy crisis played a large part in this, since the Soviet Union had increased its oil prices to its satellites by 100 percent and no longer revised its prices every five years but annually, in line with world prices.

Although Moscow still sold its oil to COMECON countries at lower prices than world prices, the countries were forced considerably to increase their deliveries to the Soviet Union to compensate for the increase in energy prices. The Soviet Union, by contrast, would not accept that the prices of the goods it received, particularly industrial plant, went up.

SOVIET OIL RATIONED BY THE SATELLITES

The socialist countries were able to cover all their coal and natural gas requirements, as well as 75 to 80 percent of their oil needs (thanks to the Soviet Union). But the Soviet Union had already announced that it would not be able to increase its deliveries of oil in line with the increase in consumption. Since the saving of energy and the move to nuclear power were very slow, the socialist countries would have to buy on the international market, even though there were difficulties in paying in hard currency.

Oil reserved for the brother countries at special prices payable in finished goods would only increase by 10 percent over the next five years (up to a total of 400 million tons). In 1980 COMECON prices were 50 percent lower than the market prices but given the extra deliveries paid for in hard currency at full price, the average cost of a ton a oil supplied by the Soviet Union — according to a Polish leader — was about 25 percent lower than world prices.

THE SOVIET LET-DOWN

The Soviet Union, which conducted more than half its external trade with other socialist countries, did not find the support it hoped for in this captive market. The new prices it set for 1975, after the first oil shock which made it an energy giant, allowed it to double the value of its energy sales to COMECON. But the Soviets thus set up a growing imbalance in their favor and accumulated a useless surplus, since it was in nonconvertible units of account. The drop in oil prices at the end of 1985 provoked the opposite phenomenon at the point when the commercial and economic impasse became obvious in the Soviet Union.

THE BREAK-UP OF COMECON

After a stay in Moscow, a Polish tourist was not allowed to bring back a color television, coffee, or caviar. The Soviet visitor to Poland could not bring back goods in short supply at home: children's clothes, toilet paper, and spare parts for cars. When a Czech tourist returned from East Germany he would be searched by customs: he was not allowed to bring back any electronic games.

In the East the customs war raged. Since November 1988, when the Czech leadership published a list of 80 products not to be exported to the brother socialist countries, in order to stop the plundering of Prague shops, there were numerous border incidents within the socialist community. In fact the instrument for economic integration, COMECON, like its member countries, was in a profound crisis.

In Moscow the Eastern "Eurocrats" were being made redundant — the number of work committees was reduced — and in vain they tried to reach an agreement on COMECON's future. It was judged to be inefficient by all the member countries and not compatible with current reform programs. While the European Community prepared for the single market in 1993, it was everyone for himself in the East.

Neither the supranational model conceived by Khrushchev in 1962, nor a more flexible system combining planning and market mechanism contained in the complex program of 1971, had led to the integration of the member countries' economies. The coordination of national plans remained a formal operation and multilateral cooperation an unrealizable ambition. The great joint investment projects envisaged in the early 1980s only led to modest efforts, mainly in energy. The 1985 program of cooperation in scientific and technical matters — an Eastern Eureka — did not produce any significant results, according to Eastern Europe.

Eventually COMECON turned out to be a simple trade body — nothing to do with a common market. Trade was strictly bilateral. Every year agreements were signed between members. The countries fixed the numbers of products to be imported and exported, the object being to find an equilibrium between the two. Prices were set in "transferable" rubles, a simple unit of account; the sum was fixed, according to the 1975 Moscow rule, on the basis of the average world price for the preceding five years.

For all the member countries, the problems with this organization were obvious. East Germany complained about the poor quality of the products supplied by some of it partners; the Czechs about late deliveries. Having grown impressively in the 1970s (more than 8 percent between 1971 and 1975), COMECON internal trade petered out (average annual growth of 3.2 percent between 1981 and 1985) to stagnate after 1988.

The figures depended on the rate of exchange used and the relative evolution in prices. But the trade crisis within COMECON, and more generally of cooperation within the zone, was evident in other ways. For example, as soon as it was possible (that is when Moscow gave the go ahead) East European airlines bought Western aircraft (Hungary, Poland, and maybe Romania bought Boeing, East Germany and Czechoslovakia bought Airbus). For almost 40 years the "international socialist division of work" meant the East European airlines had had to buy a Soviet fleet.

The actual inefficient functioning of COMECON was also considered an obstacle to the reforming countries' plans. Josef M. Van Brabant, a UN economist, explained it thus in a conference on East bloc reforms "the bilateralism and the almost barter system (which characterizes COMECON) are in themselves incompatible with the economic decentralization" advocated by Poland, Hungary, and the Soviet Union. His analysis was adopted by the reformers. "The market economy can only be set up in Hungary if trade relations with the other Eastern countries (almost half of our trade) is conducted between companies, on the basis of world prices," judged Laszlo Csaba, a Hungarian economist.

The Soviets were no more happy with COMECON than the Hungarians. In 1989 an expert official argued against the "oil for plant" model which dominated relations between the Soviet Union and its partners. Despite the Soviet Union's leading role in the area, COMECON reform seemed very difficult. The texts adopted in 1987 and 1988, notably the "collective concept of the international division of work for the years 1991 to 2005," made the objective a "single market." But the Romanians were clearly against this. The East Germans adopted the objective but officially declared their opposition. The perestroika of COMECON actively sought after by the Soviet Union, Poland, and Hungary, would be much discussed.

Many countries were in favor of immediate reforms in bilateral relations within the organization. Already Prague and Moscow had decided in March 1988 to impose the world market laws on direct relations between Soviet and Czech firms (payments would be in crowns or rubles based on a rate of exchange laid down for these operations). Similar agreements were signed between Czechoslovakia and other countries. But they only affected a marginal share of Czech external trade.

Moscow, Budapest, and Warsaw relied more on opening up trade with the West and being part of the world division of work than on COMECON reforms to regain economic growth. The reforming countries wanted to develop trade with the West. They would accept certain necessary conditions (the suppression of the monopoly of external trade and decentralization), they also looked forward to easier access to foreign markets. In particular, Hungary did not want to be considered to be a country with a state-run economy, which it no longer thought it was.

The EC-COMECON declaration of June 25, 1988 allowed bilateral negotiations between the European Commission and Eastern countries to begin. A trade and cooperation agreement was signed with Hungary on September 26 that year and signaled the removal of all obstacles to Hungarian exports to the EC by 1995. A less ambitious accord was signed with Czechoslovakia. Discussion with Bulgaria and Poland were well advanced. Finally, preliminary discussions were taking place between the Soviet Union and East Germany. The Soviet Union announced it wanted to be part of GATT, which Hungary, Poland, and Romania had already joined.

The reforming countries wanted to become trading countries like the others and to be considered part of the world financial system. After Romania, Hungary, and Poland, the Soviet Union wanted to join the IMF and the World Bank. They all agreed to respect the constraints, notably to make their currency convertible in the near future. The reformers also hope for international finance to help them transform their economies. As Jean-Pierre Broclawski showed in a study published by *Le Courier des pays de l'Est* (June-July 1989),"some Eastern countries, especially since 1985, again became active participants on the world international markets." This was particularly true of the Soviet Union.

Was there a risk that foreign loans would be a substitute for reform rather than a stimulus? Had this not been the case with Gierek's Poland and Kadar's Hungary? In any case, while Romania and East Germany refused to get into debt, the Soviet Union — globally hardly in debt to the West — decided otherwise. Gorbachev decided to borrow from the West to finance, temporarily, purchases of some consumer goods.

From this point reformers were counting on direct investments. The debate on the dependence this would create had vanished. Western capital not only brought in technology but know-how, especially in management and the Soviet Union, Poland, and Hungary tried to lure it in. Investors were offered increasingly conservative laws. In the Soviet Union, companies with mixed capital (Soviet and Western), only authorized since 1987, multiplied prolifically: 300 at the end of 1988, but more than 700 by mid-1989. Within the continent this was not enough. Moscow worked on the creation of three "free zones," where fiscal, customs, and welfare regulations would not apply.

Hoping to play a greater part in the world economy, the COMECON reforming countries were turning to the West. To achieve efficiency, they wanted the world market — the capitalist market — to impose its law on their economies. They also thought that COMECON should function according to the rules of the market. But on this point there were loud voices of dissension among the socialist community. Both politically and economically the empire was collapsing.

THE WEIGHT OF THE DEBT

According to the report published by the International Finance Institute (IFI), a private organization in Washington D.C. financed by the leading international banks, the debt of the 7 Eastern European countries (excluding the Soviet Union) stood at $116.82 billion at the end of 1989, against $93.75 billion in 1985. The debt contracted by these countries was the equivalent of a quarter of Latin America's debt. Some $56.1 million had been due at the end of 1989 to commercial banks. According to the IFI, the banks were "too conscious of their unfortunate experience in Latin America" and were very cautious with the East, whose solvency had deteriorated. The IFI thought that the governments and the international financial organizations should be in the first instance the main source of loans.

THE SOVIET UNION
PLANNING WITH FREE MARKET UPHEAVALS
THE SOVIET ECONOMIC CRISIS

The Soviet Union could boast that it has escaped zero growth prevalent in many Western countries, but the rhythm of its economic development slowed down with every year. Results were well short of the modest targets set by the plans. Real Soviet growth oscillated in the 1980s between 2 and 3 percent, while it had stood at 5 percent in the 1960s and 4 percent in the first half of the 1970s.

Oil production in 1984 (615 million tons), while being the world's largest, was less than the previous year (616 million tons). This had negative consequences, for the associated industries (petrochemical and plastics) as well as external trade, the Soviet

Union earned most of its hard currency from the sale of hydrocarbons. There were even political repercussions, since the COMECON countries would have to pay more for their oil while their supplies would not increase.

STATISTICS: MANIPULATIONS AND CONFUSION

Soviet statistics were partly manipulated because they integrated data without cross checking — let alone verifying — the volumes of production or monetary values (in rubles). The wholesale prices were sometimes discreetly inflated (while drops in the price of consumer goods were always published and commented on), which increased artificially, even only marginally, the GNP.

ACKNOWLEDGING THE PROBLEMS

After 1986, Gorbachev admitted the Soviet Union's enormous backwardness. In public he stated that many Soviet products were inferior to world norms. He said out loud what any Western visitor would notice after visiting a shop. The Soviet Union produced abundant oil, coal, steel, synthetic textiles, cotton, wool, leather, etc. But it was still incapable of supplying its citizens with household goods, shoes, and clothes that they wanted to buy. The chain of production often functioned to supply rejects, after several months collecting dust on a shelf. The Russians call these unsellable goods, gray, tawdry dresses, leaky shoes that did not always match, household machines that would never work, "stay at home."

GENERAL WASTAGE

Deficient Agriculture

In a Western industrialized country, a bad harvest did not provoke a crisis. In the Soviet Union it did. Of course, the Soviet people were not going to be without bread this winter or the next. But they would without doubt lack flour and above all meat. A bad harvest meant insufficient food for cattle and livestock was slaughtered on a large scale. All the leaders who discussed the agricultural crisis stressed the difficult weather conditions of the preceding year. Canada and parts of the United States had equally bad conditions as the Soviet Union, yet they did not suffer so severely. Mr Baibakov, the president of Gosplan, blamed the irrational utilization of agricultural equipment and fertilizer, poor returns in irrigated lands, and losses between harvesting and storage. These losses regularly accounted for 10 to 15 percent of the harvest.

The Debate on Intensification

In 1984 people began to point out that the Soviet Union was about to run out of material and human resources. This posed a few ideological problems and the Soviet leaders added Marxist optimism to the Russian tradition of territorial expansion — Siberia was the equivalent of the North American frontier. Those who were not too professionally bound up with dogma realized that the country's reserves, although considerable, were not inexhaustible and that in some areas growth had become difficult and in any case costly.

The celebrated economist of the Novosibirsk Institute, Abel Aganbegyan, showed that the labor force had grown by 11 million during the period of the Xth five year plan (1976-80) but the XIth plan (1981-85) required an increase of 3 million. At the same time the progressive exhaustion of energy and mineral resources in the European part of the Soviet Union made continual growth more dependent on deposits east of the Urals, which were more expensive to extract.

The most "modern" leaders, like Gorbachev, thought that they should not wait for further increases in labor or raw materials, but they should improve what they had, use the available resources better, which meant a more effective fight against waste, better managed deliveries from one factory to another, etc.

These views were not universally held. The massive irrigation and drainage projects to divert several Siberian rivers and the flooding of entire regions of old Russia presented during the plenary session of the Central Committee, held on October 23, to discuss agriculture, went against Agenbegyan's theses on "intensification": many still believed that arable land needed to be extended and that industry needed more natural resources. The bureaucrats liked the massive works like the BAM, the laying of another rail line a few hundred kilometers to the north of the Trans-Siberian Railroad, officially opened — even if it had not yet completed — on October 1, 1984.

Incomplete Factories

One of the great weaknesses of the Soviet economy was the delays in building industrial plant. According to official statistics, 80 percent of investments in this area were stuck on incomplete sites, and this trend was on the increase. It did not seem that the priority given to renovating factories to create new units of production, as well as the concentration on a few objectives, had borne any fruit.

A Difficult Workforce

Despite exhortations to work harder and better, calls for socialism and work discipline, and the fight against bad timekeeping, productivity remained the basic problem.

A System which does not Reflect the Real Scarcities

Despite the economic reform of 1965 which should have given factories accounting autonomy, production results continued to be measured in all inclusive figures. The more manufactured goods incorporated raw materials, the more expensive they were, and the more production seemed high. Thus, as a Pravda economist wrote, the "wastages were not merely elements of dysfunction"; they were part of the system. Members of the "people's control" noted that many factories did not pay the fines which were inflicted or else paid them without making any changes.

MANY INEFFECTIVE REFORMS

The 1965 Reform

To remedy the defects in the Soviet economy, new methods were needed to assess factory results and also new incentives for workers. This had been part of Kosygin's 1965 reform. These measures were only partially put into practice. Thus the index of global production continued to be the basis of all calculations of increased production, productivity, wages, and bonuses. Since early 1978, factories' activity should have measured by the volume of production that was delivered, taking into account the level of satisfaction given to customers; but this innovation was only introduced by a few pilot factories.

The 1979 Reform

Adopted in July 1979, the reform was a hotchpotch of half-measures. Sometimes it followed up the 1965 reform, sometimes it contradicted it. It was aimed at the "technocratization" of economic management with a reinforced central administration and greater financial autonomy for factories. This 1979 reform, which was supposed to be applied in stages, was not even mentioned in the 1981-85 plan.

Repeated Failure to Reform Agriculture

The Soviet authorities had perfected, a few years before, a plan to reorganize the public sector (the collective and state farms) and stimulate the private sector (small-holdings). In 1981 there was very little restructuring: on the contrary, the address to the 26th congress seemed to mark a retreat from these lofty plans.

Andropov's Reforms

After his accession to power, Yuri Andropov launched an energetic campaign. On several occasion he denounced the Soviet economy's terrible performances and disorganization: several plans were envisaged and put into action. Factories were to be given greater autonomy in planning, wages would be set according to the quality as well as the quantity of the work, whereas quantity had been the principal goal of all the five year plans. Also to increase production, factories would have rely on their own resources: they would have to build up their own development funds. Another innovation was that certain plants would be allowed to set their own prices, in order to adapt to the market.

Andropov's economic experiment started off in a few industrial ministries and regions in 1983 and then spread out, as planned, in 1985. It should apply to all industrial enterprises in the country by January 1, 1987. A decree, published in Pravda on August 4, 1985, reaffirmed the plan's objectives and laid down a series of concrete measures. To recapitulate, it involved the reduction of intermediaries between Gosplan and enterprises, to increase the latters' autonomy. Only accounting autonomy was encouraged, not decision-making, since Gosplan retained control of industrial matters.

PERESTROIKA

The keyword in 1986 was *perestroika*, which can be roughly translated as restructuring. This expression applied to all the Eastern countries. The introduction of the market to help the consumer and real control of management were the fundamental planks of the new economic way forward. Glasnost or openness was the political dimension of this transformation. Freedom of expression, political pluralism, free elections were at the heart of the introduction of democratic forms, previously denounced as bourgeois. In 1990 Boris Yeltsin and many others left the Soviet Communist Party, the final nail in the coffin of the single party state. This breath of liberty led to resurgent nationalism and the Baltic countries and Ukraine demanded or declared independence. One must not forget the religious and cultural particularisms of the Muslim republics, some close to Iran. Helene Carrere d'Encausse's "L'empire éclate" became a visible reality.

The 1987 Reforms
The year 1987 saw perestroika, the restructuring of the Soviet economy, in full swing. More radical than the 1965 reform,

it was aimed at giving enterprises real financial autonomy and to democratize management.

In industry, Yuri Andropov's 1984 attempts at reform, which were followed up by Constantin Chernenko, were put into action from January 1, 1987 by Gorbachev, who wanted to go even further. After 1986, a system of complete financial autonomy was introduced in certain industries (car, petrochemical, computers, etc) and in 36 enterprises. Profit became the principal indicator of results in 1986, and the firms had to find their own funds for investments.

The law on state enterprises, adopted on June 30, 1987 by the Supreme Soviet, stated that "enterprises must meet consumers' needs, their satisfaction in good time was the norm for all work collectives." This was a real revolution. Enterprises had to be governed by the 3 principles: autonomy, self-financing, worker-management control. Bosses would no longer be appointed by an administrative office, but elected by work collectives. Long-term loss-making enterprises would be closed down. The law on individual work and cooperatives came into force in April 1987. It legalized some of the black market activities, to make up for lack of stocks and improve services to the people.

The last area of attack for the Gorbachevian reformers was foreign trade. Some 20 ministerial departments and 70 industrial enterprises could now trade abroad directly. The Soviet Union wanted to become part of the world economy as an equal partner. After early 1987, Western companies were able to create joint ventures with Soviet enterprises. There were numerous restrictions: the Western partner could not have a majority holding or take profits out.

Disappointing Results

There was no point in hiding the fact that the provision of consumer goods was inversely related to breakthroughs in democratization. "When I open the refrigerator, I can look for perestroika but I don't find it." Every Muscovite responded with a heartfelt lament "It's worse than before."

The year 1988 saw the law on state enterprises, giving great autonomy, especially financial, come into action. Some enterprises found the transition, called *khozrazchiot*, very difficult. The ministries continued to impose "state orders" on important enterprises, which limited their autonomy, if not stifled it. Besides the transition to khozrazchiot was not accompanied by any training of management or personnel, which provoked some confusion. A new feature was that the press published a list of 30 enterprises declared insolvent, which was a step to closing down the unprofitable enterprises advocated by Gorbachev. But there was no law on bankruptcies so enterprises were kept going by the ministries on which they depended.

The other disappointment was the role of the private sector, particularly in the provision of services. The private and cooperative sector — non-agricultural — employed on July 1, 1988 less than a million people (out of a working population of 125 millions) and contributed less than 0.5 percent to the volume of goods and services sold to the population by state bodies.

As for joint ventures, through which the Soviet Union expected technological input and investment, they did not live up to expectations. Out of 143 mixed enterprises in existence on paper in December 1988, only 12 were fully operational. At the end of 1988 the government published a decree on foreign trade, whose principal attribute was that foreign investors could hold more than 49 percent of these joint ventures. But there was still a question mark over the transfer of profits, which made Western investors hesitate.

Controversial Reforms

This ambitious reform came up against many obstacles. The central ministries and certain local apparatchiks tried to oppose measures aimed at taking away their rights. Enterprise directors were not keen either: reforms meant they would have to manage differently, using skills difficult to acquire. They would have to respond to market forces.

The bureaucrats and their representative at the Politburo and in government created obstacles to the setting up and functioning of cooperatives by making them part of ministerial plans, and by taxing them heavily and exposing them to a Mafia racket, from which the police did little to protect them. Similarly they tried to impede the leasing of land to farm workers, by making them work in the collective and state farms. Thus Igor Ligachev, the Politburo member with responsibility for agriculture, refused to stop the subsidies to unprofitable collective farms and state farms (almost 70 percent of the total).

The workers were not always well-disposed to the reforms. For the first time in 1987, the Soviet press reported two strikes by workers unhappy with a new pay structure linked to results. Many experts stated that nothing would change without price reforms, which was being hotly debated in the highest circles. There was no definite price reform plan, even though many claimed it was crucial.

Before tackling the economic crisis, which was now called a "system failure," you had to be clear what you wanted to replace it with and the price people were willing to pay. There was a fierce struggle between the free marketeers, who believed in total economic freedom and were numerous but discreet, and those who believed in an alliance between the market and the welfare state and who were more visible and influential. The former did not advocate miracles but thought the Soviet Union should go straight into real prices, a convertible ruble, the ending of all subsidies, and the closing down of unprofitable enterprises. Although this was logical they could not respond to the criticisms of those — led by Gorbachev — who said that with an average wage of 220 rubles and 40 million Soviet citizens living below the poverty line, it would provoke massive civil unrest.

POLAND
THE REFUSAL TO REFORM PRICES WITHOUT FREEDOM

In 1976 Polish workers forced the government to step down over price increases. The year 1976 was notable for a deep political and social crisis, which forced the government to reconsider its economic priorities for the current five year plan. At the end of June the situation exploded after the government's decision to raise the price of basic foodstuffs, meat (up 69 percent), butter (up 50 percent), sugar (up 100 percent), etc. There followed a wave of strikes and demonstrations which even led to a few deaths at Radom, and the government suddenly backed down. Learning from these events, Edward Gierek, the First Secretary of the Communist Party, set new priorities: improve the supply of the internal market, devote a larger part of national income to consumption, and diminish the rhythm of investments.

THE 1980 GDANSK ACCORDS

Following the increase in the price of meat on July 1, 1980, there was social unrest, which rapidly turned into a major crisis for the regime. Poland was looking for a new economic model which encompassed membership of COMECON and public opinion, which demanded a break with the past. For three years the Polish economy had been in recession, aggravated in 1980 by a catastrophic harvest, the diverse effects of long strikes, and a rise in the foreign debt which exceeded $20 billion. In 1980 national income dropped by 3 percent. On September 15, 1980 the Gdansk accords legalized independent trade unions, including Solidarity.

DECEMBER 13, 1981: A STATE OF WAR

The results of 1981 were generally negative. Coal production — necessary to meet internal demand and exports — dropped noticeably. There were severe shortages of many foodstuffs. It was necessary to import food using hard currency, which was in short supply. Poland had the biggest state budget deficit in its history. The value of national money had dropped. For every zloty in three paid in wages there were no goods to buy. The dollar was changed for ten times the official exchange rate and was used for all legal as well as illegal transactions. Poland's indebtedness to Western countries, at $27 billion, had increased.

The military seized power on Sunday December 13, justifying their actions by the need to avoid economic collapse. According to the state of emergency all men aged between 18 and 54 years had to work a 42 hour week. The Council for National Salvation also announced on December 31 that all retail prices were free, which led to the trebling of the price of certain basic necessities (meat, butter, sugar, coal...).

1985: THE CONSOLIDATION OF THE POLISH DEBT

In 1975 Poland bought much plant abroad and increased its debt. In 1985 the Western debt stood at $26.8 billion, the largest of all the socialist countries. The effects of rescheduling the guaranteed debt reached in 1985 would not be felt for some time. Poland would have to repay every year nearly $1 billion, almost a sixth of its imports to the Western countries.

THE 1980S: OBVIOUS ECONOMIC FAILURE

The economic plans which promised autonomy, self-financing, and worker-management control, combining the market laws and planning, faced opposition from hard-line members of the party. The bureaucrats feared for their jobs and did not hide their opposition to General Jaruzelski's economic advisers, deemed to be too market-oriented.

The execution of the economic reforms faltered over the lack of support from the population for the regime's objectives. There was general unhappiness mainly because from 1979 to 1983 the Polish standard of living had dropped by 40 percent. Since November 1, 1983 certain goods had to be rationed, because of the agriculture's catastrophic situation, and this added to the gloom. As well as indebtedness, the country suffered from the repercussion of the American sanctions policy. The Polish leaders became even more partisan over further integration within COMECON. However there were limits to solidarity between member countries (including the Soviet Union), who faced many difficulties and were no longer inclined to help Poland.

On November 29, 1987 the people voted against reforms. The economic situation continued to decline because the plans no longer worked and the market had not taken over. As Waldemar Kuczinski put it "1989 was the worst year since 1981. Production dropped, as did the GNP, the external trade surplus, and hard currency reserves. The mining of coal diminished, because the miners now had Saturday off. As for farm workers, they no longer wanted to sell their wheat. There was a good harvest, but they kept it as if it were money. They no longer had any confidence in the zloty."

THE CONSERVATIVE CLIMATE OF THE 1990S

On September 12, 1989 Solidarity came to power when Tadeusz Mazowiecki's government was sworn in. Since 1989 there had been many attempts to revitalize the economy. The diagnosis was this: the old businesses that employed 5 million people needed to be closed down as soon as possible and smaller and average size units needed to be set up. A large part of the state sector was being privatized, and 290 licenses had been granted by the end of the year to set up new businesses with foreign capital. The 1990 budget was prepared in collaboration with IMF specialists. It forecast a substantial drop in state subsidies.

On December 1 the government launched a state loan of 5 billion zlotys ($1.5 billion). Subscribers would either get preferential prices in the acquisition of shares in future privatized businesses, or receive interest at inflation-linked rates. Setting up a market economy, privatizing the state sector, establishing the basis for the zloty's convertibility, building up trade with the West, encouraging the establishment of small and average businesses and joint ventures, eliminating subsidies, controlling wages: Mazowiecki's government found it hard to instil these new precepts. It was not easy for Solidarity to make the idea of austerity popular: Waldemar Kuczinski stated "Our priority is a stabilization policy which will stop inflation. But how can you have a drastic deflationary policy in a country on the road to democracy, which is still 90 percent state owned?"

For the moment the main task was the privatization of the state sector, which was in the hands of the economist Krysztof Liss, who had advised foreign companies on investments in Poland. "Mr Privatization's" objectives were the creation of a stock exchange, and putting property in the hands of the greatest possible number of small concerns.

The non-communist government expected a lot from the small private businesses, willing to take initiatives and risks. At the end of 1987 there were only 5,000 small businesses and before the change of government there were 23,400. Andrzej Kaczorowski belonged to the burgeoning class of new entrepreneurs, which was separate from Solidarity and its sympathizers. At 34 years of age, he had the best furniture factory in Warsaw and employed 77 people, in an increasingly prosperous business. By offering original and personalized goods, he outperformed state businesses, which were subject to crisis and underinvestment, and just about good for exports to the Soviet Union. Kaczorowski began his business just after martial law had been declared, to escape from the communist system. He suffered from supply problems, administrative restraints, fiscal obstacles, and the nomenklatura's nervousness but he thought he had benefited from the change in mentality, which had also taken place among the communists. Kaczorowski did not indulge in the excessive spending of the 1970s entrepreneurs. All his profits went back into the business.

This was also Tadeusz Gutt's line — he was the boss of Kangaroo — which sold colorful travel bags in Poland and Scandinavia. Nearly 40, he also started out under martial law, in the early days. He gave up his studies at the Lodz film school and left for six months to make some money in the West. On his return to Warsaw, he was immediately successful. A Swedish computer firm, run by Polish emigres, suggested a subcontract. It bought the textiles, he would make the goods which the company would sell in northern Europe. In early 1989 Gutt set up the Compensa firm, which offered foreign entrepreneurs investment opportunities in Poland. Although not part of Solidarity, in 1982 he transported packages from churches to prisons. He knew he was part of a productive class which only wanted to prosper. Enterprise could be a fertile breeding ground for those who would make things happen.

THE BRUTAL APPRENTICESHIP
TO CAPITALIST AUSTERITY

The cure for economic ills was hard. Almost 100,000 car drivers had to hand in their number plates because they could no longer afford gasoline and insurance. Taxi fares had to be multiplied by 100, and taxis could not find paying customers. Gas, electricity, heavily subsidized before, became a major component of the family budget, after increases of over 400 percent. In the evening there were still cold cuts in the meat shops as people looked at the prices and left without buying. On the sidewalks of Marchelewskiego Avenue people bought butter at 2,000 zlotys instead of the usual 3,000 in the state shops.

Many were anxious about the second phase of the reforms. Zbigniew Bujak said "People were calm about the price increases, but the second phase, that of the business bankruptcies and unemployment will be even more shocking and dangerous. People can cope with a drop in living standards.... I well remember the time when I only ate bread, margarine, and sugar. But we had the extraordinary luxury of a secure job." Government estimates showed that unemployment would go from 400,000 to 1 million in 1990. In January the first mass dismissals occurred. Jacek Kuron, an incorrigible dissident, became the Minister for Employment; not content with giving his name to "Juron soup kitchens," he began work on a social welfare plan.

HUNGARY
1968: THE NEW ECONOMIC MECHANISM

This reform allowed businesses to choose their objectives and suppliers. Businesses had to increase that part of their profits that went to the self-financing of investments. As well as the fixed state prices, the prices of some goods were set at what the market would tolerate, while others were allowed to be set within certain limits.

ONE STEP BACK

From 1972, the Communist Party recentralized the economy by bringing 54 large enterprises within its control, and giving the ministries back their leading role by distributing large subsidies, which skewed competition.

1979: RENEWED REFORM

After 1976 businesses could dismiss workers and they had to pay for wages from their own funds. The number of ministries was reduced as well as their role: they could no longer intervene in the management of businesses but could set medium term goals. In the early 1980s the private and semiprivate sector in Hungary flourished as the state's role diminished. After August 1981, some small businesses could employ up to 100 people, and different types of association were allowed and even encouraged, particularly in agriculture, light industry, and hotels.

This new freedom led to visible inflation. Price increases in 1979 were the highest for 30 years and the price index rose by 8 to 9 percent. These measures were surprisingly wide ranging but for consumers it seemed the price increases were the tip of an iceberg, representing the second phase of the 1968 reforms. After lengthy discussions, reforms were officially renewed in October 1979 under the direction of the party, but without the sanction of the forthcoming party congress.

This rush was explained by the degradation of certain basics: the terms of trade had declined (20 percent between 1974 and 1978), import prices had increased more than exports prices; the need to devote large sums of money (more than 40 percent of investments) to the exploitation of raw materials and energy, given the stagnation and increasing cost of imports from the Soviet Union; internal imbalances created by an inadequate pricing system.

The new reforms were aimed at revising the pricing system by using the pressure of external prices. Thus the hunt for lame ducks could be carried out more efficiently. Also wage differentials in terms of productivity and professional qualifications were encouraged.

Monetary freedom was the last element in the creation of the market. In 1981 a single exchange rate replaced the tourist and commercial rates. It was adjusted every week to take into account the world market fluctuations.

THE DIFFICULTIES OF BECOMING
PART OF THE WORLD ECONOMY

Lacking raw materials, whose import constituted a costly drain, Hungary was vulnerable to any downturn in the world economy. The delays in modernizing several key sectors (steel) and the weak productivity of the whole adversely affected an economy sensitive to the repercussions of a world crisis, because of the importance of external trade in the makeup of national income (more than 40 percent). The price of imported raw materials continued to increase but the sale of Hungarian goods on the world market hit several obstacles.

As well as belonging to COMECON, Hungary wanted to insert itself in the international economy as a long-term solution to its problems, according to the post-1983 leaders. But this insertion demanded sacrifices: an austerity program to fight against inflation which reached 9 percent in 1983, 18 percent in 1988, as well as to ensure the modernization of several sectors and the acceleration of growth, which neared a rate of 1.5 percent in 1980 to 1985, and then dropped. Hungary's indebtedness stood at $8 billion in 1982. The IMF, which Hungary joined on May 6, 1982, gave it credits totaling $580 million to finance an economic restructuring program.

TOWARD A MARKET ECONOMY

"To go from a socialist to a market economy is no easy matter," explained a Hungarian expert, adding with a certain irony "much has been written on the transition from capitalism to socialism, but nothing has been thought about the opposite, the passage from socialism to capitalism." Again in 1989, Hungary took the road of economic reform and the objective was a market economy.

The first step was to reduce the role of the state by three means: budget reform, a deregulation policy, and a privatization program. Besides a simultaneous drop in taxes and spending, notably all the subsidies to the lame ducks and consumer prices, the current program contained a substantial reform of those institutions which were financed by a central budget (schools, universities, hospitals...). All bureaucratic rules surrounding business management had to be eliminated. This was the context for the current policy of freeing prices, wages, private commerce, and imports, conducted by the government with the active support of the IMF. The monopoly of external trade had already been dismantled for many years (1,500 Hungarian companies traded abroad), a program to free imports, spread over three years came into force on January 1, 1989. Almost 40 percent of goods from the West, could be bought without authorization. Finally the most effective weapon against the state was privatization.

The privatization program faltered because of the weakness of the financial market. To reinvigorate the different markets: that of capital, work, real estate, was the second step in the reforms. All the taboos had been broken: unemployment seemed a necessary evil. In summer 1989 some 20,000 people were listed as unemployed (0.5 percent on the working population). For the moment the financial market was embryonic. Hungary put all its hopes on attracting foreign capital — an ultraconservative regime took over. While reducing its trade with the East, Hungary hoped to develop it with the West. To service a substantial hard currency debt ($17 billion), Budapest had to draw in a trade surplus of $1 billion during the next few years. Also the Hungarian leaders hoped to speed up the process of freeing up trade, as set out in an agreement between Hungary and the EC in 1988. The Hungarian way forward was less state, more market, and integration within the world economy. On October 23, 1989 Hungary stopped being a people's democracy.

ROMANIA
1975-80: THE FORCED MARCH
TO INDUSTRIALIZATION

Until 1980, the Romanian economy had developed at a rapid rate. To achieve these results, the planners had deliberately chosen to privilege accumulation to the detriment of consumption. In 1976 the rates of accumulation were between 32 and 33 percent, which was the highest rate within COMECON, barring the Soviet Union.

In 1978 the process of modernization and the expansion of the productive plant continued at a brisk pace. This development strategy was based more than ever on the absolute priority given to the industrial sector, which received 57 percent of investments in 1978. While it explained the rapid growth — the fastest in all of Eastern Europe —, this policy also produced internal imbalances, leaving some areas like transport lagging behind. These tensions were aggravated by the more difficult conditions affecting external trade. The brake on imports, sometimes decided very abruptly, several times provoked production chaos.

ECONOMIC AND FINANCIAL CRISIS

Previously a net exporter of energy, Romania became a net importer because of the stagnation of its oil production and an increase in requirements in the 1980s. Romania needed to import half its oil needs (15 million tons in 1980, of which only 1,496,000 came from the Soviet Union) payable in hard currency which was in short supply. As a consequence, Romania had to step up its exports. According to Nicolae Ceauşescu, industry did not manage to deliver 40 percent of its orders.

In 1981 its foreign debt exceeded $13 billion. With a $1.48 billion loan from the IMF (of which it was a member) and other bank credits, Romania faced the prospect of not being able to meet its financial commitments. Bucharest could not ignore the fact that its creditors' patience was exhausted. Especially since Romania's image was deteriorating because it was the most authoritarian communist regime.

PAYING DEBTS LEADS TO POVERTY: 1981-89

Since 1981 the Romanian economy had had to repay its foreign debt. The reduction of the debt happened naturally at the cost of modernizing the productive plant as well as people's living conditions.

In 1989 Romania had a war economy, which had not been seen for 40 years: shortages of basic necessities, hot water distributed on meters, electricity quotas (22 kilowatts a month per room, with the threat of cutting off supplies if this was exceeded). This general penury was the result of a weak agriculture, oriented to exports — destined for the Soviet Union — and of industrial plants being super-heavy and obsolete.

Instead of launching itself on privatizing land as the Soviet Union and Hungary had already done, Romania started another agricultural revolution in 1982-83. This aimed at collectivizing those rare villages that had not been made socialist, about 15 percent of land. At the same time systematization was put into action in March 1988 to get more than 320,000 hectares of new agricultural land — by destroying farmers' houses. Thousands of villages disappeared, without the main problem being addressed: such weak returns that the Romanian farmers' added value was ten times lower than that of French farmers.

Chemicals, petrochemicals, and metallurgy benefited for more than 20 years from the regime's support to create projects that were entirely disproportionate to the country's needs. This desire for gigantism sometimes suffered from the market's whims (the two oil shocks), from a sudden drop in the goods' quality, and from machinery that was prematurely aged for lack of spare parts and maintenance. In 1988 investments dropped by 1.3 percent. This negative result came from the brake on imports imposed by the leadership: "Debt comes first."

CZECHOSLOVAKIA
AN INDUSTRIAL COUNTRY VICTIM
OF THE OIL CRISIS

Like all industrialized countries lacking raw materials, Czechoslovakia suffered from stiff competition on international markets and from higher energy prices. The terms of trade with the West dropped by 70 percent in 1975. It was not surprising that the CP announced it had run out of hard currency. A third of Czechoslovakia's external trade was with capitalist countries. The party urged businesses to improve their competitiveness on the Western markets. Czechoslovakia had the highest per capita consumption of energy. After 1978, faced with a situation that was becoming more and more expensive, Mr Hula demanded draconian energy savings. At the same time the targets for lignite production were increased.

DISINDEBTEDNESS AND TECHNICAL BACKWARDNESS

After 1979 trade with the West was limited by a strict credit policy. Perhaps the leadership was afraid of repeating Poland's example of indebtedness. Czechoslovakia's foreign debt — about $3 to 4.5 billion in 1982 — was the lowest among the people's democracies. For a long time, Czechoslovakia had a conservative development strategy, to the detriment of competitiveness; according to the specialists the refusal to take on debt contributed to the growing technological gap with the Western world. Also this was reflected in unfavorable results in external trade: everyone complained in Prague about the lack of quality goods made for export to the capitalist world. There were no planned economic structural reforms, mainly for political reasons; the leadership was waiting for greater integration within COMECON to solve the problems that faced them.

1988: THE NEW MECHANISM

The exhaustion of the country's material and financial resources, the chronic delays in modernization had led the former leaders — opposed to political reforms — to elaborate in 1988 a new "mechanism of the economy," with increased autonomy for 150 businesses, which would take place on January 1, 1990. But the events of November 1989, the departure of Gustav Husak, the arrival of a coalition government, in which the communists were a minority, and the election of Vaclav Havel as president on December 29, 1989 led to a new scenario: the whole system had to be changed possibly to resemble that of Hungary.

Industrial restructuring, the reorientation of production (such as that of heavy industry which produced too much and for too high a price) were the orders of the day, as well as the environmental problems, caused by pollution from the industrial centers. Agriculture, which fed the people, needed better specialization, particularly in the food industry. Even before the upheavals at the end of 1989, a law had been passed to allow foreign participation up to 49 percent in joint ventures.

THE CONSERVATIVE OUTLOOK FOR THE 1990S

Professor Komarek said "There is some anxiety that the reforms' objectives have been poorly defined. We fear that what is in the pipeline may not function in a rational manner." Apart from the beginnings of labor mobility, the results of the year's Czech perestroika were rather meager. Economic growth was slightly below 2 percent in 1989, and industrial production had stagnated.

In 1989 there were good results in agriculture; this was a paradox for a country with a long industrial tradition, which only employed 7.5 percent of the working population in the primary sector. A Western observer noted discreetly "It's the experience of reforms with the support of austerity." It was true that very little was available for modernization, given the government's desire to limit foreign loans. With a gross debt in hard currency of $5.3

billion, Czechoslovakia was one of the least indebted socialist countries.

Some 2,246 state firms began to elect new directors in January 1989. Some of those elected were new to the scene but many others were old hands. Thus the new president of the important chemical company, Chemopetrol, was none other than Mr Zelenka, the former director of the development department in the Bohemian ministry of industry. Also the deconcentration of industry produced questionable results. The Slovak complex, Slovchemia, was dismantled a few years before but nothing replaced it.

The only area in which Czech reforms were realized was employment. Unemployment, a scarecrow which deceived no one in many socialist countries, became a reality in 1989 in Czechoslovakia, and some 116 departmental ministries and combines disappeared. While waiting the eventual reconversion, those who had lost their jobs were compensated according to a sliding scale, which lasted for at least a year. The appearance of unpaid unemployed would undoubtedly provoke social unrest.

While the former political leaders thought they could hedge their bets between planning and the market until given a definite direction from Moscow, the new economic leaders were not just half-hearted reformers. Komarek had worked in Moscow with Oleg Bogomolov and Nikolai Chmelev, who were among the most radical Soviet economists. As for the economic plans of the opposition group, Civic Forum, it reflected the conservatism of the country's economists. Its statement said "The reestablishment of the economy demands a market free from bureaucratic intervention, combining different forms of ownership."

The legal bases of reforms already existed. During 1988 and 1989, the country allowed the existence of mixed companies and adopted a law on the protection of investments. In early 1990 a new banking law created a real central bank and soon a network of commercial banks would be in place. Czechoslovakia's main problem seemed to be its lack of specialization, if we ignore industrial obsolescence.

While commercial results deteriorated (in 1988 the surplus on trade with the capitalist countries only reached $200 million),

Czechoslovakia had only a few products to sell, apart from chemicals and fine metallurgy. "There are industries in all sectors. The country produces at least 80 percent of the goods needed for a modern society," explained a Western economist. Despite the reforms, the path of competitiveness and internationalization will be long.

EAST GERMANY
WARM RELATIONS BETWEEN
EAST AND WEST GERMANY

In 1975 the East German economy went through a difficult time. East Germany was one of the country's that suffered most from the increase in raw materials' prices, having to pay an extra 1.7 million marks for its imports of Soviet oil. The result of this was that consumers suffered. At the same time the East German leadership could not ignore the needs of its people, who compared their standard of living with the West Germans.

After 1975 exports took on a new importance, but were hindered by the lack of outlets in the West. In 1975 debt to the capitalist countries was high: 3 million marks, of which 2 million was to West Germany. Most external trade was still conducted with the socialist partners, but in 1987 relations with West Germany continued to be important, exceeding the limits of a purely commercial transaction. There were specific ties (for East Germany trade with West Germany was internal trade) which contributed to the relative stability of the East German economy to a considerable degree. East Germany received every year about 2.5 billion Deutschmarks from diverse West German sources in loans, donations, gifts, which gave East Germany a financial ease as well as assuring the West that the interest and principal of its debt was paid and West German goods could be imported.

THE REFUSAL TO REFORM UNTIL 1989

In 1988 there were debates on reforms within the party leadership, which intimated that East Germany had no intention of copying this or that model and was looking for national solutions to its problems.

THE COMPLEXES

From 1980 to 1989 the management of East German firms was centralized into 132 complexes, which each comprised about 30 firms. The directors of the complexes were ministerial representatives. This organization allowed the state to control economic activity more effectively and to intensify production by eliminating double employment.

In September 1989 Hungary allowed East Germans to go West. On November 9, 1989 the symbol of the Cold War collapsed as the Berlin Wall was opened. In November 1989 the East German Minister for External Trade declared "The German Democratic Republic is going through a revolutionary process, but the country's economy remains solid." Be that as it may, by the end of the year it was a question of the gradual transformation of the planned economy into a market economy, after the departure of the immovable Erich Honecker, followed a few weeks later in early December by that of his provisional successor, Egon Krenz. The massive exodus of East Germans, begun in the summer, created a critical situation in certain sectors.

July 1, 1990 saw the economic and monetary union with West Germany. History speeded up with the absorption of East Germany by West Germany. The Soviet Union allowed the combined forces of East and West Germany to join NATO in exchange for economic aid from West Germany. Gorbachev agreed to remove Soviet troops from East Germany. In the second half of 1990 the political and economic unification of greater Germany accelerated. In the early 1990s East Germany was incorporated into greater Germany, solidly tied to the West.

EAST GERMANY WITHIN GREATER GERMANY

The 1990s would be dominated by the economic and political reunification of Germany. Greater Germany would benefit from its neighbors' demand for modernization. A powerful economic trade zone began to emerge based on the traditional links between East Germany and the COMECON countries and West Germany's industrial and commercial know-how.

The difference in the economic weight of the partners allowed West Germany to dominate and impose its model of the market economy. The law was dictated by efficiency and the abundance of goods convinced many. After the enthusiasm of unification, supplies had to follow. There was already perceptible friction: real estate speculation in East Berlin. It became impossible to sell East German goods, which suffered from competition with the more attractive West German ones. The differences in productivity put a brake on increases in East German wages and engendered frustrations. The relative dilapidation of East German factories triggered an investment boom and the influx of powerful neighboring groups, ready to conquer new markets. The strong demand from East German consumers made Western factories operate at full steam and paradoxically there were queues in the West, where shops, working on tight margins and stock management, attracted East shoppers with their savings. Only the fittest survived: the massive inflow of West Germany capital, takeovers of firms, and the extension of large distribution networks. In spite of the difficulties of reunification, the creation of an even more powerful economic entity was a major factor for the world economy.

THE FACTS BEHIND REUNIFICATION
(INSEE — NATIONAL INSTITUTE OF
ECONOMIC STATISTICS AND STUDIES)

Reunification would only slightly increase Germany's economic weight in the short-term. German reunification would obviously increase the economic weight of the German Federal Republic, but in the short-term not very much. It would certainly favor its growth within a more German-centered framework. Measured in national GDP in relation to the EC's GDP at current exchange rates, in 1987 West Germany's weight was 26.1 percent (ahead of France 20.5 percent, Italy 17.7 percent, and Great Britain 15.6 percent). West Germany's supremacy was less clear if one measured the GDP of each country at exchange rates, which took into account the parity of purchasing power between economies: West Germany had a 21.5 percent share (compared with 18.8, 18.5, and 18.5 for its three principal partners).

The total German GDP represented barely 25 percent of the EC's GDP (based on exchange rates of parity of purchasing power), which was not enough to assure German economic hegemony. In fact, the addition of East Germany's less than 17 million inhabitants would create a country whose population exceeded West Germany's current population by 27 percent. Since East Germany's GDP per capita was much lower than West Germany's, the total German GDP would probably only be barely 20 percent more than West Germany's GDP.

Aside from the mechanical weight of its production, the integration of East Germany would lead to a problem of "catching up" with West Germany and the EC, which was at least as difficult as it was for the Southern countries, (Spain, Portugal, and Greece) and Ireland. In fact, before they could achieve the same standard of living as the West Germans, the East German population had to acquire the culture of a market economy. In particular wage-earners could no longer expect their wages to be fixed unilaterally by the state, but had to accept that they would be set by their firms, and would increase in line with productivity gains.

Besides while West Germany's social market economy was struggling with determination against regional disparities, the integration of an East Germany, that was not only much poorer but also more lopsided than West Germany (almost all the East German industrial centers were in the south), made the necessity for a policy of substantial regional subsidies imperative. After monetary union, a unified Germany would enjoy stronger growth than the current West Germany with a more social and internal orientation of this growth. A large part of the West's investments would be in the East.

CONSOLIDATING ITS LEADING ROLE IN THE EAST

The Federal German Republic was already the main Western trading partner of the European COMECON countries (excluding inter-German trade): almost a third of COMECON's exports and almost half its imports were with the federal republic. This German dominance would be reinforced by the polarization of East German trade: almost 70 percent of its foreign trade was with COMECON, of which more than a third was with the Soviet Union. This geographic concentration was accompanied by a strong sectoral concentration, particularly in exports. More than half of East Germany's deliveries to other Eastern countries were of plant. It was as if parallel to West Germany's role on the Western markets, East Germany profited from a considerable share of the investment boom in all the COMECON countries.

Even if the comparison seems a bit summary, the complementary commercial roles played by the two Germanies on the Eastern markets could make a difference to the new Germany's export policy. The Eastern countries only represented 3.5 of West Germany's exports, but they constituted 10 percent of sales for both Germanies. This percentage had only an illustrative value because the consolidation of East Germany's exports and of West Germany's was statistically weakened by the problems of monetary convertibility.

If one added trade with Austria and Yugoslavia to East Germany's foreign trade, almost 10 percent of the total conducted with OECD countries, then there was the possibility of reconstituting (or constituting) a high density trade bloc between Germany and central Europe.

GERMAN UNIFICATION, A CHALLENGE
TO PRICE STABILITY IN WEST GERMANY

In fact econmically the shock of unification resembled a budget-inspired recovery. The economic space created by the two Germanies corresponded to a stimulation of world demand. In these circumstances the threat of inflation was tied to the size of transfers that the EC would grant East Germany in the first few years. Too timid transfers would discourage the East German people, revive emigration, and delay, if not check, any catching up with the West. Rapid and substantial transfers which would not be accompanied by a very big rise in fiscal and social deductions would lead to massive public borrowing (with a risk to long-term rates). The demand for consumer goods and investments would constrain the Bundesbank to raise its short-term rates, perhaps considerably. Any further skid (such as, an increase in oil prices or the dollar) would increase the tensions.

BONN PREPARES FOR UNIFICATION

The Bonn government adopted on July 3, 1990 the budget for 1991 and the budget plans up to 1994. Despite unification which was completed by the end of the year, West and East Germany would continue to have two separate budgets in 1991 to allow time for East Germany to put in place a financial system with the same strength as the West's.

The 1991 budget forecast spending of 324 billion Deutschmarks, an increase of 3.9 percent in relation to 1990, growth which according to the Finance Minister Theo Waigel was short of the anticipated increase in GNP. Waigel explained how the government would finance reunification. In the 1991 budget this would amount to 9 billion Deutschmarks, of which 4 billion went to the Unified Germany Fund put together by the Lander and local governments and 5 billion to finance other operations like setting up health insurance, unemployment protection, and a fiduciary agency to run East German state firms, prior to their privatization. The Unified Germany Fund would raise funds on the money markets to finance a debt which would add to the 31.3 billion deficit on the 1991 budget. This increased debt, which accounted for a withdrawal of 86 billion Deutschmarks from the public power on the money markets, was criticized by the opposition, the social democrats, who thought that "recourse to borrowing is the most expensive way to finance unity." Waigel did not worry: for him the global debt of the federal republic remained reasonable, in terms of percentage of GNP, and should not produce a rise in interest rates: he also said "supposing that interest rates remain around 8 percent, we will repay all the loans contracted to pay for unity in 2015."

The increase in spending was not all due to effecting German reunification. Germany was in the throes of an election, and the budget reflected the government's desire to ensure the well-being of the social classes, which had recently shown signs of nervousness. Beyond the economic and budget constraints, it was essential to change the way people thought and acted. To go from planned economy to the market was to learn a new socio-economic language. Instilling the enterprise spirit, diffusing methods of management and commercialism would take a long time. Capital and technology were nothing if people did not take an active part in creating a new destiny. There were risks in making a system too uniform or developing an ostentatious market logic too fast: friction and new unrest could follow from modernization, which had to happen with the people's cooperation.

YUGOSLAVIA
FROM WORKER-MANAGEMENT CONTROL TO THE MARKET ECONOMY

* Having adopted in 1976 two new laws on business partnerships and worker-management control plans, Yugoslavia faced the same problems as other Western European countries. Although it was socialist, it also had a market economy which was not immune to international upheavals.

* In 1981 the country's difficulties partly stemmed from the general recession and the rise in oil prices (Yugoslavia imported 10 million tons a year). But they also came from a planned system, which was not coordinated between the federal republics. Transformed into states within states, each republic had its industry, its agriculture, its external trade, its hard currency reserves, etc. With the general autarchy (local government was also closed in on itself), any firm within a republic needed plenty of ingenuity and skill to penetrate the barriers of another republic.

* Infrastructure — railroads, postal services, road and water links, energy, etc — were outside the federation's competence. The

tentatives of diverse committees and commissions to centralize them stumbled in 1986 on the right of veto, which each republic and autonomous region could exercise.

* Yugoslavia was characterized by the complete lack of any coordination between the development plans of the eight republics and autonomous regions.

Thus in 1987 the federal government was empowered to set the prices of certain products but not to control its application which fell within the realm of the republic's competence. The latter often only applied them partially, or in truth not at all if they were not in their interests. The republics and local governments also had the right to fix the price of other products and local services, which were not always set in keeping with the federal line. This dualism led to the wholesale disorder which characterized the price policy as well as the failure of several economic reforms.

* The poor economic situation, the persistence of ethnic conflicts between the federal republics led the party and the government to propose a large-scale reform, dubbed revolutionary, put into action on January 1, 1989. In 1988 the reform proclaimed the market economy, which meant Yugoslavia had given up the concerted economy (between the federal republics), which was now condemned as harmful and ineffective. The state's ability to interfere in the economy was considerably restricted, the possibilities of the private sector growing were increased, and it was made easier for foreign capital to be invested. After 1989 the opening of private firms and shops, which could take staff on without administrative formalities was authorized and banks became similar establishments to those in the West.

HYPERINFLATION WAS OVERCOME

Yugoslavia was special. For a long time the country had searched for a third way between market economics and centralized planning, before finding itself at the end of the 1980s in what could be called "stag-hyperinflation": during the last three months of 1989, there was an increase of more than 10,000 percent in the annual inflation rate, with quasi-stagnant production. Ante

Markovic deserved credit for having brought inflation back to 3 or 4 percent a month in April 1990.

The new plan was different from all the failed reform plans of 1985 to 1988 because it attacked the underlying causes of inflation, notably the budget deficit. The Markovic plan of September 19, 1989 thus rebudgetized the deficit, by arranging for three-quarters of it to be covered by fiscal receipts (a new tax on consumer goods and customs duties replaced quantitative restrictions on imports).

The second trick was to stabilize the dinar by fixing it to the Deutschmark. "One of the mysteries of the Yugoslav economy was the strength of consumption. It did not drop, while real income had dropped by 25 percent during the 1980s." What was the key to this enigma? In Yugoslavia three-quarters of savings were in foreign currency. When money was devalued, real income dropped, but savings increased in value, especially since interest rates were very high.

To restore confidence in the dinar, and increase the grip of monetary policy, in an economy where everyone dealt in Deutschmarks, a new dinar was established, equal to 10,000 old ones, with a fixed parity for six months in relation to the West German currency (1 mark equaled 7 dinars). Individuals' movement of money was freed and people were allowed to buy currency at authorized banks. Wages were frozen but retained the same value in Deutschmarks. This altogether original process restored confidence in money. The Yugoslavs emptied their piggy banks and changed their savings into dinars, to profit from the higher interest rates. Suddenly the restrictive monetary policy became effective again, allowing a very weak rise in credits. The persistent difficulties of the Yugoslav model, due in part to the political deadlocks at every level of a highly decentralized country, should give the recently converted Eastern countries food for thought: the market is much further than they think.

25. The New World of the 1990s

AN UPLIFT AND THE RETURN OF PROSPERITY?

At the beginning of the 1990s many newspapers ran the headline "the end of recession." There were many indicators of economic health: production increased rapidly, inflation — despite some feverish exceptions — seemed in control globally (except in Great Britain... and in the East). Investments had rejuvenated productive plant and there were new jobs. Industry itself was recruiting labor and increasing its productive capacity, while factories were running at full capacity. Economic institutes revised their forecasts upward taking into account the enormous outlets offered by the opening up of the East. The prospect of a single European market in 1993 forced companies to become more efficient and modernize. There were mergers and industry's image rose with the deflation of the financial bubble after the 1987 crash.

FINANCIERS BELIEVED IN THE RETURN OF GROWTH

Begun in 1982, the economic takeoff continued in the run-up to the 1990s. The industrialized countries had never know such an extended period of economic growth. The financial markets faithfully reflected the times. Their prosperity was unprecedented and persisted. Almost all reached record levels: New York, London, Paris, Frankfurt, Tokyo, Zurich, Brussels, Milan, and Amsterdam.

Factors particular to each country meant that the means of achieving these records were often different, but the convergence of interests grew during the last few years. This was particularly true of the end of 1989. On the finishing line all the markets were neck-and-neck, or almost. The gap between first and last was never more than 10 percent, which had never happened before.

Like economies, the stock markets were becoming global and were now almost entirely interconnected. They were symbiotic, feeding on the same hosts, sharing both the highs and the lows. Their rules and laws were being harmonized slowly. Eleven years before the leap into the third millennium, the contours of a world stock market became apparent. But it was only a sketch. Its execution would take much effort. The techniques would need finalizing and assimilating. It would take place as a function of world growth. The stock market had become the domain of the professionals, but more than ever, money was the essential ingredient.

If small investors no longer stalked the floors of the stock exchange, the golden boys did not replace them. They were still important as consumers and savers, and thus held the purse strings of the stock market. With or without the slightest growth, there was a shortage of liquidity so that institutional investors stayed put and the markets faced chaos.

Would growth continue? The year 1989 seemed to be a turning point. Having grown for seven years, the takeoff slowed down. But no expert would hazard a guess at its end. On the contrary, with the end of the Cold War and the probable savings on cuts in military budgets, economic prospects looked rosy. All were in agreement, including the OECD, and forecast at least two more years of growth, without any inflationary movement.

Some forecasters even dreamed of a rapid growth in trade with the East, which would solder the join between two cycles of growth. This was a seductive hypothesis. Although there were a few doubts, it made its way round the markets.

With the price earnings ratio (PER) having become more reasonable (about 13 to 15 as opposed to 20 to 25), thanks to the lull in 1989, the financial markets seemed well placed to see out the century in good shape, without having to worry about the failures of an often too radical and rapid modernity. After the spate of takeovers in the last decade, the 1990s could be an era of calm reorganization. In ten years the world stock market index had risen by 326 percent. Would it be possible to keep up this rate? The summer of 1990 proved it was not. The fear of war in the Gulf and of a third oil shock had a depressing effect on the stock markets.

DOGMAS IN QUESTION

All the experts were unanimous: the world economy was entering an upbeat period. After 15 years of crisis there was hope: economic prosperity was back again. Unemployment would drop and consumer demand takeoff thanks to wage sacrifices, the restructuring of the economy, and companies' competitiveness. Everyone had to press ahead on the road to international economic competition, the source of progress and happiness for humanity. This was the fundamental dogma of advanced societies, and was part of the religion of growth — the only belief of both West and the East. This ideology prevailed in all society.

In the early 1970s, while there had still been economic prosperity, there was a critical current emanating from Dennis Meadows, Edward Goldsmith, and Bernard Charbonneau. This timid movement compared with the bulldozer of the "thirty glorious years" disappeared with the crisis of the 1970s. Criticism of growth became incongruous if not improper, while the world faced inflation and unemployment. However a moment's thought would have shown that the crisis was the result of the preceding years' growth spurt. There was a price to be paid for the easy growth of those years resulting from the constant increase in the productive capacity of certain sectors on industry, the saturation of the markets, the brutal rise in oil prices stimulated by consumption, and the pressure of external costs (pollution, diverse burdens, rural exodus, etc).

THE HYPER-INDUSTRIALIZED 1990S

In 1989 friendly purchases, that is with the consent of the purchased companies, replaced the hostile takeovers of 1988. Was this a triumph of industrial reasoning over financial speculations? Were the Wall Street raiders a thing of the past? It was difficult to answer these questions, since the headlines tended to give the lie to the forecasts. Sir James Goldsmith failed to takeover the British conglomerate BAT (British American Tobacco), an indication that gigantic takeovers financed by junk bonds were still frowned upon in Europe.

There were a few major takeovers. The electronics companies, Siemens of Germany and GEC of Britain, took over the British Plessey and the French Paribas group bought the Compagnie de Navigation Mixte. The year 1989 was marked by the rapprochement of companies and their globalization. In Europe the merging of companies accelerated with the approach of 1993, the date of the single market: in finance the Victoire group took over the German Colonia, in industry the German MBB (military aeronautics and electronics) was taken over by Daimler-Benz, which consolidated its place as the largest European company. There were fears in Germany that such a large concern might dictate its law to the state. However the group replied by saying it needed to be large to compete with its rivals.

The same arguments applied to all countries and all sectors: in France, for example, where the state conducted a second reorganization of the chemicals industry. In Spain companies that were too small were judged to be inviable and sold to foreign companies — the truck company Pegazo was bought by the German Man and Daimler-Benz again. The Japanese giants continued to become international. Sony bought Hollywood's largest studio, Columbia, and Mitsubishi bought New York's Rockefeller Center. From West to East, the United States endured Japanese seizures. But the Europeans also took part in the feast on a United States, which having bought the world during the 1950s and 1960s, saw foreign investments within its territory multiply.

There were other investments: the implosion of communism led to many plans, including cable television and cars. While the Chinese market was closed after the events in Tienanmen Square in Beijing in June 1989 leading to losses and disappointments — especially in the consumer goods industry — Eastern Europe was a land of opportunity.

On the whole the dominant impression was of a dynamic world industry full of plans and innovations. The 1980s had started on the theme of the post-industrial era devoted to services, tourism, and leisure. They had ended on an upturn in steel, record car sales, and a general renewal on the technical side and in factories. The 1990s would be hyper-industrialized.

THE RISKS OF GROWTH

Nonetheless hanging onto a dogma was an infallible sign of an accumulation of problems. The facts were stark. Firstly, growth in developed countries was more and more difficult, mainly because of the globalization of the economy: the more countries had the industrial techniques and went for growth, the more international economic competition became difficult.

Secondly, continuous increase in wealth and in means was against elementary laws of physics, such as ecology. The increasing costs of growth were a constant reminder of the unavoidable nature of decline. In terms of social policy, growth eliminated more jobs, especially permanent qualified jobs, than it created. This was particularly clear on an international scale: a drop in unemployment in one country was inevitably a sign of problems in another . Furthermore the technological revolution, combined with intense economic competition, was the beginning of men's expulsion from the world of work, with the exception of a handful of managers. The EC's actual policy encouraged leaving land fallow and would lead to increasing intensification in those sectors still devoted to agriculture. The agro-industrial system led to increasingly vast farms to the detriment of the management of rural space.

Growth also led to a vertiginous loss of natural resources. The growth system was based on a mechanism of transfers of ecological costs in space and time. Thus future generations will pay a high price for our obsessional fixation. Faced with the threat of all kinds of disorder which would accompany the inevitable collapse of growth, how did the system react? Not by questioning its objectives, but by blindly seeking for increased production to restore short term balance. More than ever, the world economy functioned on this basis, only annual predictions were operational and corresponded to the absence of the system's end. Faced with the growing vulnerability of the economy and the complex technical systems, which made it function, regulations were put into effect which, in turn, justified the taking of further risks and led to new weaknesses.

Maybe there was still time to think about the post-expansion period. This would necessitate defusing a number of social and ecological time bombs, which scientific research had created in pursuing economic growth, an objective imposed by the technocracy or the market. That would also mean thinking about a controlled deceleration of the world economy, which was the only way to limit the current, and especially the future, damage. An essential element of this policy would be the progressive restoration of the local and regional economies' autonomy, particularly in the agro-food business. A world in which Africans are fed by food aid from the industrialized countries, and the cattle in those countries are fed with peanut flour in order to produce milk and meat surpluses is absurd.

GENERALIZATION WAS NO JUSTIFICATION

After 15 years of stagnation, Europe's economic outlook had improved, partly because the US economy was undergoing the longest period of growth since the war. Some attributed this to austerity programs, others to monetarism. Did this phase mean the same kind of growth as that after the war or was it a remission from a serious illness, which required major reforms?

First fact: the general rise in unemployment. Within the OECD countries, the unemployment rate remained stable for a decade: its drop in the United States after the longest growth cycle that country had experienced was offset by an increase in Europe. The services jobs created were precarious and these new jobs had nothing in common with the trade-union backed factory jobs of the 1950s and 1960s.

Second fact: the militarization of the Western economies, particularly the United States. Economically, this compensated for the weakness of effective demand, it also accelerated technical progress, and pushed the civil sector along. Politically, at home it welded the country around the ruling class, abroad it forced the opposing bloc to spend beyond their means. But by its very size, this militarization became counterproductive from the point of view of its initial objectives. The formidable increase in US military spending had, for example, immediate favorable economic consequences in terms of jobs and future distorting effects. To give a few examples there were: the budget deficits; the loss of economic competitiveness (as shown in the trade deficits) as a result of the weight given to the protected military sector and the now limited aftereffects of progress in military technology on the civil sector; the increasing inequality in the distribution of income, qualifications, and technical knowledge demanded by the armaments industry, excluding minorities.

Third fact: more than 15 years of economic stagnation. There was nothing in common between the immense capital demands following the Second World War, occasioned by the need to rebuild devastated countries and the current extraordinary transformation in consumption patterns (particularly the use of credit) and lifestyles (cars, urbanization, leisure), and today's short-term purchasing needs, which the immense commercial and advertising machine could barely stimulate.

Fourth fact: the speculation begun six years earlier continued despite severe warnings. The idea of uncoupling the financial economy and the "real" economy took into account a series of phenomena as well as obscuring, in our opinion, the present day coupling of stagnation and speculation. When savings and capital could longer be invested profitably, they were used in speculation (financial, real estate, in the arts, etc).

The piling up of huge state, company, and household debts prepared the ground for and led to the explosive growth of the casino economy, characterized by the apparent increased autonomy of the financial sector. The deregulation of the financial markets, accelerated in the last few years under pressure from the big banks, led to the proliferation of speculators' tools. The explosion of financial centers had nothing to do with any economic or industrial rationale, even if one pretended to believe that takeovers were justified by the synergies between companies or were decided by boards of directors.

Speculation prolonged growth, thanks to the ostentatious consumption of the *nouveau riches* and investments in computers and offices, but the corresponding increase in the costs of receipts and management of savings and capital meant there could not be a serious drop in interest rates. The turning back of the cycle might well be savage since the world economy was floundering in an ocean of debt — state, company, bank, individual — some of which were not worth the paper (or computer files) that guarantee them. There were two choices: a recession which could turn into collapse and vigorous inflation fed by new injections of liquidity.

Fifth fact: the economic adjustment policies practiced by the Western countries for over a decade and imposed on Third World countries with incredible brutality. The United States, Great Britain, France followed the same monetary policies based on the following creed: companies and capital holders had to make a profit, which would be reinvested and create jobs. The state's role had to be reduced because it blocked this mechanism by deducting these resources which would be invested if they were not consumed. These policies were based on three premises: that capital would be redistributed, that growth was limited by the capacity to save, and finally that there was an automatic balance between savings and investment.

In the current situation of stagnation, the policies of redistributing income in favor of the rich — in the hope that their increased savings would lead to extra investments — aggravated the problem and accentuated the division into two societies. These policies had been pursued with obstinacy on a global scale by the international financial organizations. The monetary creed ravaged countries and peoples. In Brazil the workers' purchasing power dropped by 40 percent between 1984 and 1986. Argentina was at the end of its tether. To repeat the point South Korea and the Asiatic dragons prospered because there was state intervention in all aspects of economic life.

Sixth and last fact: the absence of an indisputable leader. The history of capitalism showed that one was needed. The meetings of heads of state and finance ministers allowed rescue packages to be drawn up, as after the 1987 Crash, but they did not prevent contradictions from increasing between rich countries as well as between rich and poor countries. All proposals to get out of the impasse were based on economic recovery. The length of the crisis demonstrated the failure of stop and go, which was only able to regulate economic fluctuations, but unable to maintain the economy afloat.

We have to go back to Keynes' questioning of the capacity of the capitalist system to satisfy demand without a major reform of humankind's vital needs (employment, education, health, retirement) and its democratic demands. What needs taking into account is a devastated planet's repair and scrupulous maintenance, a growing future constraint.

THE ENERGY CRISIS: MYTHS AND REALITIES

Before the Gulf War and 16 years after the first oil shock, three years after the countershock, the energy market finally enjoyed an interlude. The specters of penury and disruption were forgotten, which for more than a decade had led the black gold market's caprices. For a while it seemed there would be abundant resources and reasonable and stable prices. Energy had stopped being a major problem for all governments and again became an ordinary raw material. Would this be a long lasting equilibrium or a brief respite? Politicians seemed to ignore it, while professionals were more perplexed than euphoric.

A priori, the situation seemed more favorable than one would have thought five years earlier. The world's resources — we know now — were more than enough to meet requirements well after the end of the century. Paul-Henri Bourrelier, president of Houilleres du Centre-Midi assured "We have at least 50 years ahead of us with fossil fuels: oil, gas, and coal."

Consumption, stimulated by the recovery and the drop in prices, took off but at a relatively moderate rhythm, lower than economic growth, thanks to the investments in energy conservation of the preceding decade. The world consumed ten times more than a century ago but only 16 percent more than ten years ago. Energy requirements may well double from now until 2030, but this is mainly to ensure the development of the poorest countries, which absorb according to the analysts, three-quarters of this growth. As for prices, the 1970s obsession, they had fallen back in real terms to their 1974 level (taking inflation into account). The 1990-93 embargo on Iraq, which represented nearly a quarter of the world's oil resources, led the price of barrel to climb up to $30.

Taking into account the distribution of fossil fuels, of which three-quarters of oil reserves are in OPEC countries and half gas in the former Soviet Union, the West will certainly face increases in its energy bill around the year 2000. However the leaders seem to have forgotten too quickly the lessons of the crisis, and with the newfound abundance have gone back to the obliviousness which previously resulted in tension. Everywhere the efforts to save energy and develop alternative sources have been dropped, especially since in the short-term they are no longer economically viable, given current energy prices. Public opinion is mistrustful of nuclear energy, which is also very expensive, and its expansion is at an end.

The result is that the consumption of fossil fuels is on the increase, and research, exploration, and plant-building is halted. The most expensive production in safe zones (that is outside OPEC and the former Soviet Union) diminishes. Thus US oil production dropped by 10 percent since 1985, while consumption increased by 15 percent — and the GNP by 11.5 percent. The euphoria of winter 1990 will be short-lived. Yet again the experts' estimates were jeopardized by geopolitical tensions, which were difficult to quantify in econometric equations.

THE FUTURE IS WIDE OPEN

For the West the 1950s and 1960s were years of industrialization and enrichment, but they were also years of international setbacks and a cultural crisis. At the summit of its power, the West had a bad conscience and had doubts about itself and its modernity. The 1970s and 1980s had been years of many different kinds of economic crisis — the difficult closing down of old industries, the oil shocks, the chaos of the international monetary system, income demands bringing down productivity gains — as well as the exhaustion of ideologies and political programs. More dangerous again, they were years of abandoning collective and personal plans for the future, and the falling back on consumption, and rampant individualism. Some people hoped that 1988 marked the start of a third period of a new future where one could speedily build a new economic, political, and cultural area. This would be a new society where there would be a new balance between social and political considerations, within each country and on a world level.

The moment had come to bring together the numerous and diverse indicators, which forced us to define our present situation in terms of the future. The past was difficult to break with but we had to engage with the future. The old industrial countries had great difficulty disposing of the old, declining industries and were unable to resolve the major social problems of their crises. In France, the politicians made the situation worse by giving in to the pressure of consumers, who would not accept the consequences of recession, particularly the oil shocks. The pressure of demand meant an economic depression was avoided but at the cost of reducing savings and leading to a dangerous reduction in productive investments: the future was sacrificed to the present.

By contrast the rapid growth of the Japanese and South Korean economies contributed to an acceleration of investments in research and development and the creation of jobs in the modern sectors in the world as a whole. Massive state intervention and calls for entrepreneurial spirit combined to stimulate supply-side economy, prioritized technological, economic, and financial modernization of productive plant.

The priority on production explained the decline in union power, often locked in defense of old industries, particularly in Great Britain, Belgium, and France, or in achieving increased consumption and redistribution of wealth, which ignored production problems, with the exception of Italy. This went alongside the spectacular reversal of attitudes, which were now very positive about companies. They were no longer considered centers of economic and social power in industrial society but as agents of modernization and defenders of economic frontiers, on which the country's economic survival depended in a technologically dangerous international environment.

The new vigor of the Western economy coincided with difficult changes in the former Soviet system and forced Japan, the United States, and Western Europe to fight against world imbalance, where money, having moved from the center to the periphery, was now moving back to the center. Countries sank deeper into poverty and Latin America and other countries that had valiantly fought against the 1981 crisis became exhausted. Democracy, which had gained ground, might be severely weakened in all the countries where it proved unable to reduce inequalities, which were on the increase. The exodus of capital from Third World countries to the United States and other developed countries had to be stopped by reductions in debt, works programs which created jobs, and by new investments.

Politically, the years 1988-89 was marked more impressively than any other by the collapse of authoritarian and modernizing regimes which had been brought to power during this century by anti-capitalist and anti-imperialist revolutions. The 19th century was dominated by the claims of a London-based capitalism which sought to impose on the world one type of economy, society, and culture, in the name of reason, progress, and self-interest. The 20th century saw the revenge of the oppressed classes — workers, colonies, women, etc. But these liberation movements also ran out of steam, either by fracturing or by being transformed into totalitarian power.

For half a century the Soviet model exercised great influence; in 1988 Gorbachev dealt it the final blow, acknowledging that the Soviet Union was inefficient, arbitrary, and based on lies. That same year, the Poles were the first to show that Jonah survived in the whale's stomach, the Czechs made themselves heard again, the Burmese rejected the isolation imposed on them by their brand of socialism, and the Algerians, massacred by the army in their cities, showed the world that the national liberation movement had become a military dictatorship, incapable of responding to the people's needs.

None of these events justified reactionary nostalgia. The communist revolutions and the anti-colonial struggles had transformed our century irreversibly but after years of bad conscience, the West had rediscovered the conviction that it had a right to defend its institutions and values. The time of revolutions was over, that of democracy had arrived.

ILYA & EMILIA KABAKOV   THE CANON

Texte von / Texts by Norman Rosenthal und / and Maria Baibakova
Übersetzung / Translation: Ursula Wulfekamp

GALERIE THADDAEUS ROPAC SALZBURG / PARIS

2.3

Canons and *Broken Glasses*
Norman Rosenthal

Dem geneigten Leser mag bekannt sein, dass der Verfasser dieses kurzen Essays über die neuesten Gemälde Ilya und Emilia Kabakows ein sehr entfernter und unbedeutender Verwandter des angeblich apokryphen Malers namens Charles (Shalom) Rosenthal ist, von dessen Existenz und Bedeutung die Kunstwelt erst durch die Kabakows erfuhr. Das malerische Werk der Kabakows, die ja vorwiegend als Installationskünstler bekannt sind, trägt sogar unverkennbar Einflüsse Rosenthals, und wie Sie sicher nachvollziehen können, bin ich dem Paar sehr dankbar, dass sie dem Werk meines Vorfahren, der von 1898 bis 1933 lebte, zu internationaler Anerkennung verhalfen. Denn wenn Mitglieder des Rosenthal-Clans einen Beitrag zur Kunst leisteten, dann nahezu ausschließlich als Kunsthistoriker, Kritiker oder Kuratoren. Vier dieser Art könnte ich heute namentlich nennen, die auf beiden Seiten des Atlantiks tätig sind. Doch abgesehen von Charles Rosenthal machte meines Wissens keiner als kreativer Geist von sich reden, alle anderen sind Kunst-Schmarotzer. So ist es überaus tröstlich, schließlich und endlich einen richtigen Künstler in der Familie zu finden – und zwar einen, dessen künstlerische Position in all ihrer Ambiguität und Schizophrenie als weitsichtig bezeichnet werden muss und als wesentlich für unsere so genannte ›post-moderne Ära‹, zu deren herausragende Vertreter die Kabakows gehören.

Aus diesem Grund fällt es mir schwer, beim Schreiben dieses kurzen Diskurses über die als

As the reader may know, the writer of this short text on the newest paintings by Ilya and Emilia Kabakov is a very indirect and obscure descendent of the allegedly apocryphal painter known as Charles (Shalom) Rosenthal whose reputation and importance was brought to the attention of the world of art by the Kabakovs themselves. Indeed the painterly work of the Kabakovs, who are probably best known as installation artists, has been clearly influenced by Rosenthal and as you might imagine, I am very grateful to them, for bringing the work of my very distant ancestral cousin, many times removed, who lived from 1898 – 1933, to international recognition. For, to the extent that, some members of the Rosenthal clan have made any contribution to the art world, it has been principally as art historians, critics or as curators. I can name today at least four others on both sides of the Atlantic. But apart from Charles Rosenthal, I can recall no creative individual. All the rest are art leeches, so that it is reassuring finally to find a true artist in the family, and he is one whose original artistic position, with all its intrinsic ambiguity and inherent schizophrenia can be shown to be far sighted and instrumental for our so called ›post modern age‹ of which the Kabakovs are exemplary representatives.

It is, thus, difficult not to write this short discourse on these paintings by Ilya and Emilia, which are entitled *Canon 1–10* without a small sense of family pride. In addition, there are three

Canon 1–10 bekannten Gemälde Ilyas und Emilias nicht einen gewissen Familienstolz zu empfinden. Außer dieser Serie gibt es zudem drei weitere Gemälde, dynamische Landschaften mit dem Titel *Broken Glass 1–3*. Diese greifen auf eine andere geometrische Hypothese als *The Canon* zurück, doch dazu mehr später. Der Familienstolz ist vielleicht typisch für Kinder von Immigranten, unerklärlicherweise insbesondere für Kinder jüdischer Immigranten, die oft durch grausame Umstände zur Flucht gezwungen waren, ihre kulturellen Wurzeln in der Heimat zurücklassen – im Fall der Kabakows Mütterchen Russland – und sich in der Fremde einleben mussten, ob nun in Paris, London oder auch New York – Orte, die zumindest auf eine lange Tradition der Meinungsfreiheit zurückblicken. Manchmal könnte man versucht sein, sich zu fragen, ob diese Meinungsfreiheit nicht allzu groß ist, etwa wenn man bedenkt, dass selbst Anarchie toleriert wird. Heute wird der Begriff Anarchismus vielfach missverstanden. Den Beginn des Anarchismus kann man in der Mitte des 19. Jahrhunderts ansetzen, die Jahre nach den Revolutionen 1848 in Russland. Es war die Zeit von Schriftstellern wie Turgenjew, dessen frühe Romane *Ein Adelsnest* (1858) und *Väter und Söhne* (1862) neben den Schilderungen vom Leben der Adeligen auf ihren Landsitzen vielfach auch Anspielungen auf den Anarchismus enthalten. Ähnliche Gedanken finden sich auch im Nihilismus, mit dem sich russische Schriftsteller wie etwa Alexander Herzen ebenfalls gerne befassten und der den Boden für die Russischen Revolutionen 1905 und 1917 bereitete. Bei diesen politischen Umbrüchen spielten die Künstler eine erstaunlich bedeutende

other paintings – dynamic landscapes called *Broken Glass 1–3*. These latter are based on a different geometrical hypothesis to *The Canon*, which we will discuss later. This family pride and drive is perhaps inherent to all children of immigrants, especially for some inexplicable reason, to those of Jews, who, driven by often terrible circumstances are made to flea their native lands, to abandon their cultural roots, in the case of the Kabakovs, Mother Russia, and then to settle elsewhere, in Paris or London or maybe New York – places that at least have a long tradition of freedom of expression. Sometimes it might be thought that this freedom of expression exists almost to a fault – a tolerance even of Anarchy. Anarchy, these days, is a very misunderstood term. It began in many ways in the mid-nineteenth-century after the revolutions in Russia of 1848, at the time of writers such as Turgenev, whose early novels *The House of the Gentry* (1858) and *Fathers and Sons* (1862) strongly allude to it amongst their descriptive scenes of Russian landed gentry life. These are analogous ideas to Nihilism, also much developed by Russian writers, such as Alexander Herzen, that provided a fertile territory for the Russian revolutions of 1905 and 1917. In this, artists were to play a surprisingly important role in implementing, for better and, of course, ultimately as we know, with a privileged hindsight of history, for worse. Which is what I suggest, although I have not spoken to the Kabakovs about this, is what these paintings are partly about. In them, there is an ambivalence between completion and incompletion that is their principal subject matter.

For this *Canon* does not speak of a full life. Rather, it speaks of choices taking place on

Rolle, gleichgültig, ob dieser Wandel nun zum Besseren war oder, wie wir mit dem Privileg des historischen Rückblicks sagen können, letztlich zum Schlechteren. Und eben davon handeln diese Gemälde zum Teil, so mutmaße ich, obwohl ich mit den Kabakows nicht darüber gesprochen habe. In den Bildern findet sich eine Ambivalenz von Vollständigkeit und Unvollständigkeit, die das eigentliche Thema darstellt.

Denn dieser *Canon* verweist nicht auf ein erfülltes Leben. Vielmehr erzählt er von Entscheidungen, die auf einem leeren Feld oder Raster getroffen werden und potenziell so oder so ausfallen können; ein Großteil des Rasters, bisweilen fast die gesamte Leinwand, bleibt sichtbar. 2004 schlossen die Kabakows eine Gemäldereihe mit dem Titel *Under the Snow* ab, in der Fragmente gemalter Bilder unter einer weißen Schneedecke hervorlugten, oder vielleicht so, als würden sie vom Flugzeug aus durch eine Wolkendecke gesehen. In Russland hat Schnee, ob er nun im Winter zum ersten Mal fällt oder im Frühling taut, große symbolische, wenn nicht gar epische Bedeutung und impliziert auch das Überleben der Kunst und der Kunstschaffenden während der Ära Stalins und später unter Breschnew, die sich im metaphorischen Sinne unter der Schneedecke verbergen mussten, wenn sie nicht nach Sibirien in die Verbannung geschickt oder ihnen ein noch schlimmeres Schicksal bereitet wurde, weil sie sich unbefugt einer Äußerungsfreiheit bedienen wollten. Zur Zeit Chruschtschows setzte in der Kultur ein gewisses Tauwetter ein, das allerdings nicht lange währte.

Schnee ist weiß, Weiß ist Schnee, doch Weiß birgt auch andere Möglichkeiten, wie es zum

an empty field or grid that potentially can always go any number of different ways, leaving much, if not most of the grid, visible. Recently, in 2004, the Kabakovs completed a series of paintings called *Under the Snow* in which fragments of painterly images were shown peeping from under a white snow covering, or maybe seen as though from an airplane through a partially cloudy sky. Snow, both its arrival, and its disappearance is full of symbolic, even epic, meaning for Russia and implicates also the survival of art and artists, who have often metaphorically hidden under the snow as was necessary during the period of Stalin and later, Comrade Brezhnev if they were not sent to Siberia or even to a worse fate in their attempts at freedom of expression. In the time of Khrushchev, there was something of a cultural thaw, but it was short lived.

Snow is white, white is snow, but white has other possibilities, as indeed the paintings of Charles Rosenthal show us, done supposedly in the 1930's in Paris, where many other Russian artists had also emigrated long beforehand. But even Marc Chagall had by 1930, long since given up his radical position, substituting it for a quasi-Russian sentimental Impressionist style. In the case of Rosenthal, he flirted with avant-gardism, if I understand him correctly, but he was never fully able to embrace it. Rather he still could not help remembering Russian Realism and Impressionism recalling the best work of artists such as Repin, Surikov or inspired by the likes of the landscape painter Vasily Polenov and indeed by the much famed Russian Jewish semi-Impressionist painter Isaac Levitan. The latter enjoyed great fame, even during his short life-

Beispiel die Gemälde Charles Rosenthals nahelegen, die vermutlich in den 1930er Jahren in Paris entstanden. Dort hatten schon lange vor ihm zahlreiche andere russische Künstler Zuflucht gesucht. Doch selbst Marc Chagall hatte 1930 seine radikale Position aufgegeben und war zu einem quasi-russischen sentimental-impressionistischen Stil übergegangen. Was Rosenthal betrifft, so kokettierte er, wenn ich ihn recht verstehe, mit der Avantgarde, vermochte sich aber nie ganz zu ihr bekennen. Der Grund war, dass er sich nicht den Einflüssen des Russischen Realismus und des Impressionismus entziehen wollte und ihm immer wieder die besten Werke von Künstlern wie Repin und Surikow in den Sinn kamen; dass er sich inspirieren ließ von Landschaftsmalern wie Vasili Polenow und auch von dem bekannten russisch-jüdischen Maler Isaak Lewitan, der in halb-impressionistischer Weise malte. Lewitan genoss in seinem kurzen Leben (1860 bis 1900) großes Ansehen und hatte Ausstellungen nicht nur in ganz Russland, sondern auch in München, Chicago, Paris und anderen Städten weltweit. Ein solcher Triumph war Rosenthal nie vergönnt, doch die Kabakows konnten in den letzten Jahrzehnten große Erfolge feiern. Ziemlich zu Beginn seiner Karriere zeigte Ilya in einem Kunstzentrum im Westen Londons eine seiner *Book Environments*, und dort sah ich sein Werk das erste Mal. Das war Anfang der 80er Jahre, wenn ich mich recht entsinne. Die Schönheit seiner Werke war bezwingend, doch als Engländer wünschte ich mir schon damals, ich könnte Russisch lesen.

Wie ich bereits erwähnte, ist Ilya Kabakow, und jetzt gemeinsam mit Emilia, nach wie vor am

time, 1860 – 1900, exhibiting not only all over Russia, but also in International exhibitions in Munich, Chicago, Paris and elsewhere. Rosenthal never had this success, unfortunately, but the Kabakovs have, during their careers in recent decades, done brilliantly. Even quite early on in his career, Ilya showed one of his *Book Environments* in an arts centre in West London, where I saw his work for the first time sometime back in the early eighties, if I recall correctly. The beauty of the work was more than apparent. But, as an Englishman, of course I wished even then, that I could read Russian.

As I implied earlier, Ilya Kabakov, and now with Emilia, are still most famous for their installations, in which the audience is totally immersed in scenes of Soviet Russian life. One of my favourites was a wonderful reconstruction of a cinema shown in the Jeu de Paume in Paris. I think it was in 1999 or 2000. In it, happy Soviet style early 1950's short films in a wonderful Technicolor that exists no longer, showed boys and girls, their eyes shining, singing beautiful Stalinist songs about the joys of work and the harvest. It reminds one of a moment in 1934 when Stalin himself is said to have said, around the time when Zhdanov was announcing the universal policy of Soviet Realism at the first All Union Congress of writers: »Life becomes better, comrades, when life is jollier, you work better.«

But in exile, Rosenthal, it seems found it difficult, for the most part, to work and to achieve beautiful completion. Indeed, in his immortal words: »The more I draw, the more I hear a prohibition of the white surface.« In these new paintings by the Kabakovs one can feel a similar inhibition but

meisten durch ihre Installationen bekannt, bei denen der Betrachter in Szenen aus dem Leben in Sowjetrussland eintaucht. Mit am besten gefiel mir die großartige Rekonstruktion eines Kinos, die im Jeu de Paume in Paris aufgebaut war, 1999 oder 2000, glaube ich. Dort wurden Kurzfilme der 1950er Jahre gezeigt, gedreht in einem fröhlichen frühen sowjetischen Stil und in einem großartigen Technicolor, das es heute gar nicht mehr gibt. In den Filmen sangen Jungen und Mädchen mit leuchtenden Augen wunderschöne stalinistische Lieder über die Freude der Arbeit und der Ernte. Das beschwört einen Moment 1934 herauf, als Stalin selbst angeblich sagte – etwa zu der Zeit, als Schdanow anlässlich des ersten Allunionskongresses der Schriftsteller den Sowjetischen Realismus zur verbindlichen künstlerischen Methode erklärte: »Genossen, das Leben wird besser, wenn es lustiger ist, ihr arbeitet besser.«

Im Exil jedoch fiel es Rosenthal offenbar häufig schwer, zu arbeiten und Schönheit zum Abschluss zu bringen. So seine unvergessene Äußerung: »Je mehr ich zeichne, desto mehr höre ich ein Verbot der weißen Fläche.« Bei diesen neuen Bildern der Kabakows spürt man eine ähnliche Zurückhaltung, doch ist sie bewusst und streng kontrolliert. Bei den Gemälden handelt es sich um große, weiß grundierte Leinwände, auf die mit Bleistift oder vielleicht auch grauem Ölstift (ich habe die Werke selbst noch nicht gesehen und kenne sie bislang nur von Fotografien) ein Raster gezeichnet ist. Nun weiß jeder, der ein wenig von Kunst versteht, dass das Raster – das Quadratnetz – seit undenklichen Zeiten die klassische Methode ist, ein großes

it is self-conscious and fully controlled. The paintings are as one can see, large primed white canvases on which has been drawn a grid (I have not seen the real works myself, only photographs so far) done with pencil, maybe grey oil stick. Now everyone who knows about art, knows that the grid is something that since time immemorial has been used as a classic way of making a large painting from a small sketch. A drawing is made of the composition, then a grid is drawn over the composition and on to the canvas as a way of enlarging and transferring it, and then ultimately filling it with colour. The Impressionists of course, avoided this way of making art for the most part, preferring to make work directly in the open air, transferring what they could see on to the canvas. But in these paintings of the Kabakovs, something different seems to be happening. The grid is there, to be sure, reminding me not so much of Mondrian or Malevich, but more of the mostly forgotten Swiss artist, Richard Paul Lohse, 1902 – 1988, who started his life doing still lifes and landscapes before painting rigorously grid like abstractions, of which Donald Judd said that, »they marked the end of the European cultural tradition, a good end, and there is much that is still beginning to happen.« The grids of Lohse are full of colour. The grids of the Kabakovs are white with one, occasionally two squares filled or partially filled with pale compositions recalling sometimes French Impressionism, and Russian nineteenth-century, as well as sometimes Soviet Realism using a somewhat blanched colour world that from time to time evokes the early paintings of Malevich that usually speak to us of pre-revolutionary Russian peasant and country life.

Gemälde nach einer kleinen Skizze anzufertigen.
Über die Zeichnung der Komposition wird ein
Raster gezogen, ebenso wie auf die Leinwand.
So kann der Entwurf proportional korrekt ver-
größert und übertragen und schließlich mit Farbe
gefüllt werden. Die Impressionisten vermieden
diese Art des Malens natürlich und zogen es vor,
im Freien zu arbeiten und das, was sie vor Augen
sahen, direkt auf die Leinwand zu übertragen.
Doch in diesen Gemälden der Kabakows scheint
etwas anderes vor sich zu gehen. Das Raster ist
nicht zu übersehen, und es erinnert mich weniger
an Mondrian oder Malewitsch, sondern vielmehr
an den nahezu vergessenen Schweizer Künstler
Richard Paul Lohse, 1902-1988, der zu Anfang
seiner Laufbahn Stillleben und Landschaften
malte, bevor er strenge, raster-artige Abstrak-
tionen schuf, über die Donald Judd einmal sagte:
»Sie bilden das Ende der europäischen Kulturtra-
dition, und zwar ein gutes Ende, und es gibt vieles,
was noch im Entstehen begriffen ist.« Lohses
Raster sind bunt, die der Kabakows sind weiß,
ein oder bisweilen zwei Quadrate sind ganz oder
halb mit zartfarbigen Kompositionen gefüllt, die
zuzeiten an den französischen Impressionismus
und das russische 19. Jahrhundert denken las-
sen, manchmal auch an den Sowjetischen Realismus; die etwas verhaltene Farbwelt beschwört
gelegentlich die frühen Gemälde Malewitschs
herauf, die zumeist das bäuerliche Leben im vor-
revolutionären Russland schildern. Die Kabakows
vermitteln poetische Beschwörungen einer
untergegangenen impressionistischen Welt,
die Welt Monets, Pissarros und Sisleys, eine russische Erinnerung an *Inondation*, *Champs des
Fleurs*, *Cathédrales* (bei denen es sich vermutlich

The Kabakovs give us poetic evocations of a lost
Impressionist world, a world of Monet, Pissarro
and Sisley, a Russian remembrance of the
Inondation, Champs des Fleurs, Cathedrals (that
are probably factories) and scenes on the river
bank (the Moscow River as the Seine at Asnières)
the chess players faintly recollecting Cezanne's
Card Players.

This brings one to Cezanne, who arguably
was the first artist, except perhaps Michelangelo,
especially in his later work, to focus so much on
the idea of completeness/incompleteness that is
so important for twentieth-century Modernism.
For Russian artists, Cezanne became central,
as did the two great collectors of French art in
Moscow around 1900 – Sergei Shchukin and
Mikhail and Ivan Morosov. My friend Albert
Kostenevich, curator of nineteenth-century French
painting in the Hermitage, St Petersburg, wrote
in the catalogue of an exhibition, *From Russia*
I recently organised in London, »that it would be
no exaggeration to say that Russia, no less than
France, was the country where Cezanne became
and remained for a long time, an object of the
most zealous adoration.« Artists famous in the
world today, Larionov, Goncharova, Tatlin, Chagall
and Malevich all came under his spell as did, for
us, lesser-known members of the Russian avantgarde such as Vrubel, Mashkov, Konchalovsky,
Altman and Grabar to name only a few names
still well-known and loved within Russia. But not
one of them understood, nor did Charles Rosenthal, the issue of finished/unfinished that brings
up so many aesthetic and perceptual problems
that are ultimately so central to painting, as well
as to sculpture and to installation art today. It

um Fabriken handelt) und Szenen am Flussufer (die Moskwa als die Seine bei Asnières), die Schachspieler erinnern vage an Cézannes *Die Kartenspieler*.

Und damit sind wir bei Cézanne, der sich womöglich als erster Künstler, vielleicht mit Ausnahme Michelangelos, vor allem in seinem späteren Werk mit dem Konzept von Vollständigkeit/Unvollständigkeit beschäftigte, das doch wesentlich für die Moderne des 20. Jahrhunderts ist. Für russische Künstler war Cézanne eine zentrale Bezugsgröße, ebenso wie die beiden großen Sammler französischer Kunst in Moskau um 1900 – Sergei Schtschukin und Michail und Iwan Morosow. Mein Freund Albert Kostenewitsch, Kurator für französische Malerei des 19. Jahrhunderts in der Eremitage in St. Petersburg, schrieb im Katalog zur Ausstellung *From Russia*, die ich kürzlich in London ausrichtete: »Es ist keine Übertreibung zu behaupten, dass Cézanne in Russland nicht minder als in Frankreich ein Objekt hingebungsvollster Verehrung war und lange Zeit blieb.« Heute weltberühmte Künstler wie Larionow, Goncharowa, Tatlin, Chagall und Malewitsch erlagen alle seinem Bann, ebenso wie uns weniger bekannte Mitglieder der russischen Avantgarde wie Wrubel, Maschkow, Kontschalowski, Altman und Grabar, um nur einige zu nennen, die in Russland heute noch geachtet und geliebt sind. Aber niemand, auch Charles Rosenthal nicht, begriff das Konzept vollendet/ unvollendet, das derart viele ästhetische und perzeptorische Fragen aufwirft, die letztlich zentral für die Malerei insgesamt sind, aber auch für die Skulptur und die heutige Installationskunst. Es wirft ein Schlaglicht auf die Frage, was denn die

brings to the fore the issue of what is indeed the reality of an art object, how it is to function, how much is really necessary.

For Cezanne, and in terms of his generally perceived importance to art history, in a lesser way of course for Rosenthal, the crisis was of monumental proportions. In the case of the Kabakovs, the issue is relaxed, sovereign even. It is one of post modernism, where there is no need to cover up the canvas in order for the art itself to be ›completed‹. On the contrary, through the grid strategy, in which image fragments (or maybe they are not fragments, but whole) appear, the viewer is able to make the painting as small or as large as he or she wishes. The canvas now becomes something of a perceptual enlarging machine, also visible in the three very large so-called *Broken Glass Paintings* in which fragments of Pointillist, or maybe very early Duchampian landscapes with small houses can be detected through a intersected geometrical diagram drawn across the huge canvas. Furthermore, there is a strong awareness of American Minimalist art. One might think especially of Carl Andre, with whose flat, industrial steel square plates on the floor the *Canon* paintings have a real affinity. But into them, the Kabakovs introduce fragments, souvenirs, memories of times past, of the realities of Soviet life which they have now left behind. That Soviet life had of course many drawbacks is axiomatic. But if one was that way inclined, one was able to find high-level private refuge in art. Both Ilya and Emilia who grew up separately in Russia and met in the West, did that. In music one might think of Shostakovitch as an exemplary figure, in literature, for example Akhamatova or

Realität eines Kunstobjekts nun ist, wie es funktionieren soll und ob es wirklich notwendig ist.

Für Cézanne und natürlich auch für Rosenthal – was angesichts Cézannes allgemein anerkannten Bedeutung für die Kunstgeschichte zweifellos weniger gewichtig ist – war es eine Krise von monumentalen Ausmaßen. Die Kabakows jedoch gehen das Thema gelassen, ja souverän an. Es ist natürlich ein Thema der Postmoderne, in der nicht die Notwendigkeit besteht, die Leinwand zu füllen, um ein Kunstwerk als »vollständig« zu bezeichnen. Im Gegenteil, durch das Raster, in dem Bildfragmente (oder vielleicht sind es auch keine Fragmente, vielleicht sind sie vollständig) auftauchen, kann der Betrachter das Gemälde nach Belieben vergrößern und verkleinern. So wird die Leinwand quasi zu einem optischen Vergrößerungsapparat, wie auch bei den sehr großformatigen so genannten *Broken Glass Paintings*, in denen Fragmente pointillistischer oder vielleicht sehr früher Duchampscher Landschaften mit kleinen Häusern in einer streng geometrischen Grafik auszumachen sind. Überdies lässt sich eine Anerkenntnis der amerikanischen Minimal Art nicht leugnen. Man denke insbesondere an Carl Andre, mit dessen auf dem Boden liegenden flachen Industrie-Stahlplatten die *Canon*-Gemälde durchaus Ähnlichkeit haben. Doch bei den Kabakows werden sie um Fragmente ergänzt, um Souvenirs, Erinnerungen an vergangene Zeiten, an die Realität des Lebens in der Sowjetunion, das sie hinter sich gelassen haben. Dass es im Leben in der Sowjetunion viele Fallstricke gab, ist bekannt. Doch mit der entsprechenden Neigung konnte man auf hohem Niveau eine private Zuflucht in der Kunst finden. Das taten sowohl Ilya als auch

Pasternak amongst many. All were artists who did not emigrate. The world of the visual arts was more difficult. Just because its reality needs public display and distribution, it was difficult for it to flourish even in later Soviet times, and with very rare exceptions (I would name Aleksandr Deineka, who died in 1969 and did very grand decorations for the Moscow Metro system), it found expression in children's book illustration and in environments carried out in the dingy apartments of Moscow and Leningrad. It was, in many ways, the most secret form of all the arts.

All art is a souvenir of a situation, and these paintings on their grids and diagrams are remembrances of times when art had to be hidden, when public ›art‹ could only depict chess games of happy workers in their fields, the happy artist in her studio, the citizen enjoying the riverside view on a summer Sunday. Perhaps there is something to be said for these Socialist Realist certainties. Whether these happy positivist certainties should count as art is another thing.

The Kabakovs bring with these new paintings – *The Canon 1–10* and *Broken Glass 1–3* – all the selectivity of our, perhaps, more complex post-modern culture.

Emilia, die zwar beide in Russland aufwuchsen, sich aber erst im Westen kennen lernten. In der Musik könnte man als Vertreter einer solchen Existenz vielleicht Schostakowitsch anführen, in der Literatur etwa Akhamatowa und Pasternak. Sie alle waren Künstler, die nicht emigrierten. In der Welt der visuellen Kunst nahm das Problem größere Dimensionen an. Da ihre Realität der Öffentlichkeit und Verbreitung bedarf, konnte sie in der Sowjetunion selbst in späteren Jahren nicht florieren, und mit sehr wenigen Ausnahmen (ich würde etwa Alexander Deineka nennen, der 1969 starb und für die künstlerische Ausgestaltung der Moskauer U-Bahnhöfe großartige Entwürfe vorlegte) fand sie nur in Kinderbuch-Illustrationen Ausdruck und in dunklen Wohnungen in Moskau und Leningrad. Sie war in vieler Hinsicht die geheimste aller Kunstformen.

Jede Kunst ist eine Erinnerung an Umstände, und diese Gemälde auf ihren Quadratrastern und geometrischen Mustern sind Erinnerungen an Zeiten, in denen die Kunst verborgen werden musste, in denen die öffentliche ›Kunst‹ lediglich friedliche Schachpartien zwischen fröhlichen Arbeitern auf ihren Feldern darstellen durfte, die glückliche Künstlerin in ihrem Atelier, den Bürger, der an einem Sommersonntag den Blick auf den Fluss genießt. Vielleicht sind diese Gewissheiten des sozialistischen Realismus nicht ausschließlich negativ, doch ob diese glücklichen, positivistischen Gewissheiten als Kunst zu gelten haben, ist eine andere Frage.

Mit diesen neuen Gemälden – *The Canon 1–10* und *Broken Glass 1–3* – zeigen die Kabakows die ganze Trennschärfe unserer vielleicht komplexeren postmodernen Kultur.

14.15   *Canon 1*, 2007   Öl auf Leinwand, 289 x 189 cm / Oil on canvas, 113.8 x 74.4 inches

16.17

18.19   ***Canon 2***, 2007   Öl auf Leinwand, 282 x 189 cm / Oil on canvas, 111 x 74.4 inches

20.21

22.23   *Canon 3*, 2007   Öl auf Leinwand, 189 x 282 cm / Oil on canvas, 74.4 x 111 inches

24.25

26.27   **Canon 4**, 2007   Öl auf Leinwand, 282 x 189 cm / Oil on canvas, 111 x 74.4 inches

28.29

30.31   **Canon 8**, 2007   Öl auf Leinwand, 282 x 378 cm / Oil on canvas, 111 x 149 inches

34.35   ***Canon 9***, 2007   Öl auf Leinwand, 256 x 328 cm / Oil on canvas, 100.79 x 129 inches

Kabakov und das Nicht-Narrative
Maria Baibakova

Kein Vertreter der zeitgenössischen russischen Kunst, der in den vergangenen fünfzig Jahren tätig war, ist so schwer auszuloten wie Ilya Kabakow. Seine Werke entziehen sich jeder kunsthistorischen Kategorisierung und Medien-Typisierung. Als in Amerika lebender gebürtiger Russe, der international Anerkennung genießt, ist seine nationalen Verankerung eher vage, und die Gestalten seiner Werke mögen sich zwar seiner Biografie verdanken, sind aber kein wahrer Spiegel seines Lebens. Für Kabakows Ablehnung des Narrativen als kontinuierliche und lo-gische Storyline ist sein Leben ebenso Beweis wie sein Werk, und *The Canon* von 2007 thematisieren und bestätigen diese Einstellung einmal mehr.

Der Ursprung von Kabakows problematischem Verhältnis zu narrativen Strukturen liegt in den Gefahren des Doppellebens, das er führte: Einerseits war er ein offiziell anerkannter Kinderbuch-Illustrator und angesehenes Mitglied der sowjetischen Gesellschaft, andererseits ein inoffizieller Künstler, dessen Arbeitsweise vom Regime streng verurteilt wurde und der aus Gründen der persönlichen Sicherheit vor jeder Entdeckung zurückschrecken musste. Als Begründer der Moskauer Konzeptkunst eignete er sich eine formale Methode der Darstellung an, die seine problematische Beziehung zum Narrativen erkennen ließ.

Diese Methode beruht auf der Verwendung von negativem oder ›leerem‹ Raum. Kabakow setzte ihn erstmals in seiner *Russian Series* [Abb.

Kabakov and the Anti-Narrative
Maria Baibakova

Ilya Kabakov has been the most elusive Russian contemporary artist working in the last 50 years: his works escape both art historical and media-based categorization, his identity of being Russian and living in America with international recognition has made him a man of loose national affiliations, and the characters in his works, though inspired by the artist's biography, are never true mirrors of his life. Kabakov's resistance to narrative as a continuous and logical storyline is as apparent in his life as it is in his work, and *The Canon* made in 2007 address and reinforce this issue.

The roots of Kabakov's problematic relationship towards narrative organization stem from the apprehension produced by living a double life: Kabakov was both an official illustrator of children's books and respected member of the Soviet society, and an unofficial artist who engaged in artistic practices deemed illegal by his political regime and who resisted being discovered for the sake of his own safety. As an originator and practitioner of Moscow Conceptualism, Kabakov developed a formal method of representation that relayed his problematic relationship to narrative.

This method is based on the ample use of negative or ›empty‹ space; Kabakov first used it in his *Russian Series* [Figs. 1 – 4], from 1969. The series includes four panels – three paintings and one explanatory text – and some installation elements. The panels look empty of meaning as they are overwhelmingly smothered by a

1 – 4] von 1969 ein. Die Serie umfasst vier Tafeln
– drei Gemälde und einen erläuternden Text –
sowie einige Installationselemente. Die Tafeln,
nahezu ohne jedes Bildelement, sind fast durch-
gängig beige-braun bemalt, also in der Farbe, in
der in der Sowjetunion öffentliche Gebäude ge-
meinhin gestrichen waren. Wenn das Narrative
Konnektivität, Vollständigkeit und logisches
Fortschreiten bedeutet, dann sind die Werke der
Russian Series die Antithese dazu. Die Gemälde
geben nur Andeutungen einer Geschichte, es
gibt mehrere kleine ›Seifenblasen‹, die Szenen
wie etwa ein realistisch gemaltes Haus in einem
sonnigen Dorf zeigen [Abb. 3 – 4]. Kabakow erzählt hier keine in sich geschlossene Geschichte
des Hauses in einem Dorf mit Einwohnern, die er
zeitlich und geografisch verortet, vielmehr lässt
er den größten Teil des Gemäldes leer, die Dorf-
szene wirkt wie ein Klecks, eine durch das Ver-
gessen aufscheinende Erinnerung, jedes Kontexts
und jeder Logik beraubt. Der umfassende negative
Raum, der die winzigen narrativen Eindrücke
überwältigt, wird zum Protagonisten der Werke,
verunsichert den Betrachter und weckt in ihm
das Bedürfnis, die Leere zu füllen.

Für ihr Entstehungsjahr 1969 waren diese
Gemälde radikal. Sie griffen auf die visuelle Sprache des Sozialistischen Realismus zurück, stellten
aber Szenen dar, deren Zweck im Widerspruch
zu dem der offiziellen Kunst stand. Gemälde im
sozialistisch-realistischen Stil, so war verlangt,
sollten die Stellung des Künstlers und des Be-
trachters innerhalb der sowjetischen Gesellschaft
verdeutlichen. Ihnen lag die didaktische Funktion
zugrunde, zu veranschaulichen, wie der Mensch
sich in dieser Gesellschaft zu verhalten hatte, sie

brownish-beige color reminiscent of the generic
wall paint that covered public spaces in Soviet
buildings. If narrative implies connectivity, completion, and logical progression, then the works
of the *Russian Series* are its antithesis. The paintings show only glimpses of narrative: there are
several small ›bubbles‹ in the works that depict
scenes such as a house amidst a sunny village,
painted in a realistic manner [Figs. 3 – 4]. Rather
than relaying a complete story about a house in
the village and its inhabitants with a plot situated
temporally and geographically, Kabakov left the
overwhelming part of his painting void. Instead,
the village scene appears as a blotch, a memory
on a hazy plane of amnesia, decontextualized and
stripped of logic. The ample negative space that
physically overpowers the glimpses of narrative
becomes the obvious protagonist of the paintings.
This space makes the viewer uncomfortable and
incomplete, yearning to fill the void with narrative.

The paintings were radical for 1969, mobilizing
the visual language of Socialist Realism while
creating a scene that pursued ends that were
contrary to those of official art. Socialist Realist
painting intended to clarify one's position in
Soviet society, to be didactic and to teach how one
should act in this society, and to propagate an
illusory happiness and well-being of the State
and its people. Kabakov's *Russian Series* paintings
achieve the exact opposite ends: they confuse
the viewer and make him or her question exactly
what it means to be part of the Soviet social
fabric; they refuse to engage in pro-Soviet propaganda, and they disrupt the narrative structure that
lends Socialist Realist paintings to easy readings.
The *Russian Series* is about the anti-narrative: it

Ilya Kabakov, *Russian Series*, Figure 1, 1969
Drei Tafeln / Three panels 110 x 197 cm
Eine Tafel / One panel 110 x 170 cm
Öl auf Karton / Oil on Board

Ilya Kabakov, *Russian Series*, Figure 2, 1969
Drei Tafeln / Three panels 110 x 197 cm
Eine Tafel / One panel 110 x 170 cm
Öl auf Karton / Oil on Board

sollten das illusorische Glück und Wohlergehen des Staates und seiner Bürger propagieren. Kabakows Bilder der *Russian Series* bewirken das Gegenteil: Sie verwirren den Betrachter, drängen ihm die Frage auf, was genau es bedeutet, Teil der sowjetischen Gesellschaft zu sein. Die Gemälde verweigern sich jeder pro-sowjetischen Propaganda und zerstören die narrative Struktur, der die Werke des Sozialistischen Realismus ihre unmittelbare Deutbarkeit verdanken. In der *Russian Series* geht es um das Nicht-Narrative: Die Bilder leugnen die Möglichkeit, ein klares Abbild der Welt zu liefern. Statt Klarheit und Verständlichkeit zeigen sie eine vage Welt ohne eindeutige Strukturen.

Wenn der Betrachter Kabakows Werk als Kunst sieht, die sich mit der *conditio humana* befasst, dann müssen die Gemälde der *Russian Series* als postmodern gelten, da sie sich der Möglichkeit einer universell gültigen Meta-Narrative verweigern. Der negative, darstellungsfreie Raum auf den Gemälden bietet sich als Plattform für einen Diskurs an. Indem Kabakow diesen negativen Raum zurücklässt, widersetzt er sich dem Diktat der sowjetischen Kunst, die Lebenserfahrungen des einfachen Menschen abzubilden. Um mit Craig Owens zu sprechen, demonstrieren Kabakows Gemälde der *Russian Series* die Unfähigkeit des sowjetischen Regimes, »für andere zu sprechen«.

In der *Russian Series* zeigt Kabakow dem Betrachter keine leere Fläche, das heißt, er deutet nicht an, der sowjetische Alltag könnte aus dem Kontext gerissen und beliebig umgeschrieben werden; vielmehr ist der negative Raum in der bräunlichen Farbe der sowjetischen Materialität

rejects the possibility of depicting a clear world picture. Instead of clarity and accessibility, the series represents an indiscernible world with no clear structure.

If the viewer reads Kabakov's work as art about the human condition, then paintings from the *Russian Series* are postmodern in their resistance to a metanarrative that could be universally applicable. The negative space in the paintings that is devoid of representation is a platform for discourse. By leaving this negative space, Kabakov radically rejects Soviet art's authority in depicting the common man's life experience. To use Craig Owens' terms, Kabakov's paintings in the *Russian Series* illustrate the Soviet regime's inability to »speak[ing] for others.«

In the *Russian Series*, Kabakov does not offer a blank space for the viewer and thereby does not propose that life in Soviet times can be de-contextualized and written at will; the negative space in his *Russian Series* is tainted with the brownish color of Soviet materiality and is a site of plurality of existence, but not authorship and freedom. In 1969, the artist did not feel he had artistic license to provide his viewers with an empty page or a clear platform on which each viewer can write her own individual narrative. Physical, social, and psychological spaces that were part of a Soviet subject's existence were always already politicized, hence the color of the negative space. It is in the *Russian Series* that Kabakov first generated the visual language of the anti-narrative.

The anti-narrative is a reflection of Kabakov's own life experience and it consistently appears as a formal device in his oeuvre. *The Canon*,

Ilya Kabakov, *Russian Series*, Figure 3, 1969
Drei Tafeln / Three panels 110 x 197 cm
Eine Tafel / One panel 110 x 170 cm
Öl auf Karton / Oil on Board

Ilya Kabakov, *Russian Series*, Figure 4, 1969
Drei Tafeln / Three panels 110 x 197 cm
Eine Tafel / One panel 110 x 170 cm
Öl auf Karton / Oil on Board

gehalten, ein Raum mit einer Pluralität der Existenz, jedoch ohne Urheberschaft und Freiheit. 1969 glaubte der Künstler nicht, die künstlerische Freiheit zu besitzen, seinem Betrachter ein leeres Blatt oder eine klar umrissene Plattform bieten zu können, worauf dieser seine eigene Geschichte schreiben könnte. Der physische, gesellschaftliche und psychologische Raum im Leben eines sowjetischen Staatsbürgers wurde grundsätzlich politisiert, und eben daraus erklärt sich die Farbe des negativen Raums. Das heißt, die visuelle Sprache des Nicht-Narrativen schuf Kabakow erstmals für die *Russian Series*.

Das Nicht-Narrative reflektiert auch seine eigene Lebenserfahrung und zieht sich als formales Element durch sein gesamtes Werk. *The Canon*, fast genau vierzig Jahre nach der *Russian Series* entstanden, ist ein Beleg für diese fortdauernde Auseinandersetzung.

Zwar entstanden die Serien in einem sehr unterschiedlichen Kontext, und sowohl politisch als auch persönlich herrschten für Kabakow bei ihrer Entstehung völlig andere Bedingungen, dennoch ist die Verbindung zwischen ihnen nicht von der Hand zu weisen. In beiden verwendet der Künstler das visuelle Vokabular des Sozialistischen Realismus, das sich als das geeignete Mittel erweist, um das Meta-Narrative der sowjetischen visuellen Darstellung zu hinterfragen und zu untergraben. Zudem setzt Kabakow in beiden Serien den negativen Raum als formales Stilmittel ein.

The Canon greift Themen des Nicht-Narrativen auf, indem er leere Gitterraster darstellt, von denen lediglich ein oder zwei Quadrate mit realistisch dargestellten Szenen des Alltags

made almost 40 years after the *Russian Series*, reflects this continuous preoccupation.

While the two series of works were made in radically different contexts as well as political and personal climates for Kabakov himself, the connection between them is apparent. In both the *Russian Series* and *The Canon*, Kabakov utilizes the visual vocabulary of Socialist Realist art. This vocabulary is suitable to achieving his goal of questioning and subverting the meta-narrative of Soviet visual representation. In addition, both series use the formal device of leaving negative space.

The Canon revisits issues of the anti-narrative by representing empty grids with one or two cells filled with realistically depicted scenes from everyday life. In *Canon 6*, two men are playing chess, while *Canon 2* shows people on a riverbank relaxing on benches during a pleasant summer evening. As in the *Russian Series*, the representational elements of *The Canon* appear as mere glimpses amidst a grid filled with nothing but the color white. Whereas the geometric grid of the painting proposes rhythm and order, representation does not match up. Once again, narrative appears like a disconnected recollection, devoid of context and meaning. The commentary here is clear: our lives hardly follow the orderly narrative we are socialized to expect from them. Our lives happen as sparks of meaning amidst a sea of entropy, and we cannot remember our experiences chronologically and completely. We only retain certain moments, and very often these are banal and objectively unimportant. The empty grid in *The Canon* illustrates that our lives are actually anti-narratival and not conducive to structure and logic.

gefüllt sind. In *Canon 6* etwa beugen sich zwei
Männer über ein Schachspiel, *Canon 2* zeigt
Menschen, die an einem schönen Sommer-
abend auf Bänken am Flussufer sitzen. Wie in
der *Russian Series* sind die Bildelemente in
The Canon nur kurze Eindrücke inmitten eines
Rasters, das fast vollständig von weißer Farbe
bedeckt ist. Das geometrische Raster legt zwar
Rhythmus und Ordnung nahe, diesem Eindruck
jedoch widersprechen die Darstellungselemente.
Wieder hat das Narrative die Wirkung einer frag-
mentarischen Erinnerung, der sowohl der Kontext als auch der Sinn fehlt. Die Bedeutung hier
liegt auf der Hand: Unser Leben folgt nicht einer
geordneten Bahn, wie wir es aufgrund unserer
Sozialisation von unserer Existenz erwarten.
Vielmehr vollzieht sich unser Leben als Funken-
schläge der Sinnhaftigkeit in einem Meer der
Entropie, wir erinnern es nicht chronologisch und
vollständig. Nur bestimmte Momente bleiben uns
im Gedächtnis haften, und die sind vielfach banal
und, objektiv betrachtet, unwesentlich. Das leere
Raster in *The Canon* verdeutlicht, dass unser
Leben letztlich nicht-narrativ ist und sich jeder
Struktur und Logik entzieht.

Der vom leeren Raster geschaffene negative
Raum weckt zwar keine sowjetischen Assoziationen mehr, da es nicht mit Farbe gefüllt ist,
dennoch darf man das Weiß nicht als apolitisch
verstehen. Für Kabakow ist die Farbe Weiß, ist
das Konzept eines weißen Blatts von jeher be-
ängstigend und problematisch. Seine Auseinandersetzung mit der Farbe Weiß war ein Kampf,
sie hatte für ihn etwas Erstickendes, ob in seinen
offiziellen oder seinen inoffiziellen Werken. Zu
Anfang seiner Laufbahn fühlte er sich von den

The negative space formed by the empty grids
in *The Canon* is no longer charged with Soviet
associations as it has been stripped of color;
however, its whiteness is hardly apolitical. For
Kabakov, the color white and the concept of a
white page has always been an intimidating and
problematic issue. Kabakov struggled with the
color white, which he consistently saw as
stifling, both in his official and unofficial works.
The charged modernist associations of white as
the backdrop of Malevich's constructivist compositions challenged Kabakov in the beginning of his
career, and later the white page was a nuisance
when Kabakov made children's drawings, as
Kabakov described in his essay *Notes about
Book Illustration*:

In working on a children's book, the question
always arises as to what to do with the white
background. It is active to such a degree that, as
a rule, it kills any drawing – especially a drawing
that is flat, the kind I use. A realistic drawing
can somehow hold its ground against a white
background. But a flat one, especially a colored
drawing, collapses into the white background.[1]

In *The Canon*, Kabakov actively confronts
the color white, choosing it as the protagonist of
his paintings. Consistent with his commentary
on book illustration, Kabakov once again resorts
to the visual language of realism in depicting
glimpses of narrative amidst the whiteness. Although these representational parts of the paintings do hold their own against the white at first
glance, it is the whiteness of the other cells that
presents a challenge during the viewer's con-
frontation of the work. The color white is problematic because it has dual associations: while

modernistischen Assoziationen von Weiß als Hintergrund der konstruktivistischen Kompositionen Malewitschs belastet; später, bei seinen Kinderillustrationen, wurde das weiße Blatt zum Ärgernis, wie er in seinem Essay *Notes about Book Illustration* schreibt:

Bei Kinderbüchern stellt sich immer die Frage, was man denn mit dem weißen Hintergrund machen soll. Er drängt sich derart auf, dass er meist jede Zeichnung kaputt macht – insbesondere flache Zeichnungen in der Art, wie ich sie mache. Eine realistische Zeichnung schafft es irgendwie, sich gegen einen weißen Hintergrund zu behaupten, aber eine flache Zeichnung, noch dazu eine farbige, stürzt in den weißen Hintergrund ab.[1]

In *The Canon* packt Kabakow das Weiß quasi bei den Hörnern und macht es zum Protagonisten seiner Gemälde. Gemäß seinen Anmerkungen über Buchillustrationen greift er wieder auf die visuelle Sprache des Realismus zurück und bildet inmitten des Weiß nur kurze narrative Eindrücke ab. Obwohl diese bildlichen Teile des Gemäldes sich auf den ersten Blick gegen das Weiß behaupten, stellen die weißen Quadrate doch die eigentliche Herausforderung an den Betrachter dar. Als Farbe ist Weiß problematisch aufgrund der zwiespältigen Assoziationen, die sie weckt: generell wird sie mit Sauberkeit und Freiheit in Verbindung gebracht, doch ist sie in der Kunstszene der post-institutionellen Kritik alles andere als assoziationslos. Das Weiß der Gemälde, die zwei- bis dreifache Menschengröße haben, überwältigt den Betrachter, der Mangel an durchgängiger Erzählung erregt ihn und wirkt gleichzeitig bedrohlich. Radikal formuliert, fordert das Weiß den Betrachter dazu heraus, seine

white is generally equated with cleanliness and freedom, it is hardly free of association in the post-institutional-critique art world. The white of the paintings that are twice to three times the size of human height overwhelms the viewer, and the lack of sustainable narrative in the work agitates and threatens. Radically, the whiteness dares the viewer to write his/her own narrative into the work's empty cells.

The sense of anti-narrative is produced by the absurdity of confronting a work that is made of ten percent representational painting and ninety percent void space. From its inception, the anti-narrative captivated Kabakov as a site of struggle that, for the artist, truly resonated with the human condition, and still continues to do so today.

---

[1] Ilya Kabakov, »Notes About Book Illustration«, in: *Ilya and Emilia Kabakov Present: Ilya Kabakov ORBIS PICTUS, Children's Book Illustrator as a Social Character*, The Museum of Modern Art, Kamakura and Hayama, The Tokyo Shimbun, 2007, p. 415.

eigene Geschichte in die leeren Quadrate zu
schreiben.

Das Gefühl des Nicht-Narrativen entsteht
durch die Absurdität, ein Werk zu betrachten,
das zu zehn Prozent aus darstellendem Gemälde besteht und zu neunzig Prozent aus leerer
Fläche. Von Anfang an bestach Kabakow das
Nicht-Narrative als ein Austragungsort für den
Kampf, der für ihn als Künstler die *conditio
humana* wirklich widerspiegelt, und das ist noch
heute der Fall.

1 Ilya Kabakow, »Notes About Book Illustration« [aus dem
Japanischen von Cynthia L. Martin], in: *Ilya and Emilia Kabakov
Present: Ilya Kabakov ORBIS PICTUS, Children's Book Illustrator
as a Social Character*, The Museum of Modern Art (Kamakura
und Hayama), The Tokyo Shimbun, 2007, S. 415.

46.47   **Broken Glass 1**, 2005   Öl auf Leinwand, 250 x 161 cm / Oil on canvas, 98.43 x 63.39 inches

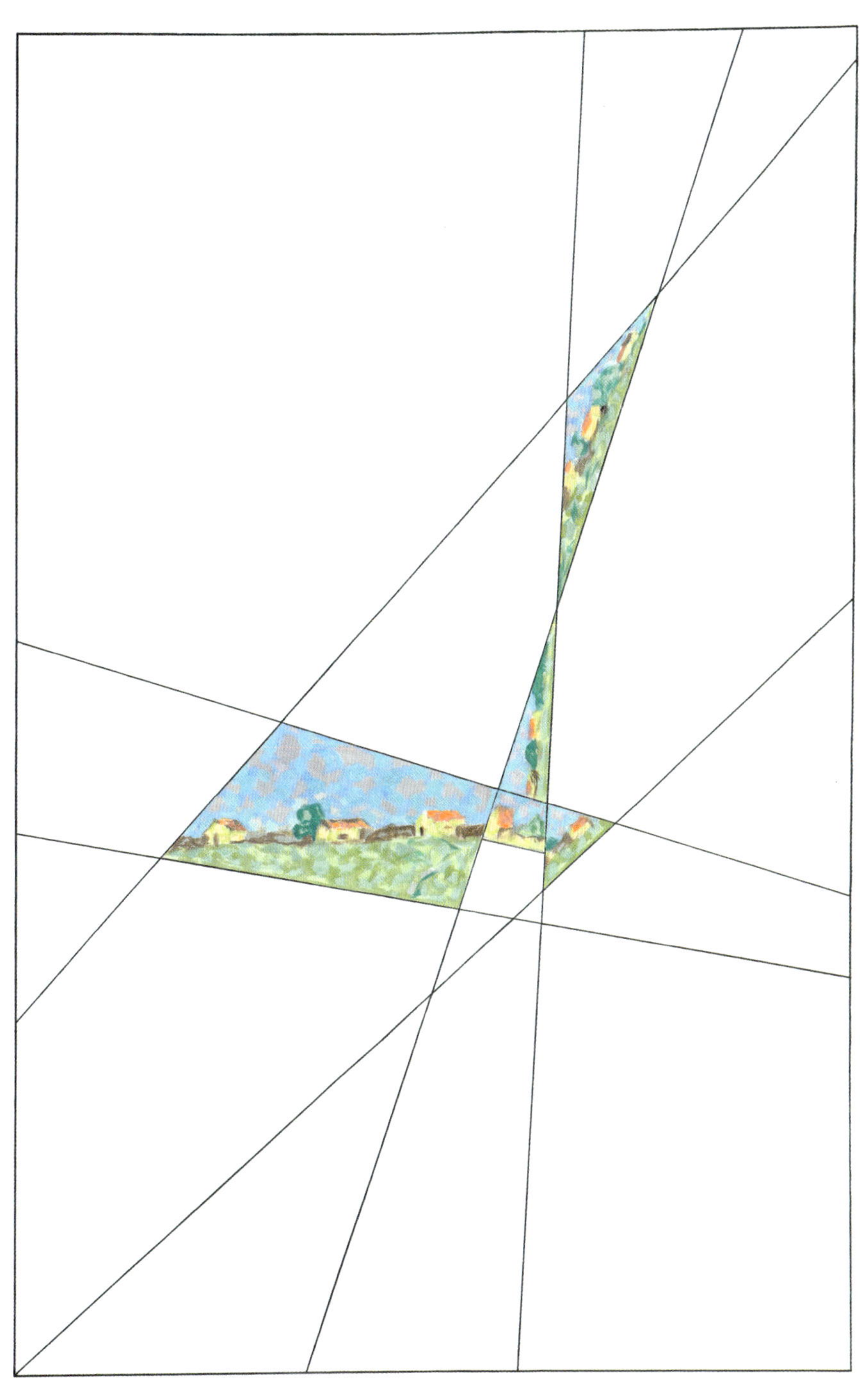

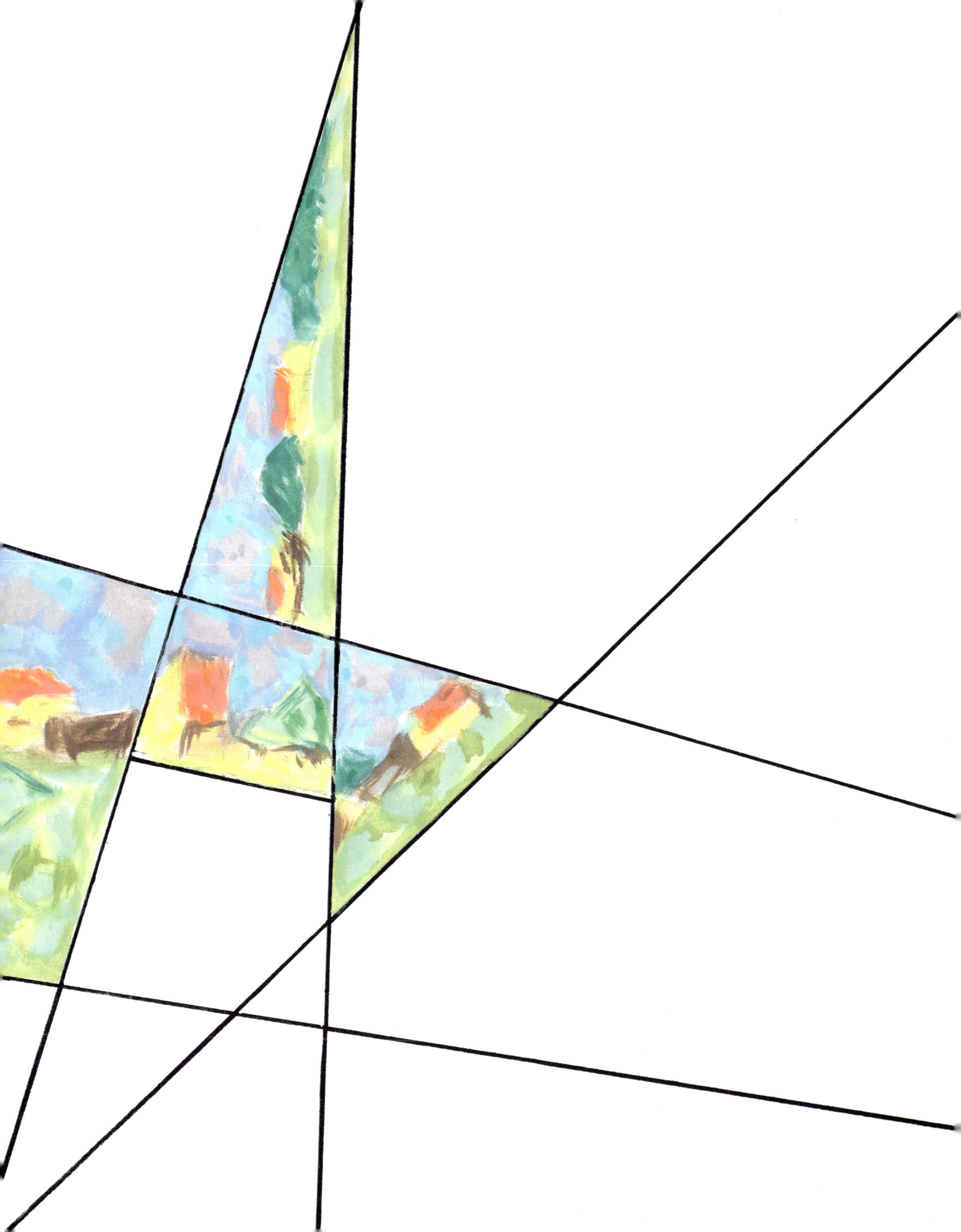

50.51   **Broken Glass 2**, 2005   Öl auf Leinwand, 250 x 161 cm / Oil on canvas, 98.43 x 63.39 inches

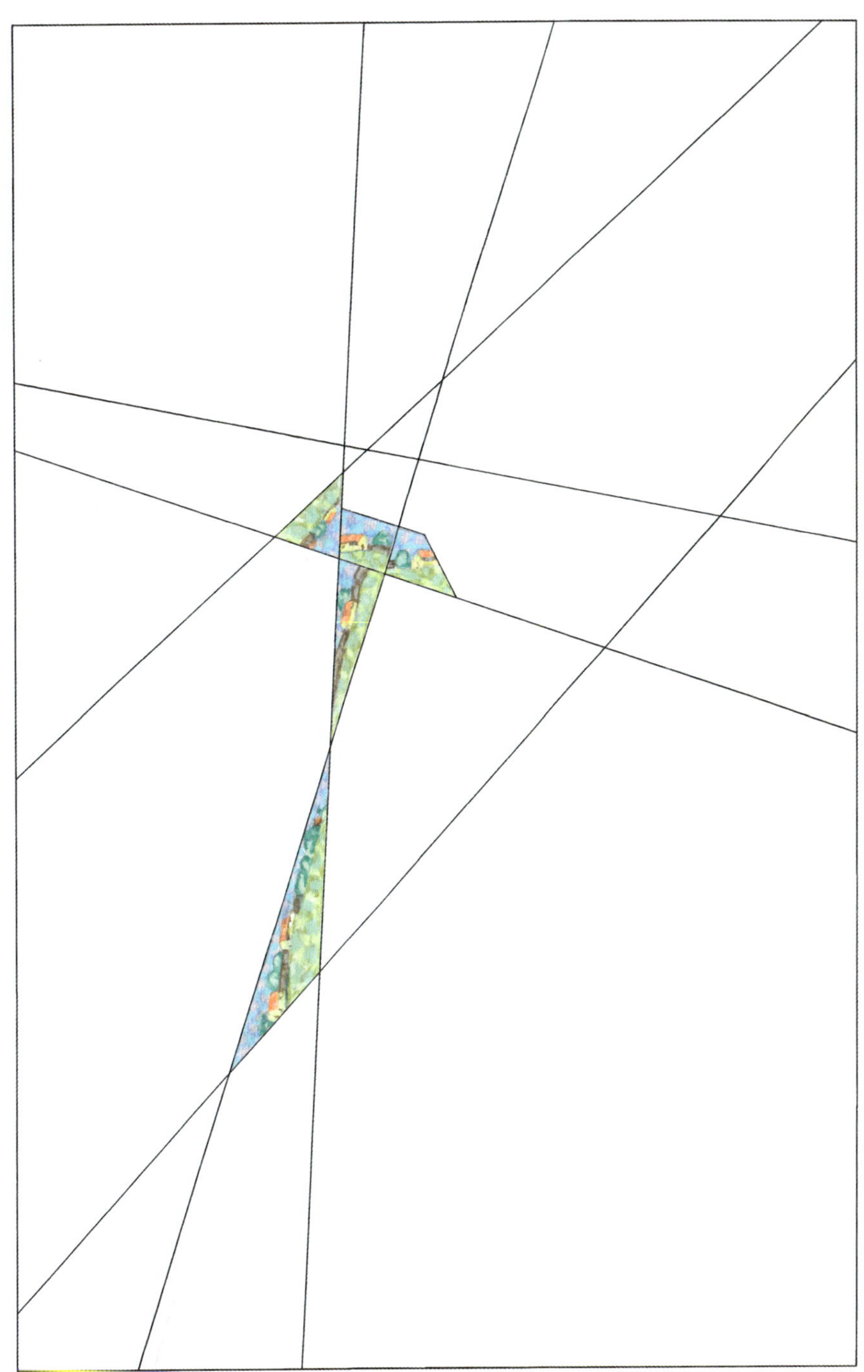

52.53   **Broken Glass 3**, 2005   Öl auf Leinwand, 250 x 161 cm / Oil on canvas, 98.43 x 63.39 inches

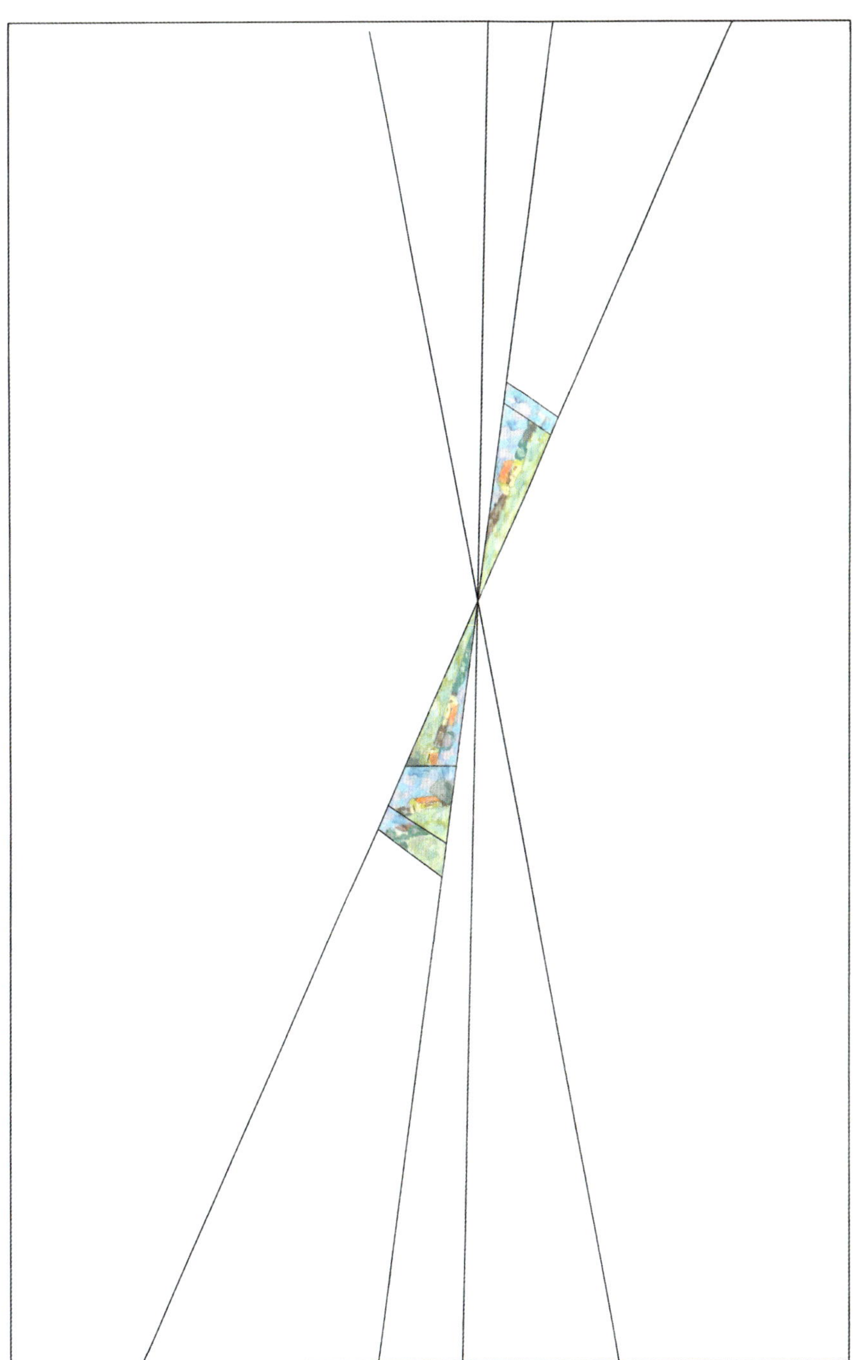

EMILIA KABAKOV

Geboren am / Born on 03. Dezember **1945** in Dnepropetrovsk (UdSSR / USSR)
1952–59 Besuch der Moskauer Musikschule / Moscow Music School
1962–66 Besuch der Musikhochschule / Music College in Irkutsk, Dnepropetrovsk (UdSSR / USSR)
1969–72 Studium der Literatur und der Spanischen Sprache an der Universität von Moskau /
Studies of literature and Spanish language at the University of Moscow
1973 Emigration nach Israel / emigration to Israel
seit / since 1975 Kuratorin und Kunsthändlerin / Curator and art dealer in New York
seit / since 1989 Zusammenarbeit mit Ilya Kabakow / Collaboration with Ilya Kabakov

ILYA KABAKOV

Geboren am / Born on 30. September **1933** in Dnepropetrovsk (UdSSR / USSR)
1945–51 Besuch der Moskauer Kunstschule / Moscow Art School
1951–57 Studium Grafik-Design und Buchillustration am staatlichen V. I. Surikov Kunstinstitut, Moskau /
Studies of graphic-design and book-illustration at National V. I. Surikov Art Institute, Moscow

Ilya und Emilia Kabakow leben und arbeiten in New York. / Ilya and Emilia Kabakov live and work in New York.

56   Der Katalog erscheint anlässlich der Ausstellung / The catalogue is published on the occasion of the exhibition

ILYA & EMILIA KABAKOV   THE CANON
30. August – 27. September 2008

Galerie Thaddaeus Ropac Salzburg, Mirabellplatz 2, 5020 Salzburg, Austria
Tel.: 0043 662 881 39 30, Fax: 0043 662 881 39 39
Galerie Thaddaeus Ropac Paris, 7, rue Debelleyme, 75003 Paris, France
Tel.: 0033 4272 9900, Fax: 0033 4272 6166
www.ropac.net

Herausgeber / Publisher: Galerie Thaddaeus Ropac, Paris / Salzburg
Redaktion / Editor: Jill Silverman van Coenegrachts

Besonders danken möchten wir / Specials thanks to: Ilya & Emilia Kabakov,
Alessandra Bellavita, Annie Belz, Eva Glittenberg, Markus Kormann, Victoria Lehnert
und den Teams in Paris und Salzburg / and the teams in Paris and Salzburg.

Umschlag / Cover: **Canon 3**, 2007 (Detail)
Übersetzung / translation: Ursula Wulfekamp
Lektorat / Proof reading: Antje Ehmann
Fotos / Photos: Ulrich Ghezzi
S. / P. 39, 41: Foto und Sammlung / Photo and Collection: John L. Stewart, New York
S. / P. 6–7: Foto / Photo: Charles Prat, Sammlung / Collection: Igor Lah, Slowenien / Slovenia
Gestaltung / Design: Linie 3, Christina & Gerhard Andraschko
Druck / Print: la linea, Salzburg

Copyright: Galerie Thaddaeus Ropac, Paris / Salzburg und bei den Autoren / and the authors

ISBN 2-910055-33-7